T0313192

Case Studies in Social Entrepreneurship
The oikos collection Vol. 4

CASE STUDIES IN
SOCIAL
ENTREPRENEURSHIP

The oikos collection

VOLUME 4

Edited by Michael Pirson

Routledge
Taylor & Francis Group

LONDON AND NEW YORK

First published 2015 by Greenleaf Publishing Limited

Published 2017 by Routledge
2 Park Square, Milton Park, Abingdon, Oxon OX14 4RN
711 Third Avenue, New York, NY 10017, USA

Routledge is an imprint of the Taylor & Francis Group, an informa business

British Library Cataloguing in Publication Data:
  A catalogue record for this book is available from the British Library.

  ISBN-13: 978-1-78353-069-4 (hbk)
  ISBN-13: 978-1-78353-050-2 (pbk)

Contents

Dear Reader,

We are proud to offer you this new volume of best global case studies in social entrepreneurship. All cases and their teaching notes have been selected in rigorous double blind review process. The authors showcased have all participated in the annual Global Social Entrepreneurship Case Writing competition sponsored by oikos in partnership with Ashoka and the Humanistic Management Network.

We hope you enjoy and can benefit from this rich teaching and learning resource.

With best regards,

Michael Pirson
Chair for the oikos-Ashoka Global Social Entrepreneurship Case Writing Competition
Partner, The Humanistic Management Network
Associate Professor and Director of the Center for Humanistic Management, Fordham University, New York, USA

June 2014

Contributors

Manish Agarwal
IBS, Hyderabad, India

Catherine Bédard
John Molson School of Business,
Concordia University, Canada

Darrell Brown
Portland State University, USA

Min Cai
Portland State University, USA

Charles Corbett
UCLA Anderson School of
Management, USA

Sarang Deo
Indian School of Business, India

Dror Etzion
McGill University, Canada

Erin Ferrigno
Portland State University

Olivier Furdelle
INSEAD Social Innovation Centre

Geneviève Grainger
John Molson School of Business,
Concordia University, Canada

Magdalena Kloibhofer
European Business School Wiesbaden,
Germany

Karin Kreutzer
European Business School Wiesbaden,
Germany

Jan Lepoutre
ESSEC Business School, France

Philippe Margery
IMD

R. Scott Marshall
Portland State University

Pia von Nell
WHU - Otto Beisheim School of
Management, Germany

Raymond L. Paquin
John Molson School of Business,
Concordia University, Canada

Lisa Peifer
Portland State University

Michael Pirson
Fordham University/ The Humanistic
Management Network

Stuart Read
IMD

Loïc Sadoulet
INSEAD Social Innovation
Centre

Bex Sakarias
Portland State University, USA

D. Satish
IBS, Hyderabad, India

Jeroen Struben
McGill University, Canada

Foreword

Marina Kim

Growth and change is the norm

I was just speaking to a professor who is on his third iteration of a social entrepreneurship course in the same number of years. Each time he taught the course he listened to the students' feedback on what could have been improved and also consulted with field experts on whether it reflected the best frameworks that needed to be addressed to prepare students for success in social entrepreneurship.

As all educators know, course content should be actively improved and iterated upon year after year. The dynamic field of social entrepreneurship is constantly changing as new models and approaches are developed, introducing challenges to keep content relevant. This is a tall order that demands a significant investment of time and effort to reach the next phase of impact in the classroom. An excellent, up-to-date course will motivate students to engage with cutting edge ideas and content and effective case studies will propel students to better understand the underlying root causes of social challenges. The same course that was taught five years ago does not fully capture the sophistication of today's social entrepreneurs, or meet the needs and expectations of the students who will be following in their footsteps.

Through our work at Ashoka, the world's largest network of social entrepreneurs, we've seen a growing interest from higher education institutions for social entrepreneurship education resources. Ashoka U was created to support educators from different disciplines interested in developing their own social entrepreneurship courses while learning from peers. Through this growing network of nearly 150 colleges and universities from 30 countries, we have derived a series of insights on curricular trends:

- **Integration across disciplines.** Courses are now being taught across many disciplines, including communications, law, engineering, social work, and public policy—not just business.

- **Global growth and new institutions.** Programs for social entrepreneurship are now embedded in more global and diverse environments–not just the most well-known universities, but also to vocational training programs as well as liberal arts and community colleges.

- **Terminology is evolving.** It used to only be called social entrepreneurship, but now social innovation, changemaking and social value creation are commonly used for courses, centers, initiatives and programs.

These areas of development indicate the increasing inclusivity of the academic field of social entrepreneurship and its future leaders.

Key challenges and promising practices to teach social entrepreneurship

Drawing on Ashoka U's birds-eye perspective of the field we have identified common challenges faced by many educators. The following suggestions will enable educators to design new, relevant, and effective courses in social entrepreneurship:

- **Scope your content to fit a single class.** Across the board we found that most courses try to accomplish too much. Instead of trying to force a certificate's worth of content into a single course, think about doing the best introductory course you can with a few, concrete learning outcomes, or instead build up to a multiple-course curricular sequence

- **Engage practitioners for input.** Most courses on social entrepreneurship do not integrate many perspectives from social innovators into the design and content. Integrate practitioner perspectives as presenters in class, partner with social sector organizations, or use case studies (including from this oikos compendium of cases!) into the content to ensure relevance and real-word application

- **Define terms clearly.** Given the progression of terminology over the past several years, it is important to get clear early in the class what exactly is meant by social entrepreneurship, social enterprise, social innovation, social impact, changemaker, intrapreneur, etc. We encourage a combination of definitions and also examples through case studies and class discussion. Having common language and common understandings of terms is a key part of adding rigor to the teaching of social innovation and social entrepreneurship

Call to action

There is already much happening in the academic environment to keep pace with the demand for social entrepreneurship programs and courses at the university level. In the 2013 Census for Social Innovation Education, administered by Ashoka U, over 200 universities reported relevant data on their institution's social entrepreneurship courses, incubators, experiential learning opportunities, staffing and budgets.

While the growth of social entrepreneurship offerings is an indicator of the gradual maturing of the field, we cannot lose sight of the need for educators equipped with the relevant course content that inspire, teach, and equip students to become leaders. We cannot lose rigor, discipline, and creativity for the sake of growth. We don't just need more courses, we need impactful ones.

Thank you for your pioneering work in the trenches of building up the next generation of socially conscious leaders. We hope that you find this compilation of social entrepreneurship cases from oikos useful in your journey for curricular innovation and excellence.

Marina Kim
Executive Director, Ashoka U

Introduction

Michael Pirson

Chances are that you picked up this book because you are interested or tasked or both to teach social entrepreneurship or social innovation related courses inside or outside a formal institution of higher learning. This book was conceived as exactly that, a resource for the increasing number of facilitators that wish to help students learn about the promise and pitfalls of social enterprise.

As our collaborators of the Ashoka U team suggested, more and more universities adopt social innovation and social entrepreneurship oriented courses. The oikos–Ashoka case competition for social entrepreneurship has been conceived at its founding in 2007 as a way to help find great material and case studies in this emerging field. We made sure that not only case studies of the highest quality get selected for this volume, but also that they come with a solid teaching note.

As a result of our yearly social entrepreneurship case writing competition, all of the cases selected for this volume have gone through a two-stage vetting process. We are therefore confident that they are among the best material professors and teachers of social entrepreneurship have to offer to their peers. The elaborate teaching notes for each of the cases are downloadable at https://www.routledge.com/Case-Studies-in-Social-Entrepreneurship-The-oikos-collection-Vol-4/Pirson/p/book/9781783530502 and we hope that they can be useful to you.

In this second volume of social entrepreneurship case studies, we wish to high-light cases from around the globe authored by teachers from around the globe. The selected cases span many industries and geographic contexts, nevertheless they are connected by a shared ambition: to highlight the power of entrepreneurship to solve social problems.

Overview of book structure

While there are many ways to present the various cases, we thought it helpful to align them according to more socially oriented entrepreneurial ventures including health and consumer products to more environmentally focused ventures. We are happy to also showcase two examples of corporate social entrepreneurship that are a testimony as to how the mindset of social entrepreneurs can inspire large corporations to innovate for a better world.

Case	Author(s)	Industry	Location	Focal point	Challenge	Area
Ndovlu	Charles Corbett, Sarang Deo	Health	South Africa	Primary Care	Scaling/ Growth	Social
wellcome	Magdalena Kloibhofer, Karin Kreutzer	Health	Germany	Post-Partum Care	Scaling	Social
Madecasse	R. Scott Marshall, Darrell Brown, Bex Sakarias, Min Cai	Consumer products	Madagascar/ EU/USA	Fair trade chocolate	Sustainable marketing/ growth	Social
BioVert	Raymond Paquin, Catherine Bédard, Geneviève Grainger	Consumer products	Canada	Ecological Household cleaners	Growth/ Competition/ Mission Drift	Environment
Terracycle	Philippe Margery, Stuart Read, Jan Lepoutre	Waste management/ recycling	USA	Waste reduction	Business Model	Environment
Tropical Salvage	R. Scott Marshall, Lisa Peifer, Erin Ferrigno	Recycling	USA/ Indonesia	Upcycling of Rain Forest Wood	Growth/ Scale	Environment
Husk Power	Manish Agarwal, D. Satish	Renewable energy	India	Husk-fed gasifiers for off-grid electricity	Scaling/ Growth	Environment
Better Place	Dror Etzion, Jeroen Struben	Automotive	USA, Israel, Denmark	Clean emission mobility	Business model	Environment
Osram	Pia von Nell	Lighting, electricity	Africa	Decentralized electricity	BOP model	Corporate Social Entrepreneurship
MPesa	Loic Sadoulet, Olivier Furdelle	Mobile phone	Kenya, Afghanistan	Mobile Payment systems	BOP model	Corporate Social Entrepreneurship

Part 1. Socially oriented enterprise cases – health and fair trade

a) Ndlovu Care Group

This case discusses the situation at Ndlovu Care Group (NCG) in July 2008. The group, founded by Dutch social entrepreneur Dr Hugo Tempelman, has been running a very successful health care facility – Ndlovu Medical Center (NMC) – in the township of Elandsdoorn in rural South Africa. From the case, and the other available materials including the online video, it is clear that Dr Tempelman has exceptional charisma and passion. The case discusses NCG's plans to expand that success to other locations in the country. At the time of the case, Dr Tempelman had just received a major grant from the Dutch embassy in South Africa to fund his expansion plans. This provides a perfect opportunity to discuss questions about how to replicate an intricate organization that has taken some 15 years to build, and whether that is even possible; what management structure is needed to oversee that replication; what risks are involved and how they might be mitigated. The need to balance increased professionalization with maintaining the founder's passion runs as a thread through the case. For more information on the work of Ndlovu Care Group visit http://www.ndlovucaregroup.com.

This case addresses several teaching objectives, some focusing on the context of health care delivery in developing countries while others focusing on the challenges associated with growth and expansion in socially focused entrepreneurial ventures.

(b) wellcome

wellcome is a social enterprise operating in Germany, offering support to families in the first weeks after a baby is born. Surprisingly, previously there was no service available to families in this new and often overwhelming situation of beginning parenthood. Statistics show that especially in those weeks mothers are endangered of showing symptoms of burn-out or postpartum depression due to exhaustion. wellcome sends volunteers to help mothers in their homes and fulfill tasks such as taking care of the baby or siblings and help in the household. wellcome has realized an impressive growth since its foundation in 2006 and their teams are now present in almost every city in Germany. That was possible thanks to the social franchising strategy wellcome had developed, where existing social service providers serve as franchisees who locally coordinate and supervise the volunteers' work.

This case addresses several teaching objectives, some focusing on the context of health care delivery in developed countries while others focusing on the challenges associated with growth and expansion in socially focused entrepreneurial ventures. It also highlights the specific appeal of a franchising strategy for growth and impact generation. Ultimately students will gain the ability to critically evaluate growth strategies in terms of their economic and social mission implications

(c) Madecasse

Madécasse is one of the only chocolates produced bean to bar on the island of Madagascar. It was on Madagascar that Brett Beach and Tim McCollum spent two memorable years as Peace Corps volunteers. Brett and Tim considered a number of options for a local Madagascar business before settling on a chocolate company. Headquartered in Brooklyn, New York, Madécasse strategically partners with four farmer cooperatives and a chocolate factory in Madagascar to make single-origin, tree-to-bar chocolates for sale in high-end groceries and chocolate boutiques internationally. Brett and Tim built the Madécasse model to maximize the amount of value added to the final product in Madagascar. This business model includes strong and enduring relationships with the cocoa farmers, partnering with a chocolate factory in Antananarivo (the capital city of Madagascar), sourcing ingredients and packaging from around Madagascar, and exporting the final, fully packaged product to overseas markets.

This case describes the issues and dilemmas facing a company in its efforts to differentiate its products based on a business model that goes beyond Fairtrade in terms of the economic benefits obtained by its employees and the region. Since its inception, the company has based nearly all its sourcing and value-adding processes in Madagascar. The company has achieved 'organic' and 'fair for life' certifications for its products. But, there is some question as to whether the certifications actually enhance the efforts of the company to distinguish itself based on a '4X Fairtrade' business model. The case is designed to highlight decisions related to marketing and operations strategy, measurement of social and environmental impacts, pros and cons of eco-labels and certifications.

The case highlights the challenges of developing and implementing a socially conscious marketing strategy that reliably delivers the promises throughout its entire supply chain. Students can learn about social and environmental impact measures, certification programs and the ability to market a commodity in an innovative, sustainable manner.

Part 2. Ecologically oriented social enterprises

(a) Bio–Vert

Based in Canada, Savons Prolav is a small manufacturer of the environmentally friendly Bio-Vert brand cleaning products. Brother and sister Yan and Bianka Grand-Maison took over the family business in 2002 and have realigned the products to fit their vision: eco-friendly, effective, and affordable. After an environmental crisis in Quebec spurred environmental legislation limiting phosphate use in detergents, Bio-Vert's sales increased by 500%. But now that 'green' cleaning products are becoming more mainstream, competition is increasing from both local and national brands. The case highlights the challenge of scale and increasing competition, as the traditional differentiation of Bio-Vert brand no longer seems to be enough; a change of strategy is needed. Students can explore the alternative strategic options for the company that highlight the economic, ecological, social and mission related trade-offs. The options include distributing altered (weakened) product formulations for house brands, maintaining the status quo, or innovating towards new products with even stronger environmental characteristics. While tempted by the short-term economic benefits, the company is seeking an approach which balances its environmental values with long-term economic success.

(b) TerraCycle

In 2001, Tom Szaky, a Princeton freshman, founded TerraCycle with the hope of creating perfect eco-capitalism. His idea was a company built on waste – worm waste to be exact. To help fund his fledgling company, Tom entered and won several business plan contests – though turned down his biggest prize of $1 million because it came with strings attached that conflicted with his aspirations for the firm. Eventually, he dropped out of Princeton to pursue his dream of eliminating waste and the company expanded into upcycling, making products from waste that would have otherwise been sent to landfills. The company went on to move into sponsored waste, whereby companies would pay TerraCycle to set up collection sites, or brigades as TerraCycle called them, for used packaging associated with their products such as drink pouches, yogurt containers and cookie wrappers. TerraCycle would take this challenging-to-recycle packaging and turn it into affordable, high-quality products. Ten years later, TerraCycle's eco-friendly products had received numerous environmental accolades, partnerships with multinationals such as Kraft, SmithKline Beecham and L'Oreal, and Terracycle's upcycled products were sold at major retailers from Home Depot to Walmart. But profits continued to elude the company, and Tom found himself at a crossroads.

Each case in this four part series addresses a key managerial issue at a crucial point in the company's evolution. The series provides an excellent illustration of the transformation process entrepreneurs go through to ensure their company not only survives but also thrives during each phase of its development. The first three cases each end at a crucial decision point that will push participants to think hard about a) the role of resources (investment and non-cash resources) in new venture creation, b) the tradeoffs of ownership and control, and c) building partnerships with consumers, multinationals and government, and finally d) whether the business model needs to be adapted to sustain further growth and therefore impact.

(c) Tropical Salvage

Headquartered in Portland, Oregon, Tropical Salvage is a private manufacturer of distinctive handcrafted furniture made from salvaged, or rediscovered, hardwoods. Time O'Brien established the company in 1998 to utilize underemployed, yet highly skilled Javanese woodworkers and a nearly inexhaustible supply of salvageable (non-virgin) tropical timber from around Indonesia. Tropical Salvage uses only salvaged, or rediscovered, wood to build its line of furniture. The company estimates that the supply of salvageable wood in Indonesia is inexhaustible for meeting its own demand. Currently, Tropical Salvage contracts primary milling of the wood it salvages. By offering steady employment, Tropical Salvage positively affects an area distressed by high rates of poverty, underemployment and unemployment.

This case focuses on the assessment of an expansion plan for the social enterprise Tropical Salvage. After ten years of steady, albeit slow, growth, the founder of Tropical Salvage has laid plans for expansion that entail product diversification and/or branded retail stores. Students will analyze Tropical Salvage's operations, marketing and financing issues, and determine the extent to which the expansion plan can/should be implemented.

The case highlights alternative strategies for socially oriented growth and the development of entrepreneurial strategies that manage the tradeoff between economic, social, ecological and mission related imperatives.

(d) Husk power

Even in 2012, lack of electricity is a major issue in the Indian hinterlands. Many remote villages were not electrified and even those that were, have power supply for just a few hours in a month. This problem was acute in the state of Bihar in North India. Gyanesh Pandey, who grew up in Bihar experiencing the shortage of electricity, came up with a unique model to generate and distribute power to the poor who lived in the remote parts of India by using an indigenously developed modified gasifier system that runs on rice husk. The enterprise, Husk Power Systems (HPS), won many awards for its innovative business plan, social entrepreneurship, and for producing clean energy.

This unique and sustainable venture, made positive impact on the society, by improving the lives of individuals, by providing them continuous power supply at a comparatively low prices. It had a positive impact on the environment too. Despite low pricing, HPS achieved a healthy profit margin which not only helped it to sustain itself but also helped it to replicate the model to grow rapidly. By mid-2011, HPS had impacted the lives of 200,000 people living in more than 325 villages and hamlets by installing more than 80 power plants. HPS planned to expand its reach to 6,500 villages by increasing the number of plants to 2014 by the year 2014. This would not only create 7,000 local jobs but would also help reduce CO_2 emissions by 750,000 tons and US$ 50 million in cash for more than 5 million people.

This case addresses several teaching objectives, some focusing on the conceptualization of the original business idea and the iterative process of achieving a workable, triple bottom line solution. Furthermore, this case illustrates well the development and refinement of an impact oriented theory of change.

(e) Better Place

In a bold bid to dramatically reshape the automotive industry, start-up company Better Place is attempting to shift transportation from reliance on the environmentally destructive internal combustion engine to electric power from renewable sources. In order to overcome the limitations of current technology and utilize off-the-shelf hardware, Better Place is rolling out an extensive infrastructure to provide ubiquitous charging opportunities in the hope that this would satisfy virtually all driver requirements. In pursuing this massive transformation, Better Place is promoting a paradigm shift in the business model for personal transportation, by shifting sales from products (cars and gasoline) to services, by selling its customers "miles". The end goal is to truly make the world a better place by substantially reducing the environmental and social impacts of the transportation sector's reliance on petroleum.

The case highlights the challenges of transforming a mature industry which is central to modern society. It includes a brief history of the automotive industry to date, illustrates various unintended consequences of its expansion, as well as provides overviews of various competing automotive technologies (hybrids, hydrogen fuel cells, etc.) The case surveys the various aspects of the Better Place model, and probes its advantages and shortcomings. It also examines the Better Place rollout strategy, as an upstart entrepreneurial company attempting to grow and expand internationally at a very rapid pace. Besides a complex economic business model specifying large upfront investments in multiple dispersed international locations, key challenges include: How to convince established automotive producers (or newcomers) that EVs are the way forward? Whether and how to coordinate infrastructure and standards? And, not least, how to convince consumers to make the leap of faith and switch to an electric car.

Part 3. Corporate Social Entrepreneurship case studies

(a) Osram

Since September 2008 OSRAM, a SIEMENS subsidiary, runs a social business, which provides light to regions that do not have power supply systems, at Lake Victoria in Kenya. Via the custom developed solar stations, called O-Hubs, residents can recharge batteries for energy-saving lamps and lanterns, as well as other electrical devices for an affordable prize and in an environmental friendly manner. As energy and light nowadays represent a major prerequisite for economic growth, OSRAM sees its business model as a potential solution for developing countries and emerging markets, which cannot afford establishing a power supply system, for further economic development. Thus, OSRAM used the first year as a trial phase in order to test the new concept at the bottom of the pyramid, to standardize products and services and to find out whether the social business could be expanded to other countries and environments.

The case describes the first year of OSRAM's social business targeting the base of the pyramid in detail. Hence, students learn about corporate approaches to social entrepreneurship. They furthermore study the African market, the business model for decentralized energy solutions, challenges regarding marketing and communication.

(b) Vodafone/Mpesa

Vodafone, in partnership with Safaricom, the leading Kenyan mobile operator, has a launched a service that allows registered users to transfer money from their mobile phones to other mobile phone users. Users simply load their M-PESA account with cash, transfer the money through a secured SMS, and the recipient can convert it to cash via any local air-time reseller. While this is not the first mobile money system in the world, it is certainly the most successful so far, with 11 million registered users in just three years (50% of Kenya's adult population), tens of millions of trans-actions per month (more than Western Union globally), and over 30 billion Kenyan shillings of transfers per month (15% of Kenyan GDP). Vodafone is now rolling out M-PESA in Tanzania, Afghanistan, South Africa and Fiji.

The case seeks to explore both the internal and external factors that under-pinned the extraordinary success story. It highlights the innovation track pioneered by a large international corporate player outside the traditional corporate process, leading to the creation of new services for new markets, which – once successful – could be reintegrated into Vodafone's core business for further replication.

We want to thank all the authors contributing to this volume and truly hope that you find the case selection useful. If you have any kind of recommendation, please do not hesitate to contact us at: mailto:case@oikosinternational.org

Michael Pirson
New York/ St. Gallen April, 2014

Part I
Socially oriented enterprise cases
Health and fair trade

CASE 1

Ndlovu

The clock ticks[1]

Charles Corbett and Sarang Deo

> **Always when I come to Africa I'm sad about the useless death, the destruction and failures I see. Today I have seen that there is also hope. Ndlovu gives me a feeling I haven't had for a long time being in Africa.**
>
> ***Sir Richard Branson, 2005**[2]

1 This case was prepared by Professors Charles Corbett and Sarang Deo with Dr Hugo Tempelman and Mariette Slabbert, with assistance from Kate Winegar, as a basis for classroom discussion rather than to illustrate either effective or ineffective handling of an administrative situation. The case and teaching note were supported by funding from CIBER and the Harold Price Center for Entrepreneurial Studies, both at the UCLA Anderson School of Management, and from the Kellogg School of Management. This case was awarded 2nd prize in the Social Entrepreneurship Track of the oikos Case Writing Competition 2011.

2 Source: http://www.ndlovu.com/nl/hugoandliesje.html, last accessed October 28, 2010.

UCLA Anderson
School of Management

NDLOVU
CARE GROUP

Kellogg
School of Management

Introduction

The phone rang. Dr Hugo Tempelman could not conceal his excitement when he saw the number. "That's the call I've been waiting for!" After a short conversation, he hung up, and punched the air: "It's official! This means hundreds, no thousands of jobs, and even more lives saved." The phone call was from a representative of the Dutch Embassy in South Africa, awarding Hugo a grant of several million US$ over four years (with a guarantee for another four years if targets were met) to expand to other locations in South Africa the Ndlovu clinic and community development programs he had founded in the rural town of Elandsdoorn.

Visibly emotional for a moment, he then called his wife and collaborator, Liesje, to tell her the good news, ending with, "I know this is no time to celebrate yet, the work is just beginning." Although Hugo was tremendously excited, he also felt a heavy burden. "Hundreds of people are depending on us to get this right," he explained. He knew there were risks involved in reproducing something that he and Liesje had spent 15 years developing. What exactly should they replicate? What variation should they allow between locations, and what should be kept rigidly constant? What risks had he simply not thought of?

Hugo walked out to the clinic courtyard. As if to remind him of the gravity of their task, a hearse was being loaded with a recently deceased patient. Although such a sight was inevitable in a clinic, Hugo's emotions showed again as he whispered, "We cannot celebrate today; this is a reminder of how much work we still have in front of us."

Ndlovu: the beginnings

Born in the Netherlands in 1960, Hugo Tempelman earned his medical degree in 1990. Rather than becoming a specialist, he believed he could put his medical degree to better use in South Africa. His wife, Liesje, also liked the idea, so they moved to Groblersdal, two hours north-east of Johannesburg, and Hugo signed on as chief medical officer at the Philadelphia Hospital in nearby Dennilton. After three years he became Head of the Paramedical Services in the Department of Health of the former homeland KwaNdebele.

1994 was a watershed year for South Africa, with the first fully democratic elections after the end of the apartheid era. Hugo anticipated that he might be "too white" to continue having much impact in government service. He had noticed there were no private health care facilities in the general area. Following his dream to put his medical training to good use, he started his own private clinic to, in his words, "bring first-world health care to a third-world country."

As Hugo recalled, "we took out a second mortgage on their home for 168,000 rand,[3] bought 40,000 bricks, and planned to build a new clinic down the road from the hospital, in Elandsdoorn. On the first day of construction the builder didn't show up. I thought, 'What on earth am I doing?' I engaged some people passing by who were eager for work, and the next day the builder showed up too." By September 1994, the Ndlovu clinic opened for business with one doctor (Hugo), three employees, and Liesje handling procurement and finance. The first months were rough, with the bank asking for its money back, but by 1995, Ndlovu added a second doctor, and a third in 1997.

Most patients could not afford anything beyond primary care, so they had to be referred to the (free) government hospital for anything more. Despite this, Ndlovu expanded, first opening a nutritional unit, which was later moved to four off-site locations. A tuberculosis (TB) unit followed, growing from 94 patients in 1996 to 2,000 new patients in 2007. Hugo negotiated to get free TB drugs from the South African Department of Health in exchange for offering free care, making Ndlovu a rare non-governmental organization (NGO) in South Africa to have a formal partnership with the government.

When, in 1995, a *Mkuhulu* (respectable male elder) asked Hugo to bring him a postage stamp from Groblersdal, Hugo realized that Elandsdoorn had no post office. Hugo got the man his stamp, and got him a post office too. Inequality was still endemic in South Africa: two post offices served Groblersdal's 5,000 white people, while Elandsdoorn Moutse, with its 160,000 blacks, had none. Hugo applied to open a post office branch within the clinic pharmacy, so residents could post their letters, send and receive faxes, and collect their aspirin and antibiotics all at once. One year of bureaucracy later, the post office opened, giving Elandsdoorn its very own zip code: 0485. The old *Mkuhulu* spoke for many when he said, "Thank you! Elandsdoorn is now on the map."

Many patients, particularly those with HIV/AIDS, suffered from malnutrition. Hugo decided to help patients plant a variety of crops in their gardens to provide a balanced and nutritious diet. Hugo knew that bringing the necessary water to Elandsdoorn was not a high priority for the government. The lake behind the nearby Loskop Dam held five years of water supply for the farmers connected to the 640 km of canals flowing around Elandsdoorn, but not a drop went to the 160,000 residents.

Drinking water was also scarce in Elandsdoorn. As Liesje noted, "After school, our children swim, play soccer, hockey or cricket. The children from the townships are given a wheelbarrow and two 20-liter canisters to get water, often a 5–15 km walk away. This is their contribution to the daily struggle for survival."

Hugo and Liesje initiated the Elandsdoorn Development Trust (EDT). Donations from individuals enabled 23 projects, where EDT paid for the installation, pumps, tanks, and 10 taps for each pipe, the community being responsible for

---

3 As of summer 2008, this was just over US$20,000.

maintenance. To illustrate the community's commitment, Hugo asked, "Isn't it incredible that these pumps have never been stolen or damaged, in a country infamous for its crime?" Walking down the street from the clinic, he pointed to one of the taps providing free drinking water. "If you try to mess with that tap, the people here will kill you," he said, without exaggeration.

He summarized his approach: "We first gained the community's confidence by providing health care, then we began to understand their other needs and started to fill them." The success that Liesje and Hugo had been able to achieve was increasingly widely recognized. In 2005, they were named Knight of the Order of Orange-Nassau by Queen Beatrix of the Netherlands.

The South African challenge

The two-hour drive from Johannesburg to Elandsdoorn (see Exhibit 2) begins with the N1 motorway traversing the glitzy shopping and residential area of Sandton that became Johannesburg's new commercial district when many businesses (including the stock market) fled there from the central business district to escape the violent crime that followed the 1994 elections. The N1 continues north past Pretoria, the legislative capital, before exiting onto the R25, a two-lane highway through what feels like an endless savannah-like landscape despite the 120 km/hr speed limit. Except for the occasional baboon along the road, traffic is sparse.

The small town of Groblersdal is signposted from 100 km away, but the first signs of Elandsdoorn are the Ndlovu billboards (see Exhibit 3) with texts such as "Be Wise, Condomize," and "Women, Don't Let Your Men Dick-tate You." This explicitness is in stark contrast with the government's confused approach to HIV/AIDS education. "Some people have started referring to Elandsdoorn as 'Condom City'," laughed Hugo.

The R25 is Elandsdoorn's only paved road; the Ndlovu Medical Center is on a dirt road. There are virtually no cars or bicycles. Single-storey homes line the roads, some built with brick, others more ramshackle. The few shops and eating establishments are almost indistinguishable from houses. By contrast, the mostly white town of Groblersdal, where Hugo and Liesje and most of the senior managers and doctors of the Ndlovu Medical Center live, has a full selection of shops, services, restaurants, and paved roads.

Elandsdoorn is typical of many rural communities in South Africa: very limited drinking water, no high quality health care facilities prior to Ndlovu, no decent educational facilities, and marginal infrastructure. About 20% of its people are infected with HIV/AIDS, of whom 60% also have tuberculosis (TB). Other diseases are rife, and malnutrition is widespread. Average income is below 10,500 rand[4] per year, and unemployment is approximately 60%. The existence of a market for sputum

4 As of summer 2008, this was just under US$1,400 per year.

from TB sufferers exemplifies the desperation and lack of education: people buy and swallow this sputum to be diagnosed as TB positive, which entitles them to some government aid.

The origins of this desperation are complex, and cannot be separated from the history of serial colonization and, subsequently, the "apartheid" regime that was in place from 1948 to 1994. The first Europeans to visit South Africa were the Portuguese in 1487. In 1652 the Dutch East India Company founded a small settlement, bringing slaves from Indonesia, Madagascar and India. During the 1800s the British gained control. The discoveries of diamonds in 1867 and gold in 1884 further spurred economic growth and immigration, but also drove the indigenous population into increased subjugation.

South Africa started to gain independence in 1910, but power remained firmly with the whites. Successive governments enforced ever stricter separation between blacks and whites, sometimes tearing down vibrant but largely black towns to build new white towns. The black population was expelled from the cities and forced to live in townships, such as Soweto ("South Western Townships") outside Johannesburg. In 1976 the mostly Zulu and Xhosa-speaking black population protested a bill requiring that instruction in all schools be in Afrikaans. The crackdown and subsequent violence in Soweto left 566 dead and led to the emergence of a real resistance movement which, together with international sanctions, led to the downfall of the apartheid regime in 1994 when the African National Congress (ANC) won the first free elections and Nelson Mandela became president.

The white and black populations still enjoy vastly different living standards. The ANC-dominated government struggles to match the high hopes that existed in 1994. It is not uncommon to hear black residents say things like "at least the apartheid government got things done." (The case-writers heard this twice within a few days.)

This pernicious inequity is an inevitable source of mistrust. It was also one of the forces driving Hugo, who likes to quote Archbishop Desmond Tutu: "When the missionaries came to Africa they had the Bible and we had the land. They said 'Let us pray.' We closed our eyes. When we opened them, we had the Bible and they had the land."

Hugo believed that bringing first-class health care to an underserved community was the way to build trust, which allowed him to address other community needs without the distrust he might otherwise have encountered. Looking to the future, Hugo was optimistic based on the changes he had seen within Elandsdoorn, but he was also deeply worried about what he called the second wave of the AIDS epidemic: the 10–12% of children who were AIDS orphans, who would grow up with no parental guidance.

Ndlovu today

The umbrella organization now known as the Ndlovu Care Group (NCG) has two main locations and several satellite offices and outreach programs. The original location is the Ndlovu Care Group Elandsdoorn, in Moutse, Limpopo, that serves a population of 120,000–140,000 people. The second location, known as Bhubezi, is 400 km away in Lillydale, in the Ehlanzeni District of Mpumalanga; it serves a population of 70,000 people, and an additional 650,000 people live in the Bushbuck Ridge area within a 50 km radius.

The Ndlovu Care Group Elandsdoorn also has a mobile team (with a doctor, nurses, counselors, and administrative staff) to provide occupational HIV care on-site at farms. It runs a satellite operation, launched in 2007 in collaboration with an NGO that started its antiretroviral (ARV) program under Ndlovu's guidance. This satellite location cares for more than 500 HIV-positive patients, of which approximately 250 are on antiretroviral therapy (ART). More such satellites are planned for the future.

Ndlovu's programs fall into four main categories: the clinical operation (on-site and off-site); the Ndlovu Aids Awareness Program (NAAP); the Ndlovu Child Care Program (NCCP); and a collection of community outreach programs. Summary financial information on the Ndlovu Care Group is shown in Exhibits 4 and 5, a chronological overview of major milestones in Exhibit 6, and other selected facts in Exhibit 7.

The Ndlovu clinic

The clinic, where Ndlovu began, has grown to four doctors, seeing 140 patients per day between them. Demand still exceeds capacity; as Hugo explained, "We still have to close the gates after 140 patients; I prefer to have quarrels outside the gate than quarrels about poor service." The Elandsdoorn clinic currently has 1,800 people on HIV/AIDS treatment, and saw 1,500 new TB cases in 2007. Somewhat unusually, Hugo insists that every patient be assigned to one doctor, who is accountable for their patients' wellbeing. This is easier said than done, as Hugo also insists that a doctor should give a patient all the time s/he needs. Moreover, except for Highly Active Antiretroviral Therapy (HAART) patients, the clinic does not take appointments; it's first-come, first-served. At midnight, 20 cars may show up to collect a number that will ensure them of an early slot; by 5:00 a.m., the next batch of patients arrives (another five–ten people) to wait for their turn. The clinic runs two shifts: 7:00 a.m. to 4:00 p.m., and 9:00 a.m. to 6:00 p.m. To balance the workload across doctors, they all work until the last patient has left. To keep the flow moving, the staff gives the doctors five patient files at a time and calls five patients into the smaller waiting area next to the doctors' offices.

The clinic supervisor and administrator is Penny Mbatha, who reports to Dr Moraba. Penny has been with Ndlovu since 1997. She started at the post office, when there were only eight–nine staff members. Now Penny's duties include supervising the receptionist; supervising the data capturers who enter information from patient charts into the computer systems; checking whether the data on the charts is correct; and bookkeeping. Among other duties, she needs to check 250–300 files every day (for instance, for HAART medication she checks whether the chart has the right code, name, and amount). She catches about five errors per day, and attributes the data capturers' mistakes to the doctors' handwriting, and to data capturing being the most short-staffed function in the clinic. Before a patient can take a prescription to the pharmacist, it has to be entered in the system, which causes delay and puts the data capturers under time pressure. Penny has reduced the time she needs to spend checking these data from two hours to 30 minutes a day.

Penny spends a lot of time following up with Medical Aids (private insurance companies) and checking on payment status. If she notices that a patient has been waiting in the reception area too long, she will sometimes help that patient. Despite this daunting set of responsibilities, she thrives on her job; she says that "the hardest moments are when I cannot help, such as when a crucial medication is out of stock". She loves working at Ndlovu, although she admits it is challenging; she characterizes it as "a game you have to play; you have to lose yourself in it for the patient to win." Having grown up in the area, Penny appreciates the improvements that have been made, including the access to water and the tennis courts.

Another building has housed the prevention of mother-to-child transmission (PMTCT) program since 2003. With over 400 births per year in the clinic, Hugo saw he could help raise a new, HIV-free generation, by combining education and treatment for mother and child. To date, 98% of all newborns delivered by HIV-positive women at Ndlovu are HIV-free, in stunning contrast to the nearly 35% infection rate elsewhere.

The Ndlovu Aids Awareness Program (NAAP)

Ntwanano Shilubane, the NAAP project manager, joined Ndlovu in 2008. After earning a degree in political science and an honors degree in international politics, he started an MBA in health management, but had to put that aside for financial reasons. (He has now re-started that program, studying from home.) Prior to Ndlovu, Ntwanano worked at various NGOs in South Africa and in the UK as a project manager, and has held a variety of government positions. He got the job after a single interview with Hugo and the Ndlovu human resource manager. Initially Ntwanano reported directly to Hugo, but now reports to Mariette Slabbert, the new Chief Operating Officer (COO).

NAAP has five teams, one each for farms, communities, schools, outreach, and sports. Each team has a coordinator, who reports to Ntwanano for tactical issues such as skills audits or defining work processes, and to Roger Sibeko, the NAAP field manager, for operational issues. Roger, a Soweto native who speaks several African languages, joined Ndlovu a month before Ntwanano; before that he had held various jobs, including tourist guide, driver, researcher, and bodyguard.

The farm team works with the Department of Agriculture. When initiating a new project, the team first explains to the farm owner what they will do to educate employees. Once the farm owner agrees, they send a peer educator to hold AIDS-awareness sessions. The peer educators, or counselors, are members of the target community, who have received HIV/AIDS training from Ndlovu. After several such sessions, once the counselors think the farm workers understand enough about

HIV/AIDS, they bring a mobile VCT (voluntary counseling and testing) team to the farm. All farm workers who choose to do so undergo further pre-counseling before being tested in a private room and receiving the results within 10–15 minutes. In a typical VCT session, 100 patients might be tested, of which some 15 would test HIV-positive. To further ensure privacy, the team arranges for a Ndlovu doctor to visit the farm soon after the VCT session. They call the patients who tested positive to suggest that they meet the doctor. Of the 15 who tested positive, 5–10 might show up, in addition to 20–25 employees who visit the doctor for any other complaints, so nobody knows who is HIV-positive.

The NAAP outreach team trains peer educators in different organizations. In the past the outreach teams would go anywhere, but Roger is trying to focus on local companies which allows the teams to leave Elandsdoorn at 6:00 a.m., arrive on site by 8:00–9:00 a.m., and be back home by 7:00 p.m. They occasionally stay overnight when traveling to more remote locations if the company invites them to. While explaining the importance of peer educators, Roger contrasts the VCT session at the farms with the VCT program he saw at one of the mines: employees waited for their test results in a common area. Even though the results were not announced in public, the staff would tell some employees "you go through that door" while sending others another way. The NAAP outreach team is now training some of the peer educators at that mine. The NAAP community team is similar to the outreach team, but typically stays within a 50 km radius.

The NAAP school team works in partnership with the Department of Education, but had to adopt a different approach because performing VCT on-site at schools is not allowed. When the NAAP peer educators visit a school, the teacher will spend some time on general life skills, while the peer educators discuss issues specific to HIV/AIDS. After several such sessions, the NAAP school team will plan a VCT session off-site, for instance by arranging a sports event and bringing the children to a location where they can do the testing and counseling.

So far, the five teams operate largely independently from one another. To encourage exchange of ideas between the teams, and to address the ambiguity about the teams' domains, Roger and Ntwanano are merging the community and outreach teams, and the schools and sports teams.

Roger and Ntwanano are making several other changes. They noticed that NAAP was operating largely independently from the rest of Ndlovu, but should collaborate more closely with the Ndlovu Child Care Programs. It was not easy for Roger and Ntwanano to make the junior staff on both sides recognize this, but now NAAP and NCCP are working hand-in-glove.

Ntwanano noticed that NAAP did not have a uniform brand so he developed a consistent message and color scheme. He is re-doing the work processes, putting more detailed descriptions of those processes into "LogFrame,"[5] and translating

5 "LogFrame" is the planning tool that Ndlovu uses to monitor outputs of certain activities in order to reach objectives. It is based on *The Logical Framework Approach (LFA): Handbook for Objectives-Oriented Planning*, Norad, 1999, fourth edition.

them into a project management framework. A firm believer in documentation, he is now capturing data on the number of VCT interactions, where those people are from, and how many children they have. Roger explains how the NAAP team is working with the monitoring and evaluation (M&E) team: "One M&E lady is here at NAAP, and she is asking us to do more detailed planning. We used to have six-month plans before, for instance we would say we want to do 5,000 VCTs, distribute 10,000 condoms, etc., but the targets were often set very high, so the teams under-performed. Now, instead, we're focusing on monthly or weekly targets, and after each week or event, we do a SWOT analysis to find out why the targets were or were not met."

Roger and Ntwanano find interacting with the peer educators both rewarding and challenging. Ntwanano feels that he can make a real contribution by working with these young people, but he finds that "the peer educators often come to Ndlovu thinking this is the end of the road. The challenge is to show them that it's really just the beginning; there's so much opportunity out there." Talking with all the NAAP employees, he saw their ambitions and skills. Roger confirms that "we are doing skills audits of the peer educators, we may send some to school, not for our benefit but to empower the individual." One thing he enjoys about working at Ndlovu is that "they are asking young people how best to do their job."

Roger sometimes accompanies the teams in the field, especially when the peer educators need him as an interpreter. Every time he sees patients walking out of a VCT test trembling he is reminded of the emotionally draining side of the peer educators' work. Every month they meet with a psychologist to help them cope.

Roger and Ntwanano have ideas about how to improve NAAP, but they both wish they had more time to put those ideas into practice. In Roger's experience, "There are always unexpected things happening; for instance, the team is out at an event, but they don't have a generator, so I have to bring it; or they forgot to bring condoms so I have to drive over." Ntwanano is also no stranger to interruptions, caused by invoices needing immediate attention or the ongoing construction of the amphitheatre, another of Hugo's pet projects. All this keeps them very busy. As Roger puts it, "We start at 6:30 a.m. and knock off at 7 p.m.; if you don't have passion, you don't survive here."

The Ndlovu Child Care Program (NCCP)

Jennifer Stuart is the program manager for the Ndlovu Child Care Program. She joined in 2005, having just earned a degree in women's studies in Durban. Themba Dlamini is the NCCP project manager. Jennifer's job is more external, focused on growth, while Themba's work is more operational. Between them, they oversee programs related to dental care, nutrition, and nature.

Jennifer added a new program for orphans and vulnerable children (OVC), the only OVC program in the immediate area. She recalls how they were unique in seeking out government partnership from the start: "The first six months it was just me, there were no large NGOs doing child care in the area; there were just some small community groups. We offered these groups a place to refer children to, and started after-school and Saturday programs, where OVC children were taught life skills, drama, etc. After each event the children got together with a counselor for a debriefing; for instance, they would discuss the soccer game they just played."

The Friends of Loskop program blends science education with recreation by bringing 6,000 children to the nearby Loskop Nature Reserve to experience nature, a rare opportunity for children growing up in townships. It also, unintentionally, highlights another major challenge in South Africa: the severe water pollution caused by the local dam and mines is slowly killing the animals that the children are taught to enjoy.

Themba explains, "What is great about Ndlovu is it's a one-stop shop for children, so we really need to integrate across our programs (NAAP, child programs, and treatment). For instance, if a child is HIV-positive, he or she needs treatment, but we also need to work on awareness for family and neighbors." Jennifer agrees wholeheartedly, "The last two years we've all been working so hard, we're all on our own island." She gives two examples of missed opportunities. First, if a child is HIV-positive, some counselors refer him to the Ndlovu home treatment program which provides additional support beyond medicine and treatment. Other times, the counselors only refer the child for regular treatment, with no additional support. Second, the child care program was trying to establish relationships with schools, only to discover that NAAP was already working with the same schools.

Jennifer is optimistic that better integrating their activities with other groups at Ndlovu will yield results. Even though everybody is busy, "we hold each other accountable: if two people agree on something they'll make it happen. If something is not done when it should be you will hear about it."

Part NCCP's work is inevitably reactive, but Jennifer credits their standard operating procedures and their reliable, efficient data management system for keeping things on running. She is particularly proud of the GPS-based map of patients' locations. "Most children in our system don't have addresses, it's just 'by the third tree after the yellow shack.' We're using this simple GPS device to register the locations of each household so when the counselors return they can drive straight to the house instead of circling around forever trying to find it. Eventually each program will have a map with colored flags, for HAART, TB, nutrition, child care, and other programs."

Jennifer enjoys the atmosphere at Ndlovu. In other organizations people often feel stifled, and struggle to get support for ideas. Ndlovu is different: "Here, if you can articulate an idea and get Hugo and Liesje excited, you go do it. In this kind of work, that's crucial. This job is all about passion; it's about innovation, growing, fun, etc." She believes that the "inspired leadership of Hugo and Liesje" is what makes Ndlovu work so well. Jennifer does find that management and staff are still not close enough, and management living outside the community does not help. She also wishes the community would take more initiative and ownership. "The community wants to get paid before they do anything, but we're trying to help them help themselves."

Community development

After health and child care, "community development" covers a range of programs, some formal, and some more accidental, under the umbrella of the Elandsdoorn Development Trust (EDT). These include the water programs, the sports program, a bakery, and a diaper factory, in addition to information technology (IT) education, a scholarship program, and facility improvements for the Mologadi preschool.

Located around the corner from the clinic, the sports fields are popular with locals and used all day and into the evening. Hugo had heard that Johan Cruijff, a Dutch soccer legend, was providing funding for football fields in the Netherlands, and asked, "Why not here?" Hugo's passion must have played a role in convincing Cruijff to visit Elandsdoorn, resulting in the star donating the first Cruijff fields outside the Netherlands. Hugo laughs when he recalls Cruijff's experience: "He loved it here. Finally he was in a place where nobody recognized him."

Next to the sports fields is a fully equipped fitness center, another rarity for a township. One block further is the site where Ndlovu is building an amphitheatre and multi-purpose community facility. Hugo sketched the design for this center himself.

Ndlovu runs several ancillary enterprises for the community's benefit. The bakery was started in 1998, when Phuti Mariba, a staff member, complained to Hugo that his workers often had to travel far (and sometimes to three different shops) to get their lunch. During the conversation, Hugo learned that Phuti's wife baked up to 200 loaves of bread each day in the little oven in her kitchen, around the clock, just so that the family could survive. Together with the Dutch foundation "Bakers for Bakers," and with financial support from Herman van Veen (a Dutch entertainer), a full range of bakery equipment was shipped to Elandsdoorn from the Netherlands. A retired Dutch baker helped to set up the bakery, after which the Maribas managed it, offering Elandsdoorn warm, fresh bread for the first time. The bakery now has 16 employees and bakes about 3,000 loaves every day, in addition to selling cakes, sandwiches, and cold drinks.

The diaper factory has more tragic roots. Many women only find out that they are HIV-positive when they become pregnant, and their husbands often leave them immediately. Therefore, an unintended consequence of Ndlovu's HIV/AIDS programs is that there are now HIV-positive single mothers with no source of income. When an opportunity arose to buy a machine for producing disposable diapers, Hugo jumped on it. Five women now work in the factory, producing 600 diapers a day, giving the maternity clinic a regular supply of diapers, and selling them at lower prices than the local supermarket.

Touring Elandsdoorn with Hugo as guide is quite an experience. Everybody seems to know him, he is constantly stopping for a chat, asking how people are, or just joking with them. While driving, Hugo also pointed out two of the local entrepreneurs that he helped launch. "That's a car wash. One day, Mafika walked up to me and said, 'Mr. Hugo, the Ndlovu cars are dirty, may I wash them?' I kept on refusing but he insisted. In the end I let him, and he did a good job. I loaned him some money, and now he has his own car wash." Pointing to another house, he continued: "That's where Vusi lives. He's a real entrepreneur. He wanted to paint. He already had a VAT number[6] and five employees lined up, but no jobs. We let him do some painting, after that he got a big job in Johannesburg. He needed money to buy equipment, and we loaned him 28,000 rand.[7] When he returned to pay me back, he then borrowed even more to buy a car."

Funding

To support these activities, Hugo has tapped into several sources of funds. Some activities are fully or partly self-sustaining; for instance, the clinic does charge for some services, and the bakery and diaper factory are or will be self-supporting. The majority of funding comes from governments and NGOs, but such grants typically only cover treatment and medication and not the broader community development activities that Hugo is committed to. For such other activities, Hugo has incorporated non-profit organizations in the Netherlands and in Germany.[8] "We are very transparent—I show donors that we can live a comfortable life here. After one year, we had two million rand, and another foundation is going to give two to three million more. We keep the money there [in Germany] until we need it here." The Friends of Loskop is funded through this foundation. As Hugo puts it, "It's neat, but not life-saving, so nobody wants to fund it; we got the Dutch and German foundations to support it."

The biggest challenge, in Hugo's view, is the impossibility of creating reserves in a charity setting. He has raised enough funds to buy himself some flexibility, however, so when one budget is exhausted he can sometimes reallocate funds from elsewhere.

Managing the growing Ndlovu ecosystem

Although Ndlovu had changed dramatically since its early days, Hugo's first three hires were still there. One started as a cleaner and was now managing the data capturing department; another started as a translator but then moved to the pharmacy.[9]

---

6 All firms must have a Value Added Tax number in order to be incorporated.
7 As of summer 2008, this was about $6,400.
8 Vivi Eikelberg, the public relations representative of Herman van Veen, the Dutch entertainer who funded the bakery and was popular in Germany, had made a documentary about Ndlovu. Hugo attended the premiere in Berlin with an audience of 600 wealthy people. She then created the "Tempelman Stiftung," using his name only because it was better for marketing.
9 Hugo recalls discovering that she was severely shortsighted and unable to read prescriptions. She worked completely from memory, recognizing patients, or hearing the prescription being dictated. Hugo drove her to buy glasses; he remembered how ecstatic she was on the way home to be able to see oranges in the trees.

In the early days, Hugo hired only unqualified people and trained them himself. He was convinced that attitudes were more important than specific skills. Mariette, the COO, continued that philosophy: "I hire attitudes; I train skills." That started to change when the first computer arrived in 1996, and the clinic needed different skills. It changed even more when the clinic switched from 12-hour to around-the-clock operation in 1998. Ndlovu needed more nurses and more professional staff. This started to create a split within the organization due to the strong hierarchical tradition within the nursing profession, where seniority was advertised with military-style stripes. Referring to these stripes as "fruit salad," Hugo's experience was that more stripes often meant less willingness to do real work. Hugo would rather hire locals and have money flow back into the local community than import capacity from elsewhere.

An extreme example of Hugo's recruiting style was the 31-year-old job candidate with 16 years missing on his resume, which Hugo guessed correctly corresponded to a prison sentence. The candidate declined to give details but reassured Hugo that he had not killed or raped anyone. Hugo liked the man's attitude and hired him. After a few good years at Ndlovu the man moved on to a respectable job in the area. Asked whether this was symptomatic of a broader retention challenge, Hugo counters, "Quite the contrary, you should make yourself a training house so people can get themselves a better life. All NGOs want at least five years experience, so Ndlovu is a great place for people to start."

Hugo admitted that this approach to hiring does have its limitations. "We can only grow local people to a certain level. If you try to go beyond that, you disappoint them, and that is risky. In this culture, you cannot show anger or disappointment with an employee in front of others."

On the other hand, Mariette found that "a big surprise to me is that everyone here understands reality, employees know when they cannot grow further. The managers here are very young but very mature." Mariette did encourage them to develop themselves as much as possible: "I provide a safety net, but they have to jump first."

Hugo's passion came with a temper, although he said, "I have learned to control my short fuse. Once, I was with a patient when the bakery called because something needed fixing. As soon as I was finished with the patient I went over to the bakery and fixed whatever it was. I was almost ready to go back to my patients when the bakery employee asked, 'Now that you're here, can you also…' I exploded, swearing profusely. I am very focused, and was prepared to step out to do precisely what they had asked for, but I was not prepared for the extra request."

The rapid growth at Ndlovu forced some changes in management style. Walking around the clinic, Hugo said, "Everything you see grew out of enthusiasm. We didn't do things systematically but relied on intuition and hard work." Liesje confirmed this: "I constantly have to curb Hugo's enthusiasm. He is the accelerator; I am the brake pedal." Hugo put it less delicately: "Liesje says I run too fast, the rest have to follow in my slipstream and clean up my sh*t." He clarified, "We did have program managers, but they all reported directly to me. We all worked extremely hard, and

I was also still doctoring at that time. Every one to two months we held manage-ment meetings at our house, from 8:30 to 10:30 p.m., followed by some good wine, because we did not want to have meetings during the day." Hugo evidently recog-nized the need to take stock: "Since November 2007, we have not started any new initiatives, we are only working on organizational development. This consolidation provides a baseline for our future growth."

That recognition did not come without pain. As Hugo recalled, "We were approached by Richard Branson, Anglo-American[10] and a third partner to open another clinic. I insisted they fund a management team to handle coordination across locations. They agreed to split the cost for the autonomous treatment center (ATC) team to manage the new clinic. This gave us the financial space we needed to hire and upgrade people. We opened Bhubezi in April 2007. Unfortunately, the third partner withdrew, so we only got two thirds of the funding, so we couldn't hire the full team yet. I was stretched too thin and started using resources from Ndlovu to support our new Bhubezi venture."

Hugo saw the writing on the wall: "I was getting sloppy, I was getting on people's nerves. It became grim. I got a wake-up call when a girl who came from the Neth-erlands left after four months because she said she didn't recognize the man who hired her."

Perhaps the most dramatic moment in Ndlovu's growth occurred a few years ago. Hugo had already hired a second doctor in 1995, and a third in 1997 who focused exclusively on seeing patients, which allowed Hugo to do many other things besides practicing medicine. Hugo relived the moment when he finally had to choose between being a doctor or a manager: "We had just hired four new management staff in three months, so our management team had doubled. I felt we needed to spend time together as a team, and rather than have Tempelman do it again, I hired a consultant to come in for a day, in January 2005. She did the usual vision and mis-sion exercises with the team, while I was thinking 'what a load of rubbish.' Later she made us all sit around an African campfire, in sequence from the most recent hire to the most senior (me), and asked us to talk about our first day on the job. After that, the consultant handed me my stethoscope, and gave me a choice: 'Hang it around your neck, or hang it up on that tree.' I was speechless, I got myself a glass of wine and a cigar and left the meeting." Recounting this moment years later, Hugo's emotions still showed. "I came back, and hung the stethoscope up on a tree. For two years I didn't go back to the office where I used to see patients. Nowadays I do occasionally see patients for half a day but absolutely no more than that."

The final blow came in November 2007 when Hugo had to fire three people in one week. Hugo believed the firings were legitimate, but the workforce went on strike. "There was a communication breakdown. Since then, we've done a lot on labor relations and capacity building, but I'm not trained for this. I'm an epidemiologist

---

10 Anglo-American is a global diversified mining group with headquarters in London, UK.

who had to climb a steep learning curve to learn how to run an organization. We had created all these new jobs but now we had to put in place processes to support those jobs."

A key step came when Hugo hired Mariette Slabbert, previously CEO of a smaller hospital in Pretoria, to be Ndlovu's chief operating officer. Hugo interviewed her in May 2008, and instantly knew he had found the right person. She joined Ndlovu in June 2008.

Mariette thoroughly enjoyed her new job. "This is a dream job for me. It's amazing to have an opportunity to step in Hugo's footsteps." As she familiarized herself with Ndlovu, she said, "The four words I heard a lot were fun, funky, holistic, and dynamic." Mariette started off by identifying organizational processes that needed streamlining. "I prepared a toolkit for the clinic, which covers VCT, wellness, and ARV, and I will do the same for other programs. I'm making standardized toolkits for the counselors, which will help them to manage their sessions and to build their confidence, and to ensure that they don't miss anything."

Hugo's vision was becoming clearer. Part of the management team needed for the expansion was in place, and now that Hugo was no longer involved in day-to-day operations he could dedicate himself to realizing his grand vision.

The expansion plan

The idea of replicating the success he had achieved with Ndlovu and Elandsdoorn had been germinating in Hugo's mind for some time, but a chance visit by the Dutch ambassador in October 2007 turned out to be a catalyst. "They were very impressed with what they saw. The ambassador took me to my office on Saturday morning and said 'tell me your dream.'" That got Hugo to start articulating his dream on paper, as the ambassador had hinted that he was interested in funding Ndlovu. Around that time, a friend of a friend who had built an investment bank was looking for work. He helped Hugo to draft a strategic plan and a 40-week change plan, an experience Hugo remembers fondly: "I really enjoyed the process of writing and reflecting. That is one of the biggest challenges of operating in the nonprofit world. Donors need to understand that time for reflection also needs to be paid, otherwise you keep drifting further from your goals." That strategic plan (see Exhibits 8 through 12) was the foundation for the grant proposal that Hugo wrote for the Dutch government. "Writing the proposal was a very useful exercise," Hugo commented, "It will allow us to replicate the Ndlovu model and create a top layer to coordinate across multiple locations."

Hugo was proud recounting the latest turn of events: "Apparently a retired investment banker somewhere wanted to give something back to the community by starting a clinic. After two years the Ministry of Health finally said, 'Okay, but follow Tempelman's model.' I hadn't heard anything about this until very recently. He and I had a great conversation but I don't have capacity now to take this on. Six months from now it would be easy, it is a great project, but I'm afraid of delivering a failure." That fear of failure did not stop Hugo: "The Memorandum of Understanding MOU is almost signed, even though it's 340 km from Ndlovu; Bhubezi is 400 km away from Ndlovu, and the two new clinics are 180 km apart."

Exhibit 10 shows the proposed organization chart for the Ndlovu Care Group, the new coordinating superstructure while Exhibit 11 shows the proposed chart for an individual local Ndlovu Care Group such as the Ndlovu Care Group Elandsdoorn, the Bhubezi clinic located in Lillydale, or other future sites. Further expansion would come from satellite locations, owned and operated by others but drawing on the Ndlovu Care Group's management expertise. Mariette anticipates opening one new location and two satellite locations per year.

Hugo has no illusions about these changes: "I told everyone that the plan would not cost jobs and could in fact help people with their careers, but I also know that not everyone will fit in." When asked where the greatest challenges will lie, Hugo and Mariette gave slightly different answers. Hugo said, "The biggest challenge is finding people in the local community with the same level of passion as you have." Mariette countered, "The biggest challenge will be retention because it takes a lot of time to train people."

Mariette was confident that they would be able to balance between letting individual sites be autonomous and sharing best practices across locations. "Our second location is also working very well; the people there are very enthusiastic. For instance, they have put an appointment system in place in Bhubezi. We will do that here too. I plan to introduce some competition between locations."

After the phone call

As the initial euphoria from the Dutch embassy's phone call began to wear off, Hugo's mind turned to the challenges ahead. Many pieces of his dream were beginning to fall in place, some slowly, others a little faster than he would have liked. There was no denying the tremendous opportunity provided by this long-term funding, but Hugo was also keenly aware that mismanaging the expansion could not only mean a missed opportunity, it could even destroy everything he had built. Leaving things the way they were was not an option for Hugo, the potential was too great. Moreover, Hugo did not have a history of shying away from risks, although he saw it differently: "I'm not afraid to put things in place, but I've hardly taken any risks. I try to foresee problems before making a decision." Hugo elaborated: "No projects have failed because we always started from community needs. Of course, we sometimes have problems. For instance, the bakery was losing money for a while, but we brought in a new manager who turned it around. Or take the sports program—at first it was not self-sustaining, so we moved it under HIV education and it is now well-funded. Changes sometime take longer than expected, but you have to change. If you stand still, you decline."

Hugo knew that expanding Ndlovu meant amplifying these challenges. And although he was optimistic and excited, he couldn't help wondering, "What am I forgetting? What will the challenges be? What can I do to reduce the risk?"

EXHIBIT 1
Hugo and Liesje Tempelman

Source: http://www.helpelandsdoorn.com/pageID_3217536.html, last accessed October 28, 2010.

EXHIBIT 2
Map of South Africa, showing Elandsdoorn

Lillydale

Elandsdoorn

EXHIBIT 3
Photos of Elandsdoorn and Ndlovu

Photo 1: Sample billboard in Elandsdoorn.

Photo 2: Another sample billboard in Elandsdoorn.

Photo 3: The parking area at the Ndlovu Medical Center.

Photo 4: Makeshift wheelchairs at the entrance to the Ndlovu Medical Center.

Photo 5: The Ndlovu Medical Center has its own fueling station.

Photo 6: Restaurant and car wash outside the Ndlovu Medical Center.

EXHIBIT 4
Balance sheet for Ndlovu Medical Trust, 2008[11]

	NOTE	2008 ZAR	2008 $
NDLOVU MEDICAL TRUST BALANCE SHEET AT			
29 FEBRUARY 2008			
ASSETS			
NET CURRENT ASSETS		4 436 950	626 688
TOTAL ASSETS		4 436 950	626 688
CAPITAL AND LIABILITIES			
CAPITAL		3 835 638	541 757
Ndlovu AIDS Awareness Program		2 274 188	321 213
Colombine maternity clinic		(176 219)	(24 890)
Highly Active Anti-Retroviral Treatment		(151 004)	(21 328)
Ndlovu Nutritional Unit		(208 872)	(29 502)
NMT TB Project		239 857	33 878
Management Ndlovu Group		704 503	99 506
Ngwenya Community Dental Program		(424 850)	60 007
Bhubezi Autonomous Treatment Center		1 578 035	222 886
LIABILITIES		601 312	84 931
TOTAL CAPITAL AND LIABILITIES		4 436 950	626 683

11 Consolidated statements are not available for years prior to 2008.

EXHIBIT 5
Income statement for Ndlovu Medical Trust, 2008[12]

NDLOVU MEDICAL TRUST INCOME STATEMENT AT 29 FEBRUARY 2008		
	2008 ZAR	2008 $
INCOME	**3 834 863**	**541 647**
Admin and Labou	1 000 249	141 278
Donations	189 425	26 755
Sunday Income	2 383 191	336 609
Ward Fees	99 170	14 007
Interest Received	162 828	22 998
EXPENSES	**26 376 112**	**3 725 440**
Accounting	28 707	4 055
Accommodation	8 820	1 246
Administration	624 390	88 191
Advertising	51 826	7 320
Bank Charges	24 977	3 528
Labour	1 209 858	170 884
Building Expenses	687 463	97 099
Consultation and medication	168 069	23 739
Computer Expenses	14 650	2 069
Counselling	97 693	13 798
Cleaning	73 475	10 378
Development	507 696	71 708
Electricity and water	88 375	12 482
Events & Promotion	612 667	86 535
Food Expenses	381 731	53 917
Strategic Planning	78 210	11 047
Interest paid	15 637	2 209
Insurance and Licences	48 602	6 865
Repairs, Maintenance and assets	445 237	62 887
Rent Paid	53 800	7 599
Laboratory Purchases	2 978 865	420 744
Leasing	16 097	2 274
Legal Fees	4 800	678
Lines	5 821	822
Medical Purchases	5 458 342	770 952
Monitoring and Evaluations	12 600	1 780
Motor vehicle Expenses	21 630	3 055
Telephone and postage	231 442	44 133
Travel and transport expenses	1 541 158	217 678
Training	462 843	65 373
Salaries and Wages	9 563 421	1 350 766
Staff Welfare	99 618	14 070
Security	97 254	13 376
Services	239 090	33 770
Subscription	114 515	16 174
Stationery and Printing	306 733	43 324
NET (SHORTAGE)/SURPLUS FOR THE YEAR	**(22 541 249)**	**(3 183 792)**
FUNDED BY : DONATIONS RECEIVED	23 335 490	3 295 973

12 Consolidated statements are not available for years prior to 2008.

EXHIBIT 6
Chronology of Ndlovu's development[13]

1994   Start and opening of Ndlovu Medical Centre a township based community general practice
1996   Opening 1st Ndlovu Nutritional Unit in Elandsdoorn
1997   Start Ndlovu Tuberculosis Program in cooperation with Provincial and National Dep. of Health
1998   Start Ndlovu Aids Awareness Program, NAAP
1999   Opening Ndlovu Maternity Clinic (24-hours)
1999   Opening of the Bakery in Elandsdoorn
2001   Opening 2nd Ndlovu Nutritional Unit and 1st water tap
2001   Expansion of Ndlovu Tuberculosis Program with defaulter-tracing
2001   Start Ndlovu Information Technology Training
2002   Opening 3rd Ndlovu Nutritional Unit
2003   Start of Dental Program under the name Ngwenya Comm. Dental Care Program (NCDCP-program)
2003   Expansion of Ndlovu Tuberculosis Program with contact tracing and community TB
2003   Start of Ndlovu Highly Active Anti-Retroviral Therapy (HAART-program)
2003   Start of Prevention of Mother To Child Transmission of HIV (PMTCT-program)
2003   Start Waste Care Program Elandsdoorn
2004   Opening 4th Ndlovu Nutritional Unit
2004   Start of mobile HAART project for farm workers
2004   Opening Sport Grounds in cooperation with the Johan Cruijff Foundation
2005   Start of a community Voluntary Counseling and Testing program (VCT-program)
2005   Start Nappy Factory Elandsdoorn
2006   Start of Orphans & Vulnerable Children Program (OVC-Program)
2007   Opening of 1st ATC satellite clinic at Vaalwater (Waterberg Welfare Society)
2007   Opening of Bhubezi, Lillydale

---

13 Source: "Strategic Plan Ndlovu: The Concept for Community Care", draft version 05-22-2008.

EXHIBIT 7
Selected facts about Ndlovu Care Group

- Number of patients seen per year at the clinic in Elandsdoorn: 11,000–12,000
- HIV patients: 11,000 known patients in the ARV program, of which 5,900 initiated on treatment, of which 3,950 currently on ARVs; 3-year retention rate of over 78%
- Maternity clinic: 350 deliveries per year
- Ndlovu Child Care Program (NCCP): 3,500 children enrolled
- Within NCCP:
  - 25–30 children enrolled at any point in time in the Ndlovu Nutritional Units, average stay 3 months
  - 160 children enrolled in the three participating pre-schools
- Ndlovu Aids Awareness Program (NAAP): worked with two farms, one was handed over to government care, the other still under NAAP with approximately 60 patients on treatment; after one year the farm's HR manager noticed a reduction of sick leave and no more HIV-related deaths

EXHIBIT 8
Excerpts from the strategic plan[14]

The vision statement of the NCG is "Empowering towards Wellness".

NCG mission: To empower communities towards Health, Childcare, and Community Development in South Africa in cooperation with other Non Governmental Organisations, Corporates, and relevant Government Departments. The NCG objective is to advance rural communities, and scale up services through the NCG Rural Advancement Program (RAP).

NCG developed an applicable and replicable Care Model for scaling up services in communities through:

14 The material here is taken from "Strategic Plan Ndlovu Care Group: The Model for Rural Community Health & Community Care Services", pp. 4–5, 17-10-2009, available online, and is largely identical to that from the earlier draft strategic plan dated 05-22-2008 that is referenced elsewhere in this case.

- Local capacity building for sustained community development and improved standard of living in rural areas

- Information, awareness, and education on health related issues to promote behaviour change, early care seeking behaviour and prevent more HIV infections

- Affordable and integrated Primary Health Care (PHC), Malaria, TB and HIV/AIDS Care to promote personal wellbeing and community health in general

- Childcare Programs to address the needs and life skills of Orphans and other Vulnerable Children (OVC)

- Research, Monitoring & Evaluation to ensure evidence based interventions and improved outcomes

- Replicating the NCG Model within the public sector and other NGO's to assist in the upliftment of health and community systems across Southern Africa.

NCG values

- Fun

- Funky

- Holistic

- Dynamic

- Innovative

EXHIBIT 9
Three-year plan for Ndlovu's expansion[15]

Step	Description	Period
	CONSOLIDATION STAGE	
1	Implement new organizational structure and appoint good management	from 2008 to mid 2009
2	Implementation of Management Cycle	from 2009
	PREPARATION	
3	Research for third Ndlovu Care Group	2009 – mid 2009
4	Get in touch with local community/ governmental organizations	mid 2009 – end 2009

15 Source: "Strategic Plan Ndlovu: The Concept for Community Care", version 05-22-2008.

Step	Description	Period
5	Find sponsor for third Ndlovu Care Group	mid 2009 – end 2009
6	Create master plan for implementation and construction	mid 2009 – end 2009
	EXPANSION	
8	Expand activities in Elandsdoorn and Lillydale	from 2008 onwards
9	Construct Ndlovu Care Group 3	from 2010
10	Appoint and train personnel for Ndlovu Care Group 3	from 2010
11	Opening Ndlovu Care Group 3	Q4 2010

EXHIBIT 10
Proposed organization chart for Ndlovu Care Group[16]

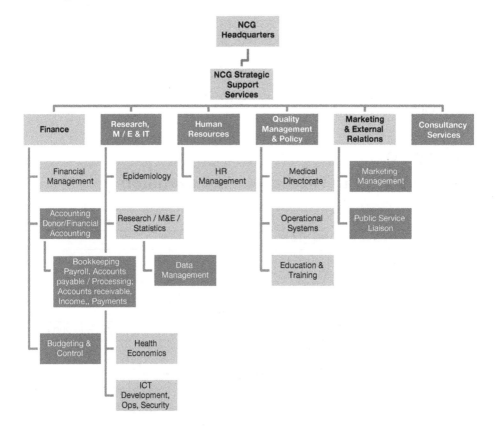

16 Source: Dr Hugo Tempelman, July 2008.

EXHIBIT 11
Proposed organization chart for a local Ndlovu Care Group[17]

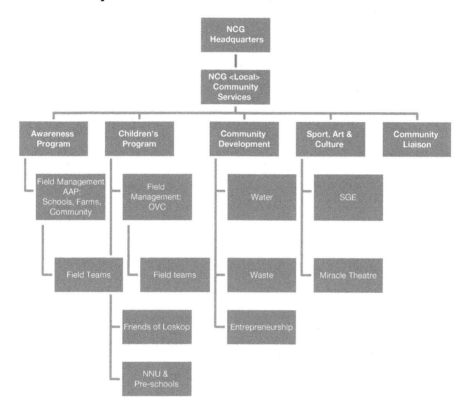

17 Source: Dr Hugo Tempelman, July 2008.

EXHIBIT 12
SWOT analysis from the strategic plan[18]

	Strengths	Weakness
Staff	Competent team Dynamic Innovative Open-minded Visionary leadership Dedicated Fun approach Expertise	Difficult to attract & retain staff Limited synergy & referral amongst departments Training & Coaching of local staff Succession planning
Financial	Spread risk through multiple funders Good financial controls	Limited government partnership – accreditation at Ndlovu Not direct PEPFAR sponsorship
Facilities	1st world facilities NCGs situated in rural areas	Reaching capacity
Marketing	Strong positive image Good reputation National Recognition: Impumelelo & CPSI NCG brand appreciated by competitors Credibility	Limited branding Weak internal communication No newsletter Professionalise all programs
Delivery	Product leadership Operational excellence Hi-tech Convenient Community involvement	Operational benchmarking – private sector customer service Infection control

18 The material here is taken from "Strategic Plan Ndlovu Care Group: The Model for Rural Community Health & Community Care Services", pp. 18–19, 17-10-2009, available online, and is largely identical to that from the strategic plan dated 5-8-2008 that is referenced elsewhere in this case.

	Strengths	**Weakness**
Product	Differentiated Holistic approach High Quality Reproducible Good outcomes	Private practice declining Not documented Cost studies

	Opportunities	**Threats**
Political	Better relationship with Government Transfer of NCG chronic care model to NDoH More funding PPP	BEE Demarcation
Economic	Popularity of HIV/AIDS with donors Export to Africa	High interest rates Global economy
Social	Operate in rural areas	Extreme poverty Trend towards alternative medicine AIDS prevalence Child headed households Poor education & health infrastructure
Technology	New technology in health	Cost

CASE 2

wellcome

Growth of a social franchise (2006–2012)

Magdalena Kloibhofer and Karin Kreutzer

wellcome offers support to families in the first weeks after a baby is born. Surprisingly, previously there was no service available to families in this new and often overwhelming situation of beginning parenthood. Statistics show that especially in those weeks mothers are in danger of showing symptoms of burn-out or postpartum depression due to exhaustion. wellcome sends volunteers to help mothers in their homes and fulfill tasks such as taking care of the baby or siblings and help in the household.

wellcome has realised an impressive growth since its foundation in 2006 and their teams are now present in almost every city in Germany. That was possible thanks to the social franchising strategy wellcome had developed, where existing social service providers serve as franchisees who locally coordinate and supervise the volunteers' work.

Teaching objectives

Students should:

- Get to know a good example of a social enterprise operating in a niche of the German social system

- Understand a social franchise strategy for growth

- Gain the ability to develop scaling strategies for social enterprises and to critically evaluate those in terms of their economic and social mission implications

Founding a social enterprise

Rose had planned her pregnancy in detail. As the director of a family service centre she felt well prepared for everything that was ahead of her. Since she was a professional expert and considered herself "well-organised" she was very much looking forward to her little baby daughter. However, after a long and difficult birth Rose felt like she had "landed on a different planet". Still exhausted from birth, she found herself confronted with sleepless nights, a baby crying for hours, tons of dirty laundry, an empty fridge and she felt her last shower was days ago. Her husband had to go back to work very soon and her family lived far away. Only years later, she realised that she might have shown symptoms of a postpartum depression—a disease that hits up to 20% of mothers (and, more rarely, also fathers). Research suggests that postpartum depressions are caused by genetic disposition and changes in women's hormones after giving birth, but that sleep deprivation and missing social support play an important role as well.

"Why is nobody here to help me?" Rose asked herself. As a professional in the area of family services, she contacted local family help organisations, only to find out that she was "too normal" to qualify for support, as she did not have any real financial or psychological problems, or extraordinary circumstances such as twins or triplets. She learned that there was no official service offered by any of the numerous social organisations directed to mothers in a situation such as her own.

Back to work, Rose decided to break the silence and speak openly about the feelings of isolation and despair she had experienced after birth—a time she had expected to be the happiest in her life. That was not easy; she was ashamed of her situation particularly because she had always regarded herself as a strong and hands-on woman. "But then", she recalls, "something special happened: other mothers also shared their stories which resembled mine". Hearing so many stories of isolation, exhaustion, and despair disturbed her, not only personally but also professionally. As an expert in the area of family services, she could not believe that there was no systematic support offer for families in the first weeks after a baby is born. That was a turning point in her life and the idea of wellcome was born.

The *leitmotiv* for starting wellcome was to create a system of support for all families irrespective of their income situation, their educational background, and their health situation. She wanted to offer support to those in need of help—anyone with a newborn child without help from the family or neighbours.

Rose has always been a leader personality with a lot of energy and spirit. She pursued a career along with a family, something unusual in her generation in which most mothers worked part-time, if at all. Holding a university degree in social work, she soon achieved a leading position in a family service centre which she decided to carry on after the birth of her daughter and, later, her twins.

In 2000, she started a first child-bed service in the two Protestant family centres in Hamburg she was managing by then. The idea felt right, but something was going wrong. She did not reach enough families, but the ones she could offer support to were all excited about the programme. Then she decided to apply to the competition "StartSocial" by McKinsey in 2002.

Out of 4,000 applications in the competition, her idea was selected among the winners and she received pro bono consulting. At that time, the common mindset was that business and social arenas were antagonistic worlds. As a trained social worker, the approach of the consultants was new to her and she felt she learned a lot from the questions they were asking. For example, the traditional logic in the social sector was that first you need funding and then you can start your project. However, the consultants told her to first think about aspects like the team, public relations, quality management, and a scaling-up strategy. The name and brand of "wellcome" was born, and important modifications to the concept put the project on a promising path. After the StartSocial consulting phase, Rose convinced McKinsey to continue to mentor her with monthly feedback meetings and individual coaching for about three years.

During that phase, the first spin-off projects were started in other cities and a first legal entity for the innovative "social franchise" was established in 2006 as a charitable, tax-exempt limited liability company (gGmbH) under full ownership of the local church district that also ran the family education centres managed by Rose. The decision for this legal form was based on the idea that wellcome should be run like a business, and not, e.g. a self-help initiative, which would have called for more participatory structures such as those of an association.

wellcome started to gain ground and spread further. However, the initial ownership arrangement proved to be holding back development. The church district was a local/regional institution, while some wellcome teams had started in other cities by then and there were nation-wide ambitions for the project already in 2006. Rose's responsibilities for running a growing number of family education centres collided more and more with her function as executive director of wellcome gGmbH. She was also traveling a lot for wellcome and therefore could often not participate in regular church meetings. Finally, in 2009, there was a sharp increase in media attention as Rose was awarded several prestigious recognitions, and all of a sudden she was well-known and, for instance, invited to high-level events where none of her direct superiors in the church hierarchy would be present. So at some point, a decision had to be taken: Should she hire a new executive to run the gGmbH, potentially risking stagnant development of the project, or should she part from her long-time employer and take the scale-up of wellcome into her very own hands? Rose boldly decided to quit her former position and take over 100% ownership of wellcome, then moved the team to downtown Hamburg and finally started a period of very strong growth. "It was just great to have that entrepreneurial freedom at last", she recalls.

Helping young families in Germany

The German welfare system is largely based on public social insurance funds covering pensions, health, unemployment and accident insurances. These insurance associations perform quasi-public functions and contributing to the funds is mandatory and usually directly deducted from an employee's payroll (and is sometimes additionally matched with employer and/or government contributions). A few large players offer the majority of social services: Workers Welfare Services (AWO), Caritas, Diakonie and the Red Cross. They operate hospitals, kindergartens, and homes for the elderly and disabled. With over 10,000 subsidiaries and local organisations, the welfare associations serve children, youth, elderly, disabled, families, migrants, and people facing situations of social distress. They receive 90% of their funding directly from the state or social insurances. This system has often been criticised for its large bureaucracy, inefficiency and inflexibility.

As Rose's personal story shows, among the vast arrays of services by insurance and welfare associations, there are no services available to "normal", middle-class mothers in the intense period after birth. However, the need for systematic help for families with small babies is there, and seems to be growing. Rose says, "Unlike two decades ago, much fewer young families live close to their parents and can rely on a tight local network of support." Until the beginning of the 20th century, women of the family and the neighbourhood took intensive care of a mother for the first six weeks after birth, e.g. cooking meals, looking after siblings and the household. Even today, in some indigenous communities mothers are supposed to lie in bed and be "pampered" by others for the first weeks. While knowledge about child care was traditionally transferred from generation to generation, today young mothers and fathers often do not have grandparents or other family members who live around the corner to offer advice and support. "It takes a village to raise a child" is an old African proverb, emphasising that raising children is actually too big a task to be just performed in a single family (let alone by a single mother or father) but that the whole community should ideally contribute.

In Germany, around 660,000 babies are born every year. Out of those, 20–25% are considered as "excessive criers", which means the baby cries at least on three days a week for more than three hours. Between 25 and 80% of the mothers suffer from "babyblues" in child-bed, and 10–20% of the mothers and even 4% of the fathers suffer from symptoms of postpartum depression. Physical challenges in the first weeks after birth include after-pains, the healing of birth-related wounds, problems with breastfeeding, and symptoms related to the quick change of hormones after giving birth. Furthermore, the number of twins and triplets is rising.

To help any mother in the first weeks after a baby is born, Rose founded wellcome. The mission of the organisation reads as follows: "We want to strengthen young families, to foster a healthy growing-up of children. We help families with small children in their everyday life through practical neighbourhood support if family and friends cannot provide this—that is our mission. Therefore, we build and support local teams of volunteers in cooperation with local welfare associations."

The brand "wellcome" stands for "wellness" and "welcome" for children and families; or, in short, "well come" in the sense of arriving safely.

wellcome's services

Young mothers (and fathers) in need of help can find out about wellcome from various sources, for example, through advice from their midwife, a poster at their childrens' physicians or a flyer at the family service centre that had offered their birth preparation courses. Once they get in touch with the local wellcome coordinator at a family service institution, she will conduct a first interview with the mother or family to explore their needs including a standardised questionnaire, will then match them with one of the volunteers of the local team and arrange a first talk or meeting. She will then continue to be available for both parties, family and volunteer, for advice if problems occur. Over the next few months,, the volunteer will visit the family about once or twice a week for a few hours and offer support in child care such as taking over the new-born so the mother can have a shower or some sleep, playing with the older kids, or even occasionally just doing some grocery shopping or helping in the household if she likes to, which is not core to the wellcome volunteer service. On average, the volunteer supports the family for 2–3 months within the first year after birth, as wellcome limits the service to the time before the child's first birthday. At the end of such a "deployment" there will be a final meeting between the family and the coordinator, also supported by a standardised questionnaire to ensure appropriate documentation and support quality management.

If there is no other network that can offer this support, the volunteer creates invaluable breaks and relief for parents who have newly arrived in a situation where the new-born needs their constant attention and frequently leaves them guessing what it might need, and frustrated at not being able to calm it down when crying or distressed—while at the same time keeping them from a good night's sleep for weeks or months at a time. Without any help in such a situation, on-going

exhaustion and frustration can even lead to anger and threaten or damage the relationship between the mother and her child.

> When my wellcome angel comes, I go have a shower and then I sleep,
> sleep, sleep… This is so important. Sleep deprivation is like torture, all
> energy is totally gone and that's not good for the mother and the child
> (Voice of a mother)

As the service is open to all and not a welfare offering only for those in financial
need, the families pay a contribution to the cost of the programme. The standard
fee of 5 euros per hour of volunteer visit is, however, very affordable, and can easily
be discounted without having to actually prove financial distress or to go through
any inconvenient bureaucracy. The small payment ensures that well-educated
and middle-class families also feel comfortable with wellcome's service instead of
feeling "stigmatised" as relying on "welfare entitlements". Furthermore, additional
value is attached to the help received in the perception of the recipients, as it is not
for free.

Building a social franchise

Thinking about the appropriate legal form for wellcome and a promising scaling
strategy, to Rose it was clear from the start that the idea would be spreading out
via a growing number of local teams that work independently. However, she soon
realised that there needed to be some form of control over how these partners
implement the concept and use the corporate identity to build a common brand
umbrella, and keep a common reputation for high-quality work. The idea of a social
franchise was born: "Wow, what we need is a franchise, almost like McDonald's",
she realised, at a time when there were no other social franchises yet in the market.

As wellcome is filling a niche in the "market" for family services, it is crucial
that each and every local team is deeply embedded in the network of institutions
offering other education, counselling, or support. Therefore, only family support
service institutions that are well-connected with other local offerings can become
a wellcome-franchisee. This idea of partnering with the subsidiaries of the large
established welfare associations in Germany enabled Rose to draw on their specific
local expertise, their network and their infrastructure (e.g. office space). This is also
important, as the local franchisee organisation must be able to direct families in
need of other help or in severe situations to competent local partners or doctors.

However, the idea of "social franchising" and charging prices for social services
was revolutionary and required a fundamental culture change in most franchisee
institutions. Especially at the beginning, Rose very often had a hard time explaining
her system, which was perceived as a "business solution" to a social problem. Social
workers in the family centres were worried that implementing Rose's wellcome

service would necessarily lead to increased "managerialism" and a marketisation of social services. Her professional background as exective director of two family service centres run by the Protestant welfare association Diakonie helped her enormously in that period. At least, she knew how welfare organisations worked and was perceived as an "insider who knows what she is talking about".

To start a wellcome-team, the franchisee institution has to fund a team coordinator with adequate professional experience who can dedicate a capacity of 5 hours per week to the programme in terms of managing and coaching the team of volunteers as well as matching and counselling the beneficiary families. They also have to pay an annual franchise fee. The franchise system was very different from common procedures in the social sector, where specific knowledge or programmes are typically spread by offering paid training courses, then allowing the newly trained and licenced individuals to use their knowledge freely afterwards, not constrained by franchise agreements, but also without any on-going support.

During a standardised foundation process wellcome's national coordinator visits a new institution several times and supports the launch of the programme. wellcome provides each team with an array of standard operating procedures, guidelines, forms, and templates which serve as the basis of their work. The future volunteer coordinator (employed by the family support institution) receives intensive training organised by wellcome. The franchisee also benefits from a strong brand and public relations efforts by Rose and the gGmbH along with standardised marketing materials for the local site.

Continuous exchange is ensured by a national coordinator, who also visits each franchisee institution for an annual evaluation meeting; regular gatherings are mandatory for all team coordinators in the same German state, and there are nationwide meetings of all state coordinators.

Asked about the difference between a conventional, commercial franchise operation and a social franchise, wellcome staff point out how the cooperation between the institutions is in fact not defined by the actual franchising contract that specifies the rights and duties of all parties, but by a shared mission and trusting partnership. wellcome does not make use of possibilities such as charging contract violation fees or even bringing contract partners to court if there are deviations or disagreements, but will by policy always interact in a cooperative way. As its franchisees are not in the network to generate profit but offer an additional service, they cannot simply be coerced into compliance to franchise rules by sanctions that would also quickly erode the basis of trust and shared goodwill of the cooperation. Therefore, Rose and her team emphasise how crucial the selection of appropriate partners is. She is convinced that "less is more" and carefully examines her franchisees before engaging into contractual relations. Only those institutions and individuals that convincingly share the mission and the idea behind wellcome will be included. wellcome seems very successful in selecting the "right" partners as hardly any franchising relationships have had to be terminated so far. In addition to the selection process, wellcome puts particular emphasis on creating and maintaining relations of trust and information-sharing from the beginning.

If there are changes or directions the team at the central gGmbH wants to roll out through the network, therefore, this can only be done by convincing and persistent communication, taking into account the perspective and concerns of the franchisees.

Human resources and leadership

Human resources

In 2009, wellcome gGmbH employs 10 women in the central office in Hamburg, most of them in part-time positions, and the franchise network comprises 127 local team coordinators across 12 German states. The local coordinators are local employees of the welfare associations (franchisees) and work approximately 5 hours a week to run their wellcome team. They are typically paid female social workers with expertise in family work. Apart from being responsible for local public relations, their main tasks are to consult the families, assign volunteers, mediate between families and volunteers, and to recruit and supervise the local volunteers. Five regional coordinators work approximately 25 hours a week. They support the team leaders and help ensure a constant flow of information between local teams and the headquarters in Hamburg.

As wellcome's support model heavily relies on the work of volunteers, successful recruiting, training, coordination and retention of volunteers is crucial. Each team coordinator is working with about 15 to 20 volunteers who mostly know each other personally and also support each other through peer-coaching in meetings. If a group grows larger, wellcome requires them to split into separate groups.

Most volunteers working for wellcome are women; 54% of them are older than 50 years. wellcome aims at offering a modern form of volunteering that is a flexible and temporary engagement in the volunteers' direct surroundings. The numbers prove that this concept works and taps into a completely new potential for community volunteering: over 50% of wellcome's volunteers volunteer for the first time and 75% are not engaged in any other volunteer activity. wellcome recruits its volunteers through articles in local newspapers and word-of-mouth. Most volunteers' motivation is to work with babies and small children. Almost all are mothers themselves and very well remember the challenges of a beginning motherhood.

One key insight Rose had gained during the intensive consulting and coaching through McKinsey at the very beginning was about how to deal with volunteers. Unlike her first concept in piloting the service, wellcome volunteers do not get any official training before they start. wellcome's philosophy is to let volunteers support the families just like a family member or neighbour would do—naturally. A local wellcome coordinator offers supervision and coaching to the volunteers whenever needed throughout the process. The approach to volunteer coordination that wellcome has chosen is also very efficient, as it combines the engagement of volunteers with limited but effective coordination and coaching by qualified professionals, who are paid for their work. As a result, they can ensure high quality services with a limited requirement of paid hours. The "package" they offer to potential volunteers (temporary engagement with children which is professionally supervised) seems to be so attractive that they are currently not facing any recruitment problems.

Leadership

Rose always considered herself a "leadership personality" and after founding the first wellcome teams in 2002, she very soon realised that she had nationwide ambitions for this. Founding, leading and growing wellcome posed particular challenges for her. With a background in social work, a lot of the business thinking and business talk of the consultants she was working with such as McKinsey and Bain was new to her. However, she found the idea of combining business strategies to achieve social impact intuitively appealing. Bridging the gap between the worlds of business and social work was one of her core goals, but also among her core challenges having to bring together actors from those still sometimes quite different arenas and more than 1,500 volunteers. For Rose, successful leadership is mainly about uniting her growing decentralised franchise organisation, bridging such different types of actors and forging a common spirit of mutual trust and belonging. With increased growth and less personal interaction with all actors involved, systems and procedures need to take over some of the functions of personal leadership in this regard, and Rose increasingly relied on her team for taking over day-to-day coordination of the programmes. Still, she herself and her Deputy Director Regine, in charge of public relations and fundraising, are often torn between daily responsibilities of running wellcome and strategically more important tasks.

Another challenge coming with growth is to lead a growing team of staff while preserving the culture that all team members had come to cherish. Rose had always maintained an open-door policy and established a participative leadership style in interacting with her mainly female colleagues, most of whom work on a part-time basis and whose needs in balancing work and child care are taken into account by flexible working hours and a working culture taking individual allocation of working time and optional home-office hours as a given. At meetings and in discussions, every voice is heard and every idea is welcome, and Rose is not the type of leader who has a hard time admitting her own mistakes or has a need to show off "superhuman" performance or self-sacrifice for the organisation. While she emphasises that people at wellcome do not mix private and professional life and relations to a great extent, a friendly and collegial atmosphere has been established and all staff are dedicated to the common mission of supporting young families. With a team that is used to steady growth, fast-paced change and/or steep increases in work requirements could challenge or overstrain the stable and familial culture.

Early on, Rose had realised that political support was crucial for making her endeavour work. Therefore, she and Regine are highly engaged with constant lobby work with politicians to ensure the daily needs of young families get the public visibility and support they deserve and that is needed to successfully run and grow wellcome. In 2007, German Chancellor Angela Merkel took on patronage of well-come nationwide, and the team has been able to secure regional patronage by the respective State Minister of Social Affairs in all states where wellcome is active. Pres-tigious awards supported the increasing national profile of Rose as a well-known player with a proven approach: in 2007, Rose was selected as a "Social Entrepreneur of the Year" by the Schwab Foundation and in 2008, she was chosen as an Ashoka Fellow by Ashoka Germany—both among the most important global support net-works for social entrepreneurs. In 2009, she received the German National Cross of Merit for her achievements.

Financing wellcome

In 2009, the financing of wellcome is still a challenge. In terms of earned revenues, every franchisee organisation pays an annual fee of 250 euros for the brand, net-work, operations manual, coaching and other services by the wellcome gGmbH. One main corporate partner supports with funding and also facilitating access to children's doctors via their distribution network, and a Childhood Foundation also contributes a significant amount; however, both commitments are not long-term. In five German states, regional wellcome coordinators have been established who are funded by the respective state Ministry of Social Affairs, which also pay a kind of "franchise fee" of 5,000 euros per year for each coordinating office.

Instead of traditional loan or equity-funded investments, wellcome's growth plans rest on a five-year scale-up grant by the German Auridis Foundation run-ning from January 2009 until the end of 2013. Reflecting on the particular situa-tion of social enterprises as filling less-profitable market niches, Rose is sceptical of a growing trend of impact investing into social start-ups before they have been established in the market, and she is certain that "If I had to repay such debt, I would need to sit as a supermarket cashier to do so". She also cherishes the freedom of entrepreneurial decision-making in strict alignment with her mission of helping young families, which she does not have to compromise to serve debt repayments or cater to shareholder interests.

Overall, the share of earned revenues in terms of franchise fees in 2009 does not seem to really qualify the "Social Enterprise" as a self-sustainable operation with its unstable mix of franchise fees, corporate partnership support, public funding and a dominating portion of grants and private donations (Exhibit 5). A pro bono consulting project delivered by Bain at year's end of 2009 resulted in the following recommendations for financial sustainability of wellcome's core programme "Prac-tical Support":

1. Increasing the number of teams to approaching 500 by 2015

2. Significantly increasing the franchise fee from 2011

Further growth in team numbers seems necessary to increase reliable income, and a raise of the franchise fee has been discussed controversially in the team. While the support and value provided to the local teams seems to justify higher fees and the income structure almost requires this step, at the same time, it seems clear that it would be very difficult to communicate a raise to the franchisee partners, some of which might even exit the franchise.

Designing a long-term growth strategy

The first growth phase of wellcome had started around 2006 with the foundation of the gGmbH. From then to 2009, the number of wellcome teams rose from 33 in 4 states and about 320 active volunteers to 127 in 12 states with a total of about 1,550 volunteers. They served 2,444 families with an impressive 43,000 hours of volunteer work in 2009. And for Rose Volz-Schmidt, the future goal in early 2009 was clear but more modest than advised by her consultants later that year: "We *can* achieve 250 teams in Germany—it will be a lot of work, but the road is clear."

As the success of the innovative concept of the signature programme of practical support was proven and the effectiveness of its approach to combine volunteer work with a sound professional infrastructure became more and more well-known, serious strategic questions started to arise regarding the further development of wellcome.

From the realisation that some families really needed selective financial help, the Families in Distress Programme for small donations had been founded in 2009. In the years of working with young families, a lot of knowledge had been collected and there were many other ideas popping up in the team and filling up Rose's desk drawers on how families could be supported with the same empowering approach that was typical for wellcome. Meanwhile, wellcome had also become known internationally and stirred interest from family service initiatives abroad such as an Irish family service centre that was eager to found a wellcome team and spread the concept in their country to support young families there.

Rose most clearly realised the need for a fundamental strategic decision when the Secretary of State of Lower Saxony congratulated here on wellcome's success and asked her: "Wouldn't that be a great solution to help senior citizens to get support at home? It would enable them to enjoy their independent live at home much longer before needing full professional home-care or move to a home for the elderly." Rose knew immediately that it would be a perfect match to apply the wellcome system to this field. She could well build a second franchise with her experience from the first, and significantly broaden the basis of her franchise fees without too much investment. But, was this the right strategy for wellcome?

Rose had to face the question of whether wellcome should continue to focus on growing and spreading its signature programme, or diversify further. And if so, what ways of diversification would fit the company? Should wellcome continue to grow by developing new ways of family support, or rather seize the opportunity to replicate its proven system for senior citizens?

ANNEX
EXHIBIT 1
wellcome timeline 2002–2009

Year	Key developments
2002	First pilot teams in Hamburg area StartSocial award Development of wellcome brand
2004	Expansion in Hamburg and State of Schleswig-Holstein
2006	Further awards Start of expansion into State of Lower Saxony Founding of wellcome gGmbH
2007	Patronage of Chancellor Angela Merkel Rose Volz-Schmidt made a fellow of the Schwab Foundation Launch of the wellcome fairy programme in Hamburg
2008	Patronage of 12 State ministers in their respective States Rose Volz-Schmidt awarded Ashoka Fellowship
2009	Rose Volz-Schmidt assumes 100% ownership of wellcome gGmbH

EXHIBIT 2
Map of wellcome teams founded in Germany up to 2009

Source: wellcome 2009.

EXHIBIT 3
wellcome growth indicators 2004–2009

Indicators / Year	2004	2005	2006	2007	2008	2009
Annual Budget (Total, EUR)	150,000	120,000	84,000	330,000	630,000	824,000
Own Revenue (EUR)*	25,000	25,000	63,000	73,000	107,000	173,000
Central Employees (FTE)	1 x 50%	2 x 50%	2 x 50%	2	2.5	6.3
Local Coordinators	26	31	33	57	87	127
Regional/State Coordinators	2	2	2	3	3	5
States w. Wellcome Teams	2	2	4	5	8	12
Wellcome Teams	26	31	33	57	87	127
Volunteers	150	220	320	617	970	1,550
Families served	240	375	560	936	1,430	2,444
Volunteer hours in families	3,500	6,950	10,500	15,000	23,300	43,000

* excluding grants and donations; including public contracts

Source: wellcome 2010.

EXHIBIT 4
Overview of the social franchise levels

Wellcome National Head Office (gGmbH)
Brand-management and quality control Centralised PR and fundraising Screening of potential franchisees, supporting foundation of new teams Development and testing of new products and services
Regional Offices at partnering welfare institutions **(mostly responsible for a state and funded by the State Ministry of Social Affairs)**
Coaching of wellcome teams within their region Building regional networks of expertise and political support Regional PR and fundraising
Local wellcome Teams at partnering welfare institutions
Team Coordinator works with volunteers to support young families Consults families and introduces them to other services/institutions where needed Local PR and fundraising

EXHIBIT 5
wellcome income composition 2009

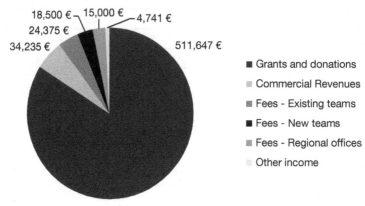

Source: wellcome 2009.

EXHIBIT 6
Income statement wellcome 2009

	Revenues	Expenses
Grants and donations	+511.647 Euro	
Operating revenues	+96.851 Euro	
Labour costs (salaries, wages plus social insurance)		−251.622 Euro
Depreciation		−6.110 Euro
General and administrative expenses		−269.100 Euro
Merchandise purchase		−33.632 Euro
Finance costs		−288 Euro
Interest earnings	+2.406 Euro	
Income tax expenses		−3.600 Euro
TOTAL	+610.904 Euro	−564.352 Euro
Annual Net Income	+56.552 Euro	

Source: wellcome 2009.

EXHIBIT 7
Revenue matrix of franchise fees / number of teams

Franchise Fee	€250	€300	€350	€400	€450	€500	€550	€600
250	62,500	75,000	87,500	100,000	112,500	125,000	137,500	150,000
300	75,000	90,000	105,000	120,000	135,000	150,000	165,000	180,000
350	87,500	105,000	122,500	140,000	157,500	175,000	192,500	210,000
400	100,000	120,000	140,000	160,000	180,000	200,000	220,000	240,000
450	112,500	135,000	157,500	180,000	202,500	225,000	247,500	270,000
500	125,000	150,000	175,000	200,000	225,000	250,000	275,000	300,000
550	137,500	165,000	192,500	220,000	247,500	275,000	302,500	330,000
600	150,000	180,000	210,000	240,000	270,000	300.000	330,000	360,000

Number of Teams

Source: wellcome 2009.

CASE 3
Madécasse
Competing with a "4x Fair Trade" business model

R. Scott Marshall, Darrell Brown, Bex Sakarias and Min Cai[1]

Lisa Johnson, Recent MBA graduate, New York City:

Amazing! I've been craving some really good chocolate and there are so many wonderful choices. Here's one that's clearly committed to endangered species. And here's one that seems to focus on the working conditions of cocoa bean farmers. And here's another that appears to be actually owned by farmers in Ghana. This one with the cool packaging says it's bean-to-bar, shade grown in Madagascar … Hmmm … Which one should I get to satisfy my craving? Well, and, be a responsible consumer?

Brett Beach, Co-Founder of Madécasse, San Francisco:

Forty-two! Wow! Unbelievable. Brett Beach, co-founder of Madécasse, counted forty-two different brands of gourmet chocolate bars arranged on the shelves of the Whole Foods Market in San Francisco. It felt great that five different types of Madécasse bars were among them. But he also couldn't help but think how difficult it is for his company's bars to stand out in that crowd.

Fast Company:

In March 2011, we named Madécasse one of the 50 Most Innovative Companies in the World for "building a chocolate company in one of the poorest countries in the world."

After his visit to Whole Foods Market, Brett Beach returned to his office and sat down at his desk. Staring at his computer screen, he watched as a series of photos appeared and disappeared. Two young boys smiling, one sporting a Spider-Man t-shirt. A group of barefoot men pushing an overloaded pick-up truck out of a hole on a muddy and rutted road. A grinning farmer in a dirty, white shirt biting into a fresh cocoa bean pod. As he watched these Malagasy faces go by, he pondered the options for his business, the business that supported these people. A fair amount of his time and attention had been spent on selecting and pursuing certifications. Certifications seemed to represent minimum requirements to play in the specialty chocolate consumer marketplace. Organic and Fair for Life certifications had been obtained. Other options included Fairtrade International and Rainforest Alliance. But the bigger concern was how to distinguish Madécasse; how to set Madécasse apart from the crowded field of gourmet chocolate bars. How was he going to convey the true value of Madécasse to consumers? Brett knew this question was at the heart of his ability to use Madécasse to help Madagascar and the Malagasy people.

Madécasse background

Lisa Johnson:

I'm really intrigued with this Madécasse brand. "Bean-to-bar"—what exactly does that mean? On the website it describes how the company works directly with the farmers and actually makes the chocolate and packaging in Madagascar. But there's no certifications … Hmmm … It seems like certifications are doing some good but they also seem to be "single-issue"—just organic or just fair trade.

Brett Beach:

Madécasse is one of the only chocolates produced bean to bar on the island of Madagascar. We start with great cocoa and end with a bar that rivals the best European chocolates. Along the way, our revolutionary approach creates 4x the economic impact of purchasing fair trade cocoa.

Good Magazine:

Madagascar can make high-quality goods … don't count Africa out.

Off the southeast coast of Africa, in the Indian Ocean, is the beautiful island of Madagascar. The world's fourth largest island, Madagascar is home to a wide range of flora and fauna, approximately 70% of which are found nowhere else on Earth.[2] The Republic of Madagascar is an agricultural powerhouse producing coffee, vanilla, sugar, cotton, cloth, pepper, cinnamon, chili, cloves as well as high quality cocoa. Despite this agricultural bounty, Madagascar is one of the poorest and least developed countries in the world. Seventy percent of the total population is rural, two-thirds of the Malagasy people live below the international poverty line ($1.25 a day), and 90% live on less than $2 a day.[3]

This widespread poverty and competition for agricultural land result in tremendous pressures on the environment. These pressures include slash-and-burn land clearing, illegal logging for precious woods or construction materials, widespread wood collection for fuel, and land clearing for mining. Deforestation and hunting have threatened many of Madagascar's endemic species, driving a number to extinction in recent decades.[4]

It was on Madagascar that Brett Beach and Tim McCollum spent two memorable years as Peace Corps volunteers. During that time, they fell in love with the country and its people. After the Peace Corps, Brett stayed in Madagascar for another four years working on development projects and a seaweed plantation. Upon returning to the United States, Brett reconnected with Tim, who was then working for American Express in sales and marketing. Recognizing the need of the local Malagasy for stable jobs and fair wages and the connection between poverty and environmental destruction, Brett and Tim discussed possibilities for creating meaningful employment for Malagasy locals and environmental, social, and economic benefits for their country. Tim recalled his Peace Corps experience:

> I left with a feeling that this [Peace Corps] is a long lasting experience that taught me a lot but I think my impact locally in Madagascar was not that great. I went from there and worked at the American Express Company for six years in sales and marketing. I got much better experience in the private sector and started to understand fundamentals of marketing and sales. As I developed that experience, I never stopped thinking about my Peace Corps experience in Madagascar and thinking "Wouldn't it be great if I can combine these two experiences? One being grassroots rural development in Madagascar, the other being commercial enterprise that's a market-driven, market-based, for-profit sort of thing?" There's tremendous value in both of those approaches but the ideal job didn't exist, meaning that there wasn't any company out there that had such an employment offer. We had to create it for ourselves, I guess you can say.

2 Wild Madagascar (2011). Retrieved from http://www.wildmadagascar.org/home.html.
3 World Bank.(2011). *World Development Indicators 2011.*Washington, DC.
4 Mittermeier, R.A.; Konstant, W.R.; Hawkins, F.; Louis, E.E.; Langrand, O.; Ratsimbazafy, J.; Rasoloarison, R.; Ganzhorn, J.U. *et al.* (2006). "Chapter 4: Conservation of Lemurs." *Lemurs of Madagascar.* Illustrated by S.D. Nash (2nd ed.). Conservation International. pp. 52-84.

Brett and Tim considered a number of options for a local Madagascar business before settling on a chocolate company. They saw three major factors to support starting the business. First, Madagascar produces some of the best cocoa in the world. They could leverage the high quality cocoa to make high quality chocolate, crucial to selling the product in the gourmet chocolate market. Second, while over 65% of the world's cocoa comes from Africa less than 1% of chocolate is made in Africa. They believed making chocolate there would create a positive social impact on local people's lives. In Brett's own words, "We provide jobs and fair wages. We help stabilize the cocoa price by partnering with the cocoa farmers. This way we keep more economic benefits within the island and create a win-win situation." The third reason was to rebuild Malagasy people's pride. The country was under French colonial rule for more than 60 years in the 20th century and a pattern of rules and behavior peculiar to the colonial system remained on the island. The Malagasy people have gone through continual political turmoil since Madagascar gained its independence from France. "By producing a branded, high-end product in Madagascar, we hope to help them regain their pride," Brett stated. With that inspiration, Brett and Tim started a small company in 2006. Brett started with Tim's support during nights and weekends until he joined the company full-time in 2008.

Headquartered in Brooklyn, New York, Madécasse strategically partners with four farmer cooperatives and a chocolate factory in Madagascar to make single-origin, tree-to-bar[5] chocolates for sale in high-end groceries and chocolate boutiques internationally. Through this partnership, the company creates benefits to locals well in excess of exporting fair trade cocoa, the typical model of "fair trade" chocolate. Since its inception, the company and its founders have received considerable attention and recognition by the media and the food industry. Exhibit 1 lists the awards and recognition received by Madécasse.

Dark side of the chocolate industry

Lisa Johnson:

Maybe I'll do a little research to learn more about the industry. I love my chocolate but I didn't realize there were so many problems with it. . . . Wow. Yikes. . . . This 2012 documentary[6] shows how child labor fuels the global cocoa industry and how these kids are handling pesticides and heavy bags of beans instead of going to school. The *New York Times* has reported on studies that show cocoa farmers live in poverty because they get only

5 Wonnacott, P. (2011). "Small Factories Take Root in Africa." *Wall Street Journal.* September 24, 2011. Retrieved from http://online.wsj.com/article/SB10001424053111190406060 4576570541250028496.html?KEYWORDS=madagascar+Madécasse.
6 Child Labour: The Dark Side of Chocolate, http://www.youtube.com/watch?v=KXW FXeIZY9g, produced by 16x9, August 13, 2012.

about 3 cents out of a $3.49 chocolate bar purchase at a US grocery store.[7] And according to the World Wildlife Fund, cocoa farming is a source of deforestation in countries like Brazil.[8]

Brett Beach

Madécasse can fundamentally change how consumption of chocolate in one place creates new economic opportunities for the people of Madagascar. Long-term farmer partnerships, in-country manufacture, and shade grown techniques support the people and the environment in a comprehensive way.

Food & Wine:

In 2010 we named Madécasse to 40 Under 40 list of people "changing the way Americans eat and drink".

The chocolate industry has been plagued by numerous issues including endemic poverty for cocoa farmers, child and forced labor in cocoa growing communities, and environmental degradation.

Farmer poverty

In the world market, cocoa is treated as a commodity and is therefore subject to considerable price fluctuations. In addition, the concentration of buyers in a few very dominant organizations gives them virtually oligopolistic power in cocoa purchasing, both at the farm and at the international level. As a result, farmers often find themselves at the mercy of the buyers and suffer from price instability.

Cocoa bean price instability, in the long term, induces periods of either under- or over-supply. As a result, farmers' decisions to invest in cocoa production depend largely on the price level prevailing in the market. A low price leads to underinvestment and, therefore, to a supply deficit in the medium term, and vice versa. Over the short term, price volatility affects farmers' husbandry patterns, such as the use of workers to harvest the beans and the use of fertilizers and pesticides. More generally, price instability is a factor that aggravates the poverty of cocoa farmers. In West Africa alone, cocoa is grown by some two million farmers, and for most of them, it remains a critical source of cash income. Worldwide, more than three million farmers depend on cocoa for a major part of their income. At times, low cocoa prices may not even cover the cost of production and thus increase farmers' poverty.

---

7 Alsever, Jennifer. (2006) "Sunday Money: Spending; Fair Prices for Farmers: Simple Idea, Complex Reality." *New York Times*, March 19, 2006: 5.

8 Edwards, Mark. "Environmental Problems in Brazil: Losing Nature at its most Extraordinary." WWF. wwf.panda.org. Retrieved April 19, 2012.

Child labor

Child labor has been a major social issue in the chocolate industry for many years. Low cocoa prices and the desire for lower labor costs drive farmers to employ children as a means to survive. Côte d'Ivoire, the leading supplier of cocoa, accounting for more than 40% of global production, is home to some of the worst offenders of child labor practices. Slave traders traffic boys ranging from the ages of 12 to 16 from their home countries and sell them to cocoa farmers, where they work on small farms across the country, harvesting cocoa beans day and night under inhumane conditions. Many use dangerous tools, face frequent exposure to dangerous pesticides, and travel great distances in grueling heat. Those who labor as slaves also suffer frequent beatings and other cruel treatment.[9]

In 2001, under international pressure, chocolate companies signed the Harkin–Engel Protocol, an international effort to stop the practice of dangerous child labor. The protocol brought together Western governments, NGOs, the chocolate industry, and the government of Cote d'Ivoire. It called for the establishment of a child-free certification system, child labor monitoring, independent verification, and programs to improve conditions. The cocoa industry missed the July 1, 2005 deadline for achieving these goals. By 2011, all eight of the major cocoa processors and chocolate manufacturers had become members of the International Cocoa Initiative, a non-profit foundation whose aim is to combat the worst forms of child labor and forced adult labor in cocoa farms. However, a recent report commissioned by the US government found that more than 1.8 million children in West Africa were involved in growing cocoa. Many continue to be victims of human trafficking or enslavement and are at risk of being injured by hazards such as machetes or pesticides.[10]

Environment destruction

For poor cocoa farmers, making a living is more important than and seems incompatible with environmental preservation. The need for short-term economic returns leads to environmentally damaging behaviors such as overharvesting economic timber species, clearing overstory in cocoa plantations, and intensive use of pesticides and fertilizer. In many countries, intensive farming of single-crop cocoa is widespread. Naturally occurring forests with a mix of cocoa and other species are cleared, resulting in unshaded farms that, while more productive, lack the shade that protects the trees and reduces the impacts of pests. In some producing countries, such as Ghana, government-initiated disease and pest control programs led cocoa farms across the country to be sprayed with insecticides and

---

9 International Labor Rights Forum. (2011). "Cocoa Campaign". Retrieved from http://www.ilrf.org/stop-child-labor/cocoa-campaign.

10 Hawksley, H. (2011). "Ivory Coast Cocoa Farms Child Labour: Little Change". BBC. Retrieved from http://www.bbc.co.uk/news/world-africa-15681986.

fungicides. While the cocoa production was increased, the use of pesticides on the farms caused the destruction of the soil flora and fauna through both physical and chemical deterioration.[11]

Global chocolate industry

Lisa Johnson:

It's really quite something that so many bars are available dealing with a variety of social and environmental issues. All the issues seem important: endangered animals, farmers' rights, local ownership. It makes me wonder what the difference is between how all the usual chocolate goodies are made compared to these brands here. And, what the real difference is between all of these, seemingly, more enlightened brands.

Brett Beach:

We're disrupting the global industry. The concentration of large corporations in the entire value chain has created a power imbalance between growers and buyers, has moved the value created by chocolate out of the grower nations, and has put profits ahead of preserving uniquely biodiverse locales.

Good Food Awards 2011:

Madécasse is redefining chocolate production ... creating a real Madagascar chocolate and a sustainable chocolate industry in Africa.

Value chain structure

The cocoa to chocolate supply chain consists of eight participants: growers, buyers, processors, manufacturers, importers, distributors, retailers, and consumers. Consolidation, mergers, and vertical integration have sometimes blurred the lines between steps in the supply chain, but all these processes occur.

Growers

Cocoa is grown in equatorial regions of Africa, Latin America, and Asia. Production is geographically concentrated, with almost 90% of the global supply coming from eight countries—Côte d'Ivoire, Ghana, Indonesia, Nigeria, Cameroon, Brazil, Ecuador, and Papua New Guinea. Exhibit 2 shows cocoa bean production by country

---

11 Ntiamoah, A. and Afrane, G. (2008). Environmental Impacts of Cocoa Production and Processing in Ghana: Life Cycle Assessment Approach. *Journal of Cleaner Production*, 16, 1735-1740. Retrieved from http://orton.catie.ac.cr/repdoc/A3660I/A3660I.PDF.

and region from 2007 to 2010.[12] Most cocoa is grown on small, family-run farms; small holdings of 1–3 hectares (2.5–7.4 acres) produce 95% of world cocoa beans.[13] The cacao tree fruits throughout the year and is generally harvested twice a year, before and after the rainy season. It takes about 6 months from pollination for a tree to produce ripe fruit. After harvest, growers open the cocoa pods and remove and clean the fresh beans (uncured). The beans ferment for 5–7 days and are then sun-dried.[14] Growers sometimes outsource the fermenting and drying to an in-country third-party; however, growers with the necessary equipment and adequate training to perform these steps receive a higher price for their beans. A cocoa pod needs to be cracked open within eight hours of harvesting or it will start to spoil. As the end of the eight-hour window approaches, farmers selling fresh cocoa are at the mercy of buyers to sell at whatever price they offer that day or they cannot sell at all. (Three kilograms of fresh cocoa produces approximately one kilogram of fermented and dried cocoa.)

Yields of dry cocoa vary considerably, based on the farming techniques and the productivity of the land. In Côte d'Ivoire the average per hectare per year is over 500 kilograms while in Nigeria and Ghana it is less than 300 kilograms.[15] A healthy cocoa tree produces 25 pods per year that result in approximately one kilogram of dry cocoa.[16]

A frequent problem in the cocoa growing sector is the low quality[17] of the cocoa delivered by farmers. Due to the many layers of middlemen between cocoa farmers and consumers, most farmers are often not aware of what quality attributes are required. They often do not know how to control, or if necessary eliminate, the development of specific characteristics; some attributes, such as flavor, are difficult or even impossible to measure on-farm. In early 2009, the International Cocoa Organization (ICCO) prepared guidelines on "Best Known Practices in the Cocoa

12 ICCO (2011). *The ICCO Annual Report for 2009/10*. London: ICCO.
13 ICCO (2007) *Sustainable Cocoa Economy: Comprehensive and Participatory Approach.* London: ICCO.
14 UNCTAD (2008). *Cocoa Study: Industry Structures and Competition.* Geneva: UNCTAD Secretariat.
15 ICCO (2003). *Trends in Global Supply and Demand for Cocoa.* (EX/116/7). London: ICCO.
16 Food and Agriculture Organization of the United Nations (2007). *Organic Cocoa Production: A guide for Farmer Field Schools in Sierra Leone.* Rome: FAO.
17 According to the second Roundtable for a Sustainable Cocoa Economy (RSCE2) Working Group, "quality" is used in the broadest sense to include not just the all-important aspects of flavor and purity, but also the physical characteristics that have a direct bearing on manufacturing performance, especially yield of the cocoa nib (Biscuit, Cake, Chocolate and Confectionery Alliance [BCCCA], 1996). The different aspects or specifications of quality in cocoa therefore include: flavor, purity or wholesomeness, consistency, yield of edible material and cocoa butter yield and characteristics. These are the key criteria affecting a manufacturer's assessment of "value" of a particular parcel of beans and the price it is willing to pay for it.

Value Chain"[18] to guide farmers to reach the highest physical quality. Focusing at first on cocoa production, the scope of the guidelines was later widened to include trade, transport, warehousing, processing, and manufacturing requirements.

Another factor affecting cocoa quality relates to the transportation of cocoa beans. Due to the predominantly small size of farms, the cocoa output of a single farmer alone cannot meet the optimal quantity for shipping in an export container. To minimize shipping costs, cocoa beans collected from different farmers, and therefore of different quality and characteristics, are mixed in the same container. This makes it difficult or impossible to differentiate high quality beans from low quality beans. The contamination of high quality beans with low quality beans results in the entire batch being considered low quality.

Buyers

Cocoa bean buyers generally purchase from farmers either in their villages or after transportation to port. Most bean purchasing and exporting companies are subsidiaries or partners of processors; independent players in this sector are rare. The international cocoa market price is the dominant influence on actual prices paid to farmers.[19] The global market price for cocoa is set on two commodity exchanges, the London International Financial Futures and Options Exchange and the New York Board of Trade.

Processors

Cocoa processing consists of roasting the beans, grinding them to make cocoa liquor, and pressing the liquor to extract cocoa butter and produce cocoa powder. It takes 75 cocoa beans (two pods of beans) to make one 2.64 oz chocolate bar. The beans arrive at the processor or factory fermented and dried. At the factory, the workers first sort and clean the cured beans and then roast them. After roasting, the beans are put in a winnower where the shells are removed and the beans are chopped to small pieces, called nibs, the essence of the cocoa bean that is full of cocoa solids and cocoa butter. The nibs are then ground to a thick, rich paste called chocolate liquor, the foundation for all chocolate products. It takes two days of processing for nibs to turn to chocolate liquor. The chocolate liquor is then mixed with other ingredients such as sugar, vanilla, and milk in a conching machine. The speed, temperature, and length of the conching determine the final texture and flavor of the chocolate. Conching smoothes the chocolate and mellows any remaining acidic tones. After the final texture and flavor are achieved, the chocolate is set to

---

18 UNCTAD (2011). *The ICCO at Work under the 2011 Agreement.* Retrieved from http://www.unctad.org/Templates/WebFlyer.asp?intItemID=53 90&lang=1.

19 Capelle, J. (2008). *Towards a Sustainable Cocoa Chain: Power and Possibilities within the Cocoa and Chocolate Sector,* Oxfam International Research Report, available at http://www.oxfam.org/en/policy. (Accessed August 10, 2011), 36pp.

a precise temperature to ensure the formation of small, stable fat crystals in the finished product. Finally the chocolate is poured into molds, conveyed in a cooling tunnel to return the chocolate to a solid state and wrapped for shipment.

Most cocoa grinding installations are located in consuming nations with 54% of global grinding done in the United States and Europe.[20] Processing is highly concentrated in three dominant companies, Cargill, Archer Daniels Midland, and Barry Callebaut, which combined grind close to 40% of global cocoa.[21] The concentration is driven by new processing technologies, economies of scale in purchasing, and the benefits of bulk shipping and just-in-time delivery to chocolate manufacturers.[22]

Manufacturers

Most chocolate manufacturers are located in consuming nations. Similar to processing, chocolate manufacturing is geographically concentrated, with 47% in the United States and Germany.[23] Additionally, chocolate manufacturing is concentrated in a small number of firms, with five companies, Mars, Nestlé, Kraft-Cadbury, Hershey, and Ferrero, responsible for 60% of the world's chocolate products.[24] The capital demands of branding and marketing drive this concentration.[25] Large resources are required to establish and maintain a strong consumer facing brand, particularly on a global scale.

Among large players in the sector, a few focus primarily on chocolate (e.g. Ferrero), but most are diversified across packaged foods (e.g. Nestlé, Kraft-Cadbury). Most firms are vertically integrated and process raw cocoa to create some of their own bulk chocolate. Chocolate manufacturers add ingredients and further blend and process bulk chocolate to create consumer products. The marketplace contains a huge variety of finished products with a wide range of chocolate content.

20 ICCO (2009). International Cocoa Organization Annual Report 2008/09. London: ICCO. Available at www.icco.org.
21 *ibid.*
22 Kaplinsky, R. (2004). *Competitions Policy and the Global Coffee and Cocoa Value Chains.* Brighton: Institute of Development Studies University of Sussex, and Centre for Research in Innovation Management, University of Brighton.
23 UNCTAD (2008). *Cocoa Study: Industry Structures and Competition.* Geneva: UNCTAD Secretariat.
24 Capelle, J. (2008). *Towards a Sustainable Cocoa Chain: Power and Possibilities within the Cocoa and Chocolate Sector,* Oxfam International Research Report, available at http://www.oxfam.org/en/policy. (Accessed August 10, 2011), 36pp.
25 Kaplinsky, R. (2004), *Competitions Policy and the Global Coffee and Cocoa Value Chains.* Brighton: Institute of Development Studies University of Sussex, and Centre for Research in Innovation Management, University of Brighton.

Retailers

Chocolate goes to retail through a broad network of distribution centers, warehouses, and retail outlets. The majority of chocolate products are sold in grocery stores. In the United States, the food, drug, and mass merchant (FDMM) channel accounts for about 40% of retail sales.[26] Other sales occur through non-traditional channels including specialty markets, direct sale by chocolatiers, the internet, and non-food retailers from bookstores to electronics merchants. Premium chocolate sales follow a similar pattern with about 35% occurring through FDMM locations.[27]

End consumers

Global chocolate consumption grew an average of 2.5% annually from the early 1990s and into the middle of the next decade.[28] Chocolate consumption continues to be low in the relatively poor growing nations, while two-thirds of chocolate consumption occurs in Western Europe and North America.[29] Exhibit 3 shows worldwide per capita chocolate consumption by selected country from 2000 to 2008. Although the volume of chocolate consumed has increased at only at a slow pace, the volume of cocoa consumed has increased more rapidly. The new trend in chocolate consumption has been characterized by the increasing appeal of premium chocolates and, in particular, of high cocoa content dark chocolate. Chocolate manufacturers have noticed the changing tastes and even companies traditionally known for milk chocolate products have been introducing new dark and high cocoa content products. The growth has been mainly driven by single-origin chocolate which grew by over 20% per annum as well as by organic certified chocolate (up by almost 20%) and dark chocolate (up by over 15%). While consumer trends indicate a heightened interest in having food produced in a socially acceptable way, consumer quality perceptions of chocolate seem to be more strongly linked to the location of manufacturing (e.g. Swiss and Belgian chocolate) than to the producer nations where the cocoa beans are grown.[30]

26 Mintel (2008). *Chocolate Confectionary: US*. Mintel Reports. July 2008. (October 10, 2011).
27 Mintel (2007) *Premium Chocolate Confectionar: US*. Mintel Reports. March 2007. (October 10, 2011).
28 ICCO (2007). Sustainable Cocoa Economy: Comprehensive and Participatory Approach. London: ICCO.
29 *ibid.*
30 UNCTAD (2008). *Cocoa Study: Industry Structures and Competition*. Geneva: UNCTAD Secretariat, 2008.

Social and environmental certifications and initiatives

Lisa Johnson:

There are some serious problems in the chocolate industry. I'm definitely willing to pay a bit more for my chocolate if I know it will bring some change. But, all of the labels on the bars are really quite something. I know about organic. Fair Trade seems pretty straightforward. But what are these other labels. I've never heard of a lot of them. And it seems really hard to know that buying one particular bar actually makes a difference.

Brett Beach:

Madécasse is 4x Fair Trade. Our system adds tremendous value to the livelihoods of the Malagasy people. Providing these opportunities is having systemic impact—better livelihoods leads to healthier people and better stewardship of natural resources. Manufacturing and performing the value added steps of chocolate production in-country creates benefits far greater than what mere premium pricing on ingredients can achieve.

New York Times:

My favorite chocolate isn't U.S.D.A. organic certified and it's not Fair Trade or Rainforest Alliance stamped. It's Madécasse...[31]

In 2009, 3% of the global cocoa volume was certified by one or more standard-setting organization. Sourcing cocoa certified to environmental and social standards has generally been restricted to niche competitors, whose target consumer markets are socially and environmentally conscious. However, mainstream competition is increasingly sourcing certified cocoa. Some of the major certifications in the cocoa sector include Fair Trade, Organic, Rainforest Alliance, UTZ and Fair for Life. In addition to the various certification systems, the World Cocoa Foundation and International Cocoa Initiative play important roles in studying and advocating for change in the production, sourcing and distribution of cocoa.

Fair trade

Like most commodities, world cocoa prices are volatile. Fair trade practices attempt to provide a level of stability to the growers by insulating them somewhat from the vagaries of a commodity marketplace and providing an assurance of a fair price for their products. Fairtrade Labeling Organizations International (FLO) sets a minimum price for cocoa. By setting a minimum price, FLO stabilizes prices and ensures that the price paid covers the costs of production. In 2010, the FLO price

31 Santopietro, Jill (2009). "Tasteful Company: Madécasse." Food. *New York Times* blog. July 10, 2009.

was US$1,600 per ton, including a fair trade premium of US$150 per ton. When the world cocoa price exceeds US$1,600 per ton, the FLO price is the world price plus the US$150/ton premium.[32] Exhibit 4 illustrates the comparative prices of cocoa on the commodity market and Fairtrade certified from 1994 to 2008.

In addition to stable prices, fair trade empowers farmers and workers. For instance, small farmer groups must have a democratic structure and transparent administration in order to be certified under the FLO standards.[33] Workers must be allowed to have representatives on a committee that decides on the use of the fair trade premium.

Organic

Organic production focuses on environmental stewardship. Organic standards and certification systems are well established around the world and are now commonly regulated by national governments. However, the International Federation of Agricultural Movements (IFOAM) still plays an important role in the organic sector by representing consumer and producer groups. Organic certification applies to the land under cultivation and there are no specifications on the size of farms. Organic standards focus primarily on eliminating the use of chemical fertilizers and pesticides, using natural methods to enhance soil fertility and foster plant resistance to disease and ensuring products are not genetically modified. Organic certified products often command a market premium but this is not guaranteed.

Rainforest Alliance

Rainforest Alliance focuses on how farms are managed, with the goal of preventing deforestation. It has a civil society based coordinating organization, the Sustainable Agriculture Network (SAN), with members from North and South America. Rainforest Alliance certifies farm units of varying size and is oriented towards large producers, though small-scale farmer certification is increasing, especially as it has moved into cocoa. Its environmental standards are the broadest of these initiatives, focusing on a wide range of farm management issues, including the protection of biodiversity and prohibition of genetically modified organisms (GMOs), but with weaker standards than organic on the use of agrochemical inputs. Its social standards focus on compliance with existing labor and safety laws and prioritize worker protection on farms.

---

32 Fairtrade Foundation (n.d.). *The Cocoa Market 1994–2008: Comparison of Fairtrade & New York Exchange Prices.* Retrieved from http://www.Fairtrade.net/fileadmin/user_ upload/content/2009/products/Cocoa_Price_Chart_94-08.pdf

33 FLO (2007). *The Benefits of Fairtrade: A Monitoring and Evaluation Report of Fairtrade Certified Producer Organisations for 2007.* Bonn: Fairtrade Labelling Organizations International.

UTZ Certified

UTZ Certified (Utz Kapeh) was founded in 1997 by Guatemalan coffee producers and the Ahold Coffee Company to certify coffee; the word "utz" means "good" in the Mayan language. UTZ originally focused on coffee; in 2009 the certification protocol was expanded to include cocoa and tea. UTZ Certified Good Inside is based on the International Labor Organization's Conventions and prohibits forced labor, child labor, and discrimination and protects the right to organize and bargain collectively. UTZ requires cooperatives to separate and appropriately label UTZ Certified cocoa beans to ensure transparency. Paying the legal minimum wage is required only after the first year of certification. In terms of pricing, UTZ states that premiums are paid to farmers for their certified products, but the price is solely based on negotiations between the buyers and farmers. Currently, certified cocoa cooperatives are in Costa Rica, Côte d'Ivoire, Dominican Republic, Ecuador, Ghana, and Peru. In 2011, the UTZ label began to appear on chocolate products in Germany; but, as of yet, there are not any chocolate products with the UTZ label in the United States.

Fair for Life

The Fair for Life (FfL) Social and Fair Trade Certification Programme was created in 2006 by the Institute for Marketecology (IMO) and the Swiss Bio-Foundation. FfL came in response to increasing criticism from consumers, producers, processors, retailers and their global suppliers that existing certification schemes did not cover the entire range of products, production situations and trade relations. The terminology "Programme" instead of "standard" reflects that FfL is based on widely acknowledged baseline standards such as the International Labour Organization (ILO), SA 8000, FLO and IFOAM Social Chapter. Fair for Life certified cocoa producers are in Brazil, Congo, Tanzania, Uganda, Peru, and Madagascar and certified processors are in Switzerland and Germany.

World Cocoa Foundation

The World Cocoa Foundation (WCF) is an international membership organization established in 2000 in Washington, DC. The WCF partners include governments of cocoa-producing countries, the US government, the EU Parliament, research institutes, non-governmental organizations, philanthropic foundations, and international development and multilateral organizations. The WCF supports programs that work directly with cocoa farmers at the farm level, prior to commercialization of their cocoa. The intent of WCF programs is to build the capacity of cocoa farmers to increase yields, improve quality, and enhance environmentally sustainable practices. It supports cocoa farmers in Africa, Southeast Asia, and the Americas.

International Cocoa Initiative

The International Cocoa Initiative (ICI) was founded in 2002 as a response to rising public opinion that the chocolate industry needed to ensure child and forced labor was not used in the production of its products. The Board is the governing body of the ICI, providing oversight and funding. There are 15 members of the Board, comprising representatives of major chocolate brands, such as Archer Daniel Midlands, Hershey Foods, and Nestlé, and civil society organizations, such as Education International, Free the Slaves, and Global March Against Child Labour. The ICI is based in Geneva, Switzerland, and has local offices in Ivory Coast and Ghana. The major activities of the ICI fall into five categories: evidence-building and research; supporting social change; knowledge management; advocacy; and partnership and capacity-building.

Global and niche competitors and their sustainability efforts

The global chocolate industry is characterized by major international firms with very strong product portfolios with most of the world's best known brands. These companies use massive advertising budgets to aggressively promote their products and they benefit from significant efficiencies provided by economies of scale and scope. Lower per unit costs of production, varied product lines, high levels of investment in technology and equipment and favorable contracts with grocery stores and supermarkets create significant barriers to entry.[34] Nevertheless, new entrants have established themselves within the industry, with a mix of gourmet and specialty products and of low-priced, non-branded segment. Other smaller players have managed to carve out regional market niches, thereby reducing the directness of competition from the major players. With the extensive coverage of the child and forced labor issues in cocoa farming, many of the large and small players in the industry have adopted practices to address both social and environmental issues in their value chains.

Kraft-Cadbury[35]

Cadbury was founded in the 1800s by a tea dealer and grocer shop owner, turned manufacturer in 1831. In the midcentury the firm expanded adding manufacturing capabilities and capacity and new products. In the 20th century, the company

---

34 IBISWorld (2012) *Industry Report C1113-GL. Global Candy and Chocolate Manufacturing.* IBISWorld.com. June 2012.

35 Kraft Foods "Corporate Home". Web. http://www.kraftfoodscompany.com, October 20, 2011; Cadbury "Chocolate". http://www.cadbury.co.uk/, October 20, 2011.

continued to grow, merged with Schweppes in 1969, and became the world's leading confectionary company in 2003 through a merger with gum manufacturer Adams (maker of Trident and Stride chewing gums). However, in 2008, Cadbury and Schweppes demerged; in effect, this split apart the confectionary and drinks businesses. In 2010, Cadbury was purchased by American food conglomerate Kraft Foods.

Cadbury sources its cocoa from Ghana, West Africa, and does not own or control any cocoa farms. The company was the largest buyer of certified Fairtrade or Rainforest Alliance beans in 2010. Prior to the merger with Kraft, Cadbury processed and produced its chocolate in the UK. A portion of Kraft's sustainability initiatives are focused on improving the lives of cocoa farmers in its supply chain. In addition to its internal programs, Kraft participates in World Cocoa Foundation initiatives, the UN Cocoa Partnership, and other multi-organization efforts. Kraft-Cadbury owns the Green and Black's brand, known for producing premium organic chocolate bars, including Fairtrade certified products.

Mars[36]

Founded in 1911 as a butter cream candy maker, Mars expanded to chocolate in 1923. Diversification into non-confectionary products such as pet food and convenient meals started in the 1930s and '40s. The Mars company is privately held and operates globally in pet care, confectionary, food, and health and life sciences.

Mars began efforts to change the chocolate supply chain in 1982 when it established the Mars Center for Cocoa Science to research more sustainable farming techniques. Continued efforts included preliminary research into sequencing the cocoa genome in 2010. On the purchasing side, Mars obtained 5% of its 2010 cocoa supply from Rainforest Alliance certified farms and publically committed to sourcing 100% of the chocolate for its Dove Dark Chocolate product by 2012.

Nestlé[37]

Founded in 1866 in Switzerland, Nestlé's first products were baby cereal and condensed milk. Chocolate joined the firm's portfolio with the 1929 purchase of fellow Swiss company Peter, Cailler, Kohler Chocolats. Today Nestlé operates 443 factories worldwide to produce food products of different types, as well as pet care and nutritional items.

Nestlé produces chocolate in 52 factories worldwide and offers a mix of global and regional brands. It purchases cocoa from Cote d'Ivoire, Ecuador, and Venezuela. Nestlé has an internal project called the Cocoa Plan dedicated, in part, to sustainable cocoa production. Additionally, Nestlé is part of World Cocoa Foundation

36 Mars. Web. http://wwwmars.com/. (Accessed October 20, 2011).
37 Nestle Global. Web. http://www.nestlecom/. (Accessed October 20, 2011).

programs and the International Cocoa Initiative. In 2010, its KitKat bars sold in the UK and Ireland became Fairtrade certified.

Ferrero[38]

Ferrero was founded as an Italian confectionary manufacturer after World War II. It is still family owned and managed. Unlike the other big players, Ferrero produces only confectionery and beverages. Ferrero sources its cocoa from Cote d'Ivoire, Ghana, and Ecuador. It is a member of the International Cocoa Initiative, works with the World Cocoa Foundation, and has an internal corporate social responsibility program. The company has set a goal of 100% certified sustainable cocoa by 2020. Ferrero works directly with local cocoa farmers in an effort to improve the prices they receive.

Hershey[39]

Hershey started as a caramel candy business in 1876 and added chocolate in 1894. Hershey introduced the iconic Hershey bar in 1900. A public company, its largest shareholder is the Hershey Trust Company, which administers the Milton Hershey School. The Milton Hershey School was founded as a school for orphans in 1909 and today focuses on providing education and social services to children in need.

Hershey sources its cocoa on the global market and produces chocolate at factories in North America (plus some joint ventures in Asia and Brazil). Like Ferrero, Hershey is less diversified than the three biggest players and sells confectionary, snack, and beverage products. It has owned Dagoba, a maker of organic, premium chocolate bars, since 2006. Hershey runs internal programs to support healthy cocoa communities and collaborates with the World Cocoa Foundation, the International Cocoa Initiative, and other inter-organization groups.

Competition—niche

The chocolate industry is filled with niche competitors. Retail chocolate display fixtures are teeming with small producers attempting to differentiate their chocolate bars. Companies tout their chocolate as: organic, shade grown, heirloom cocoa varietals, single origin, fair trade, direct trade, artisanal, and so on. There are even other companies that, like Madécasse, use an in-country manufacturing set-up that goes from bean to packaged bar within a grower nation. Five of these companies are profiled below.

---

38 Ferrero. Web. http://www.ferrero.com/. (Accessed October 20, 2011).
39 Hershey's–The Hershey Company. Web. http://www.thehersheycompany.com/. (Accessed October 20, 2011).

Omanhene[40]

Produced entirely in Ghana, Omanhene was started by an American who spent time in Ghana through an American Field Service (AFS) exchange program. Since the cooperative structure is not culturally understood in Ghana, they work outside of the fair trade system. The company uses a beyond fair trade philosophy that addresses not just the price paid, but also environmental effects, value-added manufacture, child labor, and corruption. Omanhene's approach provides higher wages for chocolate factory workers and for farmers and is concerned with the entire value chain, not just farmer payments.

Claudio Corallo[41]

Run by an Italian agronomist and his family, Claudio Corallo operates on the African islands of São Tomé and Príncipe. The cocoa is grown and dried on Príncipe, then transported by boat to São Tomé for processing. The family employs local residents to assist in transport, quality checking, and production. The company focuses on chocolate quality and innovation in growing and processing more than on the benefits they might be providing to their host nation.

The Grenada Chocolate Company[42]

Founded in 1999, the Grenada Chocolate company has co-op farms, fermentation equipment, and a factory in the Caribbean island nation. The co-op includes 150 acres of organic farms and the operation received organic certification in 2004. In addition to organic certification, the operation uses solar energy and sources ingredients from like-minded outfits (e.g. organic sugar from a Paraguay grower's co-op and biodynamic vanilla from Costa Rica). The company's goal is to have cocoa growers benefit as much as chocolate makers.

Pacari[43]

Made entirely in Ecuador, Pacari produces organic, single-source chocolate. The source farms are 100% organic certified and some are Fairtrade certified. Long-term commitments and relationships with growers have preserved traditional farming methods. Founded in 2002 by an Ecuadorian couple, Pacari employs small batch

40 Omanhene–The Cocoa Bean Company. Web. http://omanhenecocoa.com/. (Accessed July 28, 2011).
41 Claudio Corallo. Web. http://www.claudiocorallo.com. (Accessed July 28, 2011).
42 Grenada Chocolate Company "Organic Dark Chocolate". Web. http://www.grenadachocolate.com. (Accessed August 11, 2011).
43 Pacari "Ecuadorian Organic Chocolate". http://pacarichocolate.com. (Accessed July 28, 2011).

production, supports sustainability programs in grower communities, and cuts out the middlemen so that farmers receive a significant premium over market prices.

Kallari[44]

Located in the Ecuadorian Amazon, Kallari produces organic, shade-grown cocoa and chocolate. The growers' association was established in 1997, and bar production was started in 2000. Growers receive prices that are 20–60% higher than the market average and the cooperative sponsors social initiatives in farmer communities. Like Madécasse, Kallari targets customers who wish to combine an opportunity for social good (benefiting the host nation through purchase) with a high quality product.

Competing with a "4x" model: the Madécasse difference

Brett and Tim built the Madécasse model to maximize the amount of value added to the final product in Madagascar. This business model includes strong and enduring relationships with the cocoa farmers, partnering with a chocolate factory in Antananarivo (the capital city of Madagascar), sourcing ingredients and packaging from around Madagascar, and exporting the final, fully packaged product to overseas markets. It is through this holistic approach to sourcing and manufacturing in Madagascar that Brett and Tim created a business model that offers more than four times the social and economic benefit to Madagascar when compared to the standard Fair Trade model. Exhibit 5 illustrates the structure of Madecasse's value chain activities, highlighting the extent of the value chain activities that Brett and Tim have developed in Madagascar.

Cocoa Farmers

Madécasse partners with 70 cocoa farmers in the Sambirano Valley of Madagascar. These farmers belong to four different cooperatives. In selecting the farmer groups, Brett and Tim considered the possibility of building long-term relationships that benefit both the farmers and Madécasse. Creating these relationships required them to invest considerable money and time. Through these relationships Madécasse provides farmers training on fermentation and drying of cocoa beans, cocoa curing facilities, higher cocoa prices, and a stable market for the crop. Because Madécasse finances the fermenting and drying equipment and teaches growers

---

44 Kallari "A Cooperative of Kichwa Organic Artists, Cacao Growers & Gourmet Chocolate Makers". Web. http://www.kallari.com/. (Accessed July 28, 2011).

how to dramatically increase the quality of their cocoa beans, the farmers are able to increase the value of cocoa beans they are selling.

In addition, Madécasse offers farmers a price that is 20% higher than the market price for the cured cocoa beans. According to Brett, 10% of this premium is a reward for working together with Madécasse and the other 10% is for the high quality of the crop. The Madécasse partnership does not prevent farmers from selling to other channels. However, farmers generally choose not to sell to collectors or other middleman because in the past they were cheated, charged an unfavorable exchange rate, or suffered from fluctuating market prices. The partnership ensures farmers a stable market for their crops and the ability to earn an income that covers sustainable farming costs, supports their families, and improves their living standards.

The chocolate factory

Madécasse partners with a chocolate factory where the chocolate makers bring together the high quality Madagascar cocoa with craft chocolate making. Brett and Tim work with the chocolate makers to discover the perfect roast for each Madécasse chocolate. The chocolate factory employs 40 Malagasy people: 20 women and 20 men. In addition, Madécasse employs a full-time project manager to work with the chocolate factory and other supply partners in the capital city.

Fermented and dried beans are transported from farms to the factory by oxcart and truck. At the factory, the beans are roasted in 500 kg batches. The ingredients added to the chocolate liquor to create the different flavored bars are all from Madagascar and include sugar, vanilla, nuts, and spices. Madécasse chocolate sits in the conching machine for two days to achieve the desired texture and flavor. When the chocolate is finished, workers wrap the chocolate in aluminum foil, insert the foil wrapped bar into a wrapper, tie the wrapper with raffia, and pack 12 bars into a display box that goes to an outer carton ready for shipping.

These packaging steps are all done by hand in the chocolate factory. The raffia and boxes are manufactured in Madagascar. Although the wrapper paper is imported from France, the color printing is done in another factory in Madagascar where workers hole punch, fold, and glue the printed wrapper into an envelope that holds the finished chocolate bars. Thus, Madécasse's production of chocolate in Madagascar has resulted in the development of secondary industries such as packaging and utilities and thus creates a lot of additional employment in Madagascar. Exhibit 6 shows the direct and secondary employment created by the Madécasse business model. The growth of Madécasse leads to the growth of these businesses and a more stable market for other agricultural products that are used for flavoring the chocolate. In this sense, along with the benefits to the farmers, Madécasse generates much greater social impact than exporting fair trade cocoa alone.

Distribution

Finished chocolates packaged in boxes are transported in a refrigerated truck owned by the chocolate factory to meet the customs broker. After inspection and customs clearance, the product is ready to be shipped out of the country. Madécasse chocolates are shipped to international markets, mainly the United States and Europe, by two routes. Most of the chocolate is shipped by boat from Madagascar to New York. Air shipment is sometimes used for new products in which case the chocolates flies to Paris first and then to New York. Upon arrival in the United States, orders are inspected by customs and rushed to a cool room to await a refrigerated truck which takes them to a warehouse in Brooklyn, New York. From Brooklyn, the chocolate is sent to distributors and retailers around the country.

Madécasse sells the majority of its products through distributors who then sell to retailers and boutique stores. In the United States, Madécasse also sells directly to some specialty retailers and high-end grocers. As of July 2012, there were more than 1,250 stores in the United States carrying Madécasse chocolate, including 300 Whole Foods stores. A small percentage of Madécasse sales occur in other geographies through exporters and online sales.

Marketing

Madécasse focuses on the story behind the bars in marketing its chocolate products. Brett and Tim take an active role in a wide range of industry trade shows to showcase their products and tell the story themselves. The Madécasse story has been covered in several major newspapers and magazines including the *Wall Street Journal*[45] and the *New York Times* Style Magazine. Madécasse also uses its packaging to talk about the bean-to-bar story and the environmental, economic, and social impact in Madagascar. Exhibit 7 shows eight different varieties of 75 gram Madécasse chocolate bars and how a holistic story of Madécasse is conveyed through the different messages on the packaging.

In addition to consumer chocolates, Madécasse also sells baking chocolate and vanilla. The product diversification provides a means for increasing its market reach and telling its story to a broader consumer market.

Social and environmental impact

Exhibit 8 provides a 'bar-based' assessment of the social and environmental impacts and benefits to Madagascar of the Madécasse business model. According to this analysis, it takes an estimated 17.87 minutes of total actual labor to make a 75 g Madécasse bar. Farm labor accounts for 42% (or 7.51 minutes) of the total work time. This shows that employment is more than doubled by making finished

---

45 The most recent coverage in *Wall Street Journal* is Wonnacott, P. (2011). "Small Factories Take Root in Africa." *Wall Street Journal*. September 24, 2011.

chocolate in Madagascar versus exporting raw cocoa. According to Brett, minimum revenue of $14,000 is generated in Madagascar through the processing of 1 ton of cocoa, translating into a minimum of $0.88 left in county per 75g chocolate bar.[46] When comparing $0.88 per bar with the $0.13 per bar kept in country when exporting fair trade cocoa at the price of $2,000/metric ton,[47] there is a minimum of seven times more money that stays in Madagascar. This means that every time someone buys a Madécasse bar, seven times more money is going back to the country of cocoa origin.

By combining the information from employment (2x) and profit (7x), it becomes clear that the creation of finished products is 4x more beneficial for the people of Madagascar than selling fair trade, and more than 14x better than selling commodity cocoa. This higher return is at the heart of the Madécasse mission: finished products are vastly more beneficial to the cocoa-growing country than raw materials.

Madécasse not only strives to maximize the in-country social benefits but also helps preserve the natural environment. In Madagascar, cocoa grows under a shade tree which creates a bio-diverse environment with fruit trees and other edible plants such as banana, apple, papaya, pepper, and vanilla alongside the cocoa. Native species of birds and lemurs are also commonly seen in a typical cocoa forest. In regions in Madagascar where cocoa farmers cannot sustain their farming due to the exploitation of middlemen and the fluctuation of the cocoa market, they cut down these diverse cocoa forests in favor of other edible crops, such as rice. Sadly, as the cocoa forest is destroyed so is the ecology.

When they partner with Madécasse, farmers can continue cocoa farming and therefore preserve the natural and bio-diverse environment in the region. Madécasse works with farmers to increase crop yield without planting additional cocoa at the expenses of other tree species. When Madécasse grows and has greater demand for cocoa, it will increase its cocoa supply by partnering with farmers with existing cocoa farms. In the summer of 2012, Madécasse initiated organic certification to train farmers about environmental stewardship.

Ethical and organic certification

As a specialty chocolate brand, Madécasse not only competes with other specialty brands, but also numerous conventional brands. In order to catch consumers' attention and communicate with them about the company's products in a matter of seconds, the founders tried different methods and came to the conclusion that certifications will help to validate the brand in the eyes of conscious consumers.

---

46 This number represents only part of the production costs.
47 Byrne, Jane (2010). "New Minimum Price for Fairtrade Organic Cocoa will Offset Volatility, Claims FLO". Confectionery News, December 7, 2010. Retrieved from http://www.confectionerynews.com/Commodities/New-minimum-price-for-Fairtrade-organic-cocoa-will-offset-volatility-claims-FLO http://www.confectionerynews.com/Markets/New-minimum-price-for-Fair trade-organic-cocoa-will-offset-volatility-claims-FLO

The company recently garnered the Fair for Life Social & Fair Trade ("Fair for Life")[48] and Organic certifications.

Madécasse chocolates are created using organic cocoa and exceed Fair Trade in terms of the company's relationships with farmers and the chocolate manufacturer. However, the company cannot take for granted that consumers know the story. Tim expressed the challenge the company is facing in communicating with consumers, "The biggest challenge is distilling the story down to something that fits the attention span of an average consumer which is a few seconds. The Fair Trade label is very effective in a matter of a few seconds to tell if our product is an ethical product although it cannot tell our story. It increases product sales."

The future

Through their unique business model, Brett and Tim are confident they can compete with the global chocolate industry. The "4x Fair Trade" business model provides a consumer choice criterion and appeals to a market that is looking for something that builds on fair trade. Brett and Tim's connection to Madagascar allows them to network and navigate the culture in a way the five big manufacturers cannot. However, Madécasse is not unique in focusing on differentiating based on single origin specialty chocolate. And, the Fair for Life and Organic certifications are becoming more common in both the specialty and mass markets for chocolate products.

To achieve continued success, Madécasse needs to obtain high levels of customer engagement and loyalty. Survival depends on Madécasse's ability to leverage its "4x" impact. How does Madécasse create an enduring connection between developed country consumers and the people and natural beauty of Madagascar? Given the competitive dynamics in the chocolate industry, what should Madécasse do to ensure it maintains distinct brand positioning and product differentiation? Ultimately, how do Brett and Tim make sure that the value proposition of Madécasse is clearly aligned with current and emerging customer needs?

The laptop chirped as a new email arrived—it was a reminder to register for the Winter Fancy Food Show. Brett was ready to register to ensure Madécasse was well represented at this premier specialty foods exhibition; but he also knew that at least two other chocolate companies with claims to being "direct to source" and organically certified will be there. Here was another great opportunity to tell the Madécasse story and connect consumers with the Malagasy people and the unique natural beauty of Madagascar. He began the online registration process.

48 IMO (2011). *Fair For All. World Wide –Social Responsibility & Fair Trade*. Retrieved from http://www.fairforlife.net/logicio/pmws/indexDOM.php?client_id=fairforlife&page_id=home.

EXHIBIT 1
Awards and recognition

Named one of the 50 Most Innovative Companies in the World for "building a chocolate company in one of the poorest countries in the world."
Fast Company, March 2011 "50 Most Innovative Companies."

"Madécasse is redefining chocolate production ... creating a real Madagascar chocolate and a sustainable chocolate industry in Africa."
Good Food Awards 2011.

Named to 40 Under 40 list of people "changing the way Americans eat and drink ..."
Food & Wine Magazine, November 2010, "40 Big Thinkers, 40 & Under."

"... the chocolate was so good. I put the quality of all (bars) very, very high. Madagascar is one of those places where myth and reality merge."
Wine Spectator Magazine, May 31, 2010, "Made in Madagascar."

"I'm awestruck. The 70% is smooth and chocolaty with a sweet-and-sour dried cherry finish. The 63% is noticeably sweeter, buttery and rich."
New York Times "The Moment" Online edition, July 2009, "Tasteful Company."

"(madécasse vanilla powder is) more flavorful than vanilla extract and less expensive than whole beans."
Food & Wine Magazine. December 2008. "Holiday Gifts $30 and Under."

"(madécasse) hold the title of 'exclusive U.S. importer of Madagascar chocolate.' ... the island's aromatic cocoa is considered to yield the world's best dark chocolate."
Bloomberg Businessweek Online edition, November 2008,
"Bringing Madagascar to the United States."

"The unanimous favorite Madécasse Triple Vanilla Extract offered what was deemed to be the ideal vanilla flavor."
THE NIBBLE Online edition, November 2008, "The Best Vanilla Extract."

EXHIBIT 2
World cocoa beans production by country (thousand tonnes)

	2007/08		2008/09		2009/10	
	Amount	%	Amount	%	Amount	%
Africa						
Cameroon	185	4.9%	227	6.3%	190	5.3%
Côte d'Ivoire	1382	36.8%	1222	33.9%	1242	34.4%
Ghana	729	19.4%	662	18.4%	632	17.5%
Nigeria	230	6.1%	250	6.9%	240	6.6%
Others	166	4.4%	158	4.4%	154	4.3%
Total Africa	**2692**	**71.7%**	**2519**	**69.9%**	**2458**	**68.0%**
America						
Brazil	171	4.6%	157	4.4%	161	4.5%
Ecuador	118	3.1%	134	3.7%	160	4.4%
Others	180	4.8%	197	5.5%	201	5.6%
Total America	**469**	**12.5%**	**488**	**13.5%**	**522**	**14.4%**
Asia & Oceania						
Indonesia	485	12.9%	490	13.6%	535	14.8%
Papua New Guinea	52	1.4%	59	1.6%	50	1.4%
Others	55	1.5%	50	1.4%	48	1.3%
Total Asia & Oceania	**592**	**15.8%**	**599**	**16.6%**	**633**	**17.5%**
World Total	**3753**	**100%**	**3606**	**100%**	**3613**	**100%**

Source: *ICCO Quarterly Bulletin of Cocoa Statistics*, Vol. XXXVI, No. 4, Cocoa year 2009/2010.

EXHIBIT 3
Per capita chocolate consumption in selected countries

Countries/Region	2000	2001	2002	2003	2004	2005	2006	2007	2008
Selected EU Countries					(Kilograms)				
Germany	9.97	10.00	10.32	10.50	11.13	10.85	11.16	11.42	11.39
UK	9.41	9.17	10.02	10.12	10.25	10.22	10.29	10.40	10.31
Denmark	8.22	8.62	9.25	8.66	8.72	7.74	7.65	8.07	8.57
Austria	7.37	8.70	7.99	7.53	8.96	9.43	8.19	8.22	7.90
Estonia	n.a.	n.a.	n.a.	3.21	3.60	14.19	2.69	8.07	7.85
France	6.97	6.81	6.96	6.91	7.33	7.04	6.55	7.04	7.39
Finland	6.02	6.49	6.53	6.69	6.92	6.77	6.92	7.56	6.97
Belgium	8.05	7.22	8.88	8.46	9.22	10.18	8.60	9.05	6.80
Sweden	7.61	6.06	5.98	5.98	6.16	6.38	6.40	6.75	6.59
Lithuania	n.a.	n.a.	n.a.	2.06	2.78	3.80	5.70	6.34	6.08
Netherlands	4.79	4.68	4.60	4.51	4.51	2.94	n.a.	n.a.	n.a.
Poland	n.a.	n.a.	3.30	3.98	4.04	3.67	3.62	3.62	4.52
Greece	2.83	2.66	2.90	2.99	3.13	3.15	3.29	3.29	4.50
Portugal	3.62	1.57	1.67	1.85	1.52	1.18	1.32	1.32	4.45
Hungary	n.a.	n.a.	n.a.	3.05	3.15	3.21	3.72	3.72	3.47
Spain	3.93	3.77	3.67	3.43	3.47	3.22	3.27	3.27	3.30
Italy	3.62	3.67	3.94	4.00	4.17	4.26	3.37	3.37	3.26
Bulgaria	n.a.	n.a.	n.a.	n.a.	n.a.	n.a.	2.99	2.99	2.23
Other Countries									
Switzerland	10.75	11.20	10.92	10.25	10.80	10.74	10.05	10.47	10.77
Norway	8.13	8.61	8.27	8.66	9.19	9.19	8.76	9.70	9.80
Australia	5.79	5.95	4.35	4.38	4.77	4.77	5.72	5.81	5.96
USA	5.32	5.06	5.36	5.36	5.31	5.31	5.45	5.18	5.09
Brazil	1.84	1.72	1.77	1.69	2.07	2.07	2.16	2.47	2.48
Japan	2.18	2.21	2.14	2.22	2.22	2.22	2.23	2.18	2.15

Note: Data provided included consumption of white chocolate (HS17049030).

Source: ICCO. (July 30, 2010) *The World Cocoa Economy: Past and Present.*

EXHIBIT 4

The cocoa market 1994–2008: comparison of Fairtrade and New York exchange prices

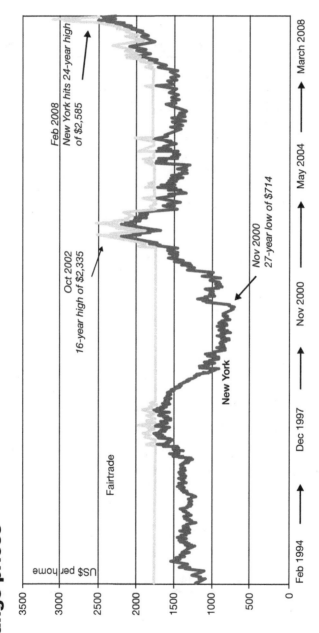

EXHIBIT 5
Madagascar-based value chain activities of Madécasse

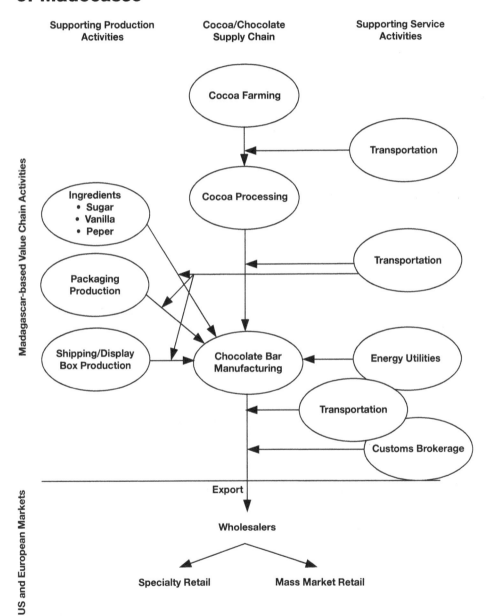

EXHIBIT 6
Analysis of socio-economic benefits of Madécasse business model

Activity	Cocoa & Chocolate Breakdown			Labor Breakdown			Work Hours to Process into Chocolate			Minutes to Process into Chocolate		
	KG of Cocoa	KG of Choc	# of 75g Bars	# of People	Hrs/Person	Total Hours	1 KG Cocoa	1 KG Choc	1-75g Bar	1 KG Cocoa	1 KG Choc	1-75g Bar
Cocoa Farm												
Dry Cocoa Production	81	97	1,293	1	160	160	1.9692	1.6495	0.1237			
Transport Farm	2,000	2,381	31,746	3	6	18	0.0090	0.0076	0.0006			
Transport Ambanja	5,000	5,952	79,358	3	24	72	0.0144	0.0121	0.0009			
Subtotal							**1.9926**	**1.6692**	**0.1252**	**119.56**	**100.15**	**7.51**
Madecasse Cocoa												
Cocoa Technicians	2,500	188	2,507	1	160	160	0.0640	0.8511	0.0638	3.84	51.07	3.83
Production Partner Management												
Madagascar Manager	2,520	3,000	39,399	1	160	160	0.0635	0.0533	0.0040	3.81	3.20	0.24
Sugar Farm												
Cultivation	1,000	1,190	15,866	4	20	80	0.0800	0.0672	0.0050			
Harvest	1,000	1,190	15,866	1	8	8	0.0080	0.0067	0.0005			

Processing	1,000	1,190	15,866	4	8	31	0.0320	0.0269	0.0020			
Transport: Farm	5,000	5,952	79,358	3	48	144	0.0288	0.0242	0.0018			
Subtotal							**0.1488**	**0.1250**	**0.0093**	**8.93**	**7.50**	**0.56**
Print Factory												
File & Plate preparation	630	750	10,000	2	3	6	0.0095	0.0080	0.0006			
Printing	630	750	10,000	3	4	12	0.0190	0.0160	0.0012			
Cutting	630	750	10,000	1	4	4	0.0063	0.0053	0.0004			
Hole Punching	630	750	10,000	1	2	2	0.0032	0.0027	0.0002			
Gluing & Folding	630	750	10,000	20	13	260	0.4127	0.3467	0.0260			
Quality Control	630	750	10,000	1	2	2	0.0032	0.0027	0.0002			
Transport	630	750	10,000			0	0.0000	0.0000	0.0000			
Subtotal							**0.4539**	**0.3814**	**0.0286**	**27.23**	**22.88**	**1.72**
Box Maker												
Production - case box	378	560	6,000	3	1	3	0.0079	0.0067	0.0005			
Production - master	907	1,080	14,400	3	1	3	0.0033	0.0028	0.0002			
Transport to Choc	1,680	2,000	26,666	2	4	7	0.0042	0.0035	0.0003			
Subtotal							**0.0154**	**0.0130**	**0.0010**	**0.92**	**0.78**	**0.06**

Activity	Cocoa & Chocolate Breakdown			Labor Breakdown			Work Hours to Process into Chocolate			Minutes to Process into Chocolate		
	KG of Cocoa	KG of Choc	# of 75g Bars	# of People	Hrs/Person	Total Hours	1 KG Cocoa	1 KG Choc	1-75g Bar	1 KG Cocoa	1 KG Choc	1-75g Bar
Chocolate Factory												
Sorting Cocoa	65	77	1,027	1	8	8	0.1231	0.1039	0.0078			
Roasting	65	77	1,027	2	1	2	0.0308	0.0260	0.0019			
Winnowing	65	77	1,027	2	1	2	0.0308	0.0260	0.0019			
Conching (grinding)	550	655	8,733	1	5	5	0.0091	0.0076	0.0006			
Tempering & Molding	731	870	11,600	5	24	120	0.1642	0.1379	0.0103			
Packaging	302	360	4,800	20	10	200	0.6623	0.5556	0.0417			
Subtotal							**1.0203**	**0.8570**	**0.0642**	**61.22**	**51.42**	**3.85**
Export												
Chocolate Production	1,680	2,000	26,666	4	4	16	0.0095	0.0080	0.0006			
Customs Broker Team	1,680	2,000	26,666	2	6	12	0.0071	0.0060	0.0005			
Madecasse Support	1,680	2,000	26,666	2	6	12	0.0071	0.0060	0.0005			
Total							**3.7585**	**3.9500**	**0.2961**	**225.5100**	**237.0000**	**17.7700**

EXHIBIT 7
Packaging and story-telling on Madécasse 75g chocolate bars

EXHIBIT 8
The Madécasse Story: "What We Do For the Planet" and "Beyond Fair Trade"

WHAT WE DO FOR THE
PLANET

MADAGASCAR
- 85% of plant and animal life exists nowhere else in the world
- Only 10% of original forest still exists

Madagascar is one of the most ecologically diverse places on the earth, Every step we take in producing a chocolate bar ensures a better natural environment in Madagascar.

Habitat Conservation
- Native species of birds and lemurs
- Indigenous hardwoods
- Protects local forests

Creating Biodiversity
- Cocoa Grown alongside fruit trees, edible plant
- Nutrient rich-soil

Natural Farming Practices
- No herbicides or pesticides
- All-natural compost
- Harvested by hand

BEYOND FAIR TRADE

LOCAL IMPACT OF FAIR TRADE (GOOD)

1. Farmers paid fair price
2. Cocoa shipped out of country

The Fair Trade concept is a great start. It pays farmers a fair price for their cocoa.

LOCAL IMPACT OF MADÉCASSE (BETTER)

1. Farmers paid above fair price
2. Purchase local ingredients
3. Invest in co-op equipment, skill training
4. Chocolate made locally
5. Wrappers printed locally
6. Chocolate hand-wrapped locally
7. Finished chocolate bar shipped

Going several steps further, the Madecasse model invests in the entire chocolate production process.

Part II
Ecologically oriented social enterprises

CASE 4

Bio-Vert

Green to what limit?[1]

Raymond L. Paquin, Catherine Bédard and Geneviève Grainger

Bio-Vert is a leading Canadian brand of eco-cleaning products manufactured by Quebec-based Savons Prolav. Run by brother and sister team Yan and Bianka Grand-Maison, Savons Prolav bases its products on their vision which includes eco-friendliness, affordability, and effectiveness. Demand for Bio-Vert's phosphate-free detergents has increased dramatically since the 2007 blue-green algae bloom outbreaks in Quebec's waterways and subsequent legislation restricting phosphate use in cleaning products. However, now that 'green' cleaning products have become more mainstream Savons Prolav faces the issue of how to adapt and grow in an increasingly crowded marketplace. This discussion considers how

1 Paquin, R., December 2012. Richard Ivey School of Business Foundation prohibits any form of reproduction, storage or transmission of this material without its written permission. This material is not covered under authorization from any reproduction rights organization. To order copies or request permission to reproduce materials, contact Ivey Publishing, Ivey Business School, Western University, London, Ontario, Canada, N6G 0N1; t. 519.661.3208. e. cases@ivey.ca, www.iveycases.com. Copyright (c) 2012 Richard Ivey School of Business Foundation.

IVEY | Publishing

Savons Prolav can remain competitive in this difficult industry segment while maintaining its environmental focus.

This case highlights the pressures that an SME with strong environmental values faces in a competitive market. It includes a portrait of the cleaning products industry, consumer patterns with regards to eco-friendly products, and a background of the provincial socio-environmental event that triggered increased demand for 'green' cleaning products in Quebec. Savons Prolav's history, business model, and core values are discussed along with potential growth options. Details on related industry, societal and marketing perspectives are provided to guide the reader through the advantages and disadvantages inherent to each opportunity.

Information and data in this case study were collected primarily from interviews with Savons Prolav employees and owners and supplemented with secondary research and public media.

Courses and learning objectives

This case can be used in a variety of undergraduate and introductory MBA settings including in Strategic Marketing, Strategy & Entrepreneurship, and Business & Sustainability. It provides students a context to explore the alignment of SME (small and medium enterprise) owners' ecological values in developing the firm's future strategy and product design and marketing. Depending on the instructor's orientation, case learning objectives may include:

- Identifying the firm's core values and managing according to the values

- Identifying market segments and attracting/educating customers

- Creating brand image and brand loyalty

- Anticipating customer needs and social trends

- Understanding an industry's behaviours and factors

- Navigating a saturated market place through differentiation

- Using an environmental differentiation strategy

Strategic Marketing Class. Students may explore how consumer patterns allow marketers to develop consumer categories, using LOHAS (Lifestyle of Health and Sustainability) to illustrate the evolution of consumer interest in green products. Students can reflect and exchange ideas on green-washing aligning products with corporate brands.

Strategy & Entrepreneurship Class. Students can step into the owners' shoes to evaluate industry-specific pressures and explore tensions between growth and organizational values. Students can identify and compare market opportunities, direct and indirect competitors, consumer expectations and core values, and explore trade-offs.

Business & Sustainability Class. This case illustrates the challenges of operating an SME with strong environmental values. Students explore some inherent difficulties in the 'green' marketplace, including performance perceptions and customer biases. Students consider alignment between the products and firm, including the relationship between eco-products' and the firm's impacts.

Introduction

As Yan Grand-Maison steered his shopping cart through the supermarket, he spotted his company's laundry detergent on the top shelf and smiled. 2008 was a record year for Grand-Maison's company, Savons Prolav, maker of the Bio-Vert brand of environmentally friendly ('green') household cleaning products (see Exhibit 1). Despite being proud of the hard work he and his sister, Bianka, had put in to reach this point, Grand-Maison knew that a local environmental threat had helped propel the recent sales growth.

In the summer of 2007, Quebec was hit by a blue-green algae crisis, which wreaked havoc on many of the province's lakes and severely limited water usage. Media coverage of the topic was intense and, in 2008, in an effort to mitigate future occurrences, the Quebec provincial government passed legislation limiting the allowable phosphorus quantity (considered the culprit of the crisis) in laundry and dishwashing detergents to 0.5 per cent.[2] As Bio-Vert products were already phosphate-free, they flew off store shelves. Demand exploded and within a year, Bio-Vert products were carried by all major provincial retailers, including Loblaws Companies Limited, Metro, Costco Wholesale Corporation and Walmart.

As he scanned the surrounding shelves, Grand-Maison's smile thinned. Another national brand had introduced a green product line which was placed front and centre on the shelf—and on sale for 50 per cent off. Just a few years ago, Bio-Vert was one of the only green options; now, Bio-Vert was one of many.

To stave off increasing competition, Savons Prolav needed to do more to differentiate Bio-Vert from its competitors. Product efficiency, the brand's prime differentiator, was no longer enough. Grand-Maison feared that Bio-Vert would disappear from the minds of consumers and retailers once the blue-green algae crisis subsided. Grand-Maison thought back to a phone call he received a few days earlier. A wholesaler was looking for a green product line to include as the house

---

2   "Moins de phosphate dans le détergent à vaisselle," *Rue Frontenac*, 2010, http://exrue frontenac.com/nouvelles-generales/environnement/24934--phosphate-dans-le-detergent-a-vaisselle, accessed November 19, 2012.

brand of a large, well-known supermarket chain in Western Canada. The offer guaranteed a significant sales volume for several years; however, the house brand was to be priced at the low end of the range and the company was therefore looking to secure source material at a "reasonable cost." Grand-Maison knew this meant diluting product formulas, which he did not want to pursue at all—but as he looked at the increasing green product options on the grocery shelves, he realized he had to act quickly to keep Bio-Vert's competitive position. Retailers would not continue to carry so many different products much longer. How could he make sure the Bio-Vert brand remained on the shelves?

Why use green household products?

Household cleaning products were undergoing a 'green' revolution in Canada in the early 21st century. The Canadian public was increasingly concerned about the health and environmental impacts of everyday products.[3] Consumers recognized the impact of their purchase decisions and were opting for products that minimized adverse effects, even if these green products sold for a premium.[4]

Water: an important resource

Quebec was Canada's largest province by area, covering 1.7 million square kilometres (almost three times larger than France). Known as "the land of lakes and forests," Quebec's 4,500 rivers and 500,000 lakes held about 3 per cent of the world's fresh water reserves, providing an abundance of inexpensive water for all of its needs: domestic, agricultural, industrial, commercial and recreational. Water had always played a key role in Quebec's economic development, helping it to expand from a single trading outpost into thousands of vibrant communities over four centuries. Since the 1980s, waterways had also played a key role in the strong local tourist industry. Some 15 million tourists—almost double the province's entire population—visited Quebec's rural areas in 2009, collectively spending C$3 billion.[5,6,7] Seeking a respite from hectic urban life, tourists flocked to the

---

3 Jessica Nadeau, "Jean Coutu: Fini les phosphates," *Canoë—Techno & Sciences*, January 23, 2008, http://fr.canoe.ca/techno/nouvelles/archives/2008/01/20080123-092253.html, accessed October 11, 2010.

4 "Green product price premiums turn off cash-strapped consumers," *Business Green*, June 18, 2008, http://www.businessgreen.com/bg/news/1802815/green-product-price-premiums-cash-strapped-consumers, accessed September 18, 2011.

5 All figures are in C$ unless stated otherwise.

6 "Quebec handy numbers," Institut de la statistique du Québec, 2010, http://www.stat.gouv.qc.ca/publications/referenc/pdf2010/QCM2010_an.pdf, accessed February 16, 2011.

7 "Le tourisme au Québec en bref – 2009," Ministère du Tourisme, Gouvernement du Québec, 2009, http://www.tourisme.gouv.qc.ca/publications/media/document/etudes-statistiques/TQ-bref-2009.pdf, accessed February 16, 2011.

beautiful lakes and rivers in the countryside. Thus, the tourism industry realized that the proliferation of unsightly blue-green algae must be kept in check.[8]

Health and environmental impacts of conventional products

Canadians spent an average of 90 per cent of their time indoors.[9] Indoor air was up to five times more polluted than outdoor air, in part because of the chemicals found in household products.[10] More specifically, many conventional cleaning supplies contained volatile organic chemicals (VOCs), vapours that evaporated into the air when certain liquid or solid products were used or stored. VOCs had adverse health effects, including eye, throat and nose irritation, headaches, nausea, liver, kidney or central nervous system damage and even cancer. Green household products did not contain VOCs; therefore, the use of these products improved indoor air quality.[11]

Laundry detergents, in particular, contained many ingredients that had potentially negative health and environmental effects; however, most consumers did not know or understand the potential impacts of these ingredients over time (see exhibits 2 and 3). As consumers became more aware of and alarmed by these issues, they created increased demand for green detergents.

While many common ingredients in cleaning products were linked to environmental and health concerns, phosphates had gained particular attention in Quebec. Due to their high efficiency and low cost, phosphates were widely used as a main component in conventional detergents. Unfortunately, for detergents to be effective, their main components or 'builders' must address a number of cleaning characteristics. Sodium triphosphate, a widely used phosphate builder, rated high in many areas; however, like phosphates in general, sodium triphosphate had poor environmental characteristics due to its spurring of excessive algae growth, adversely affecting other marine life (see exhibits 3 and 4).[12]

8 "Guide de mise en valeur des plans d'eau du Québec à des fins récréotouristiques et de conservation de patrimoine," Ministère du Tourisme, Gouvernement du Québec, 2000, http://www.bonjourquebec.com/eau, accessed February 16, 2011.
9 "Indoor air quality," *Health Canada*, 2011, http://www.hc-sc.gc.ca/ewh-semt/air/in/index-eng.php, accessed November 19, 2012.
10 "Healthy buildings, healthy people: A vision for the 21st century," United States Environmental Protection Agency, October 2001, http://www.epa.gov/iaq/pubs/hbhp.html, accessed February 20, 2011.
11 "Care for your air: A guide to indoor air quality," United States Environmental Protection Agency, September 2008, http://www.epa.gov/iaq/pubs/careforyourair.html, accessed February 16, 2011.
12 Eduard Smulders, Wolfgang von Rybinski, & Anette Nordskog "Laundry detergents, 1. Introduction," *Ullmann's Encyclopedia of Industrial Chemistry*, 2011, Wiley; Eduard Smulders & Eric Sung "Laundry detergents, 2. Ingredients and Products," *Ullmann's Encyclopedia of Industrial Chemistry*, 2011, Wiley; Josef Steber & Frederike Wiebel, "Laundry detergents, 4. Ecology and Toxicology," *Ullmann's Encyclopedia of Industrial Chemistry*, 2011, Wiley.

Until increases in blue-green algae blooms in Quebec's lakes and rivers brought environmental concerns associated with the use of phosphates to the forefront, environmental considerations were often secondary to cleaning performance among most consumers' preferences. The blue-green algae crisis peaked in 2007 (see Exhibit 5).[13]

Usually invisible to the naked eye and almost omnipresent in some form wherever there was light and water, blue-green algae were necessary to the majority of ecosystems. They performed key life-cycle functions for other marine organisms.[14] Most abundant in freshwater lakes and rivers, algae were widely known as 'pond scum,' the slimy green coating on lakes and rivers in the summer months. These blooms, which signalled an imbalance of blue-green algae, occurred when algae proliferated due to a combination of excess nitrogen and/or phosphorus (which they, and many other organisms, used as food) and hot temperatures. This process, called eutrophication,[15] happened because these algae had a higher affinity for phosphorus than a lake's other organisms. The algae essentially monopolized the food supply and grew out of balance with other organisms in the waterway.[16] Over time, this imbalance could become permanent and hinder biodiversity, limiting and altering species that survived in the water.

In addition to disrupting a waterway's ecosystem, certain types of algae blooms produced and released toxins, further damaging the ecosystem and potentially harming humans as well (see Exhibit 6).[17] In the summer of 2007, drinking, cooking and swimming were banned in a record number of Quebec's waterways and the detrimental effects of blue-green algae caught the public's attention.[18]

Sales of Bio-Vert products skyrocketed during and after this crisis, thanks in part to broad media coverage that sensitized consumers to solutions that mitigated recurrences. Despite limited capacity at its facility in Laval, Quebec, Savons Pro-lav responded quickly by outsourcing production and distribution, employing a

13 "Blue-green algae contamination a crisis: Quebec officials," CBC News, July 12, 2007, http://www.cbc.ca/health/story/2007/07/12/ot-algae-070712.html, accessed November 16, 2010.

14 John Waterbury, "Little things matter a lot," *Oceanus*, March 11, 2005, www.whoi.edu/oceanus/viewArticle.do?id=3808, accessed February 18, 2011.

15 Stéphanie Saucier, "Bientôt les algues bleues?" *Canoë Infos*, July 11, 2010, http://fr.canoe.ca/infos/environnement/archives/2010/07/20100711-184417.html, accessed November 22, 2010.

16 Luuc R. Mur, Olav M. Skulberg, Hans Utkilen, "Cyanobacteria in the environment," in Ingrid Chorus, Jamie Bartram (eds.), *Toxic cyanobacteria in water: A guide to their public health consequences, monitoring and management*, World Health Organization, 1999, pp.25-54. www.who.int/water_sanitation_health/resourcesquality/toxcyanchap2.pdf, accessed February 18, 2011.

17 "Blue-green algae (cyanobacteria) and their toxins," *Health Canada*, 2008, http://www.hc-sc.gc.ca/ewh-semt/pubs/water-eau/cyanobacter-eng.php, accessed November 17, 2010.

18 "Blue-green algae contamination a crisis: Quebec officials," *CBC News*, July 12, 2007, http://www.cbc.ca/health/story/2007/07/12/ot-algae-070712.html, accessed November 16, 2010.

strategy much like that of beverage giant The Coca-Cola Company.[19] Coca-Cola owned the patent and branding rights to its products, but independent bottling groups manufactured and distributed its products through licensing agreements.[20] Given the uncertainty of consumer demand as well as the Grand-Maisons' belief that product formulations provided 'added value' to their company's products, outsourcing made more sense than physically expanding. It also minimized capital expenditures, allowing the company to meet the current demands while remaining flexible to future fluctuations.[21]

Challenges with green household products

Despite having gained ground, green cleaning products still faced many challenges, including consumer demand, product efficiency, pricing and difficulty in discerning 'green authenticity' from 'greenwashing' (portraying a product as greener than it was).

Consumers

Many consumers were unaware of the health and environmental benefits of green cleaning products. Among those who were aware, purchasing decisions still varied based on the importance of these benefits relative to other considerations. In addition, when considering a product's complete life cycle, inefficient product use by the consumer increased the product's environmental impact—something over which manufacturers had little control.[22]

However, these consumer issues were simultaneously a major challenge and key opportunity for expanding market share for makers of green cleaning products. According to Grand-Maison, confusing information in the media surrounding green cleaning products impeded consumers' abilities to make informed purchasing decisions. To address this problem, Savons Prolav took several steps to increase consumer education on the advantages of using green products and concerns associated with conventional products. These steps included hiring Savons Prolav's first in-house environmental director, developing a more in-depth website to support

---

19 Yan Grand-Maison, personal interview, October 12, 2010.

20 "Our Business Model," Coca-Cola Ltd., no date, www.cocacola.ca/our_company_our businessmodel.htm, accessed October 18, 2011.

21 J. Lamarche, personal interview, October 22, 2010.

22 Jacob Madsen, Bryan Hartlin, Shahila Perumalpillai, Sarah Selby, Simon Aumônier, *Mapping of evidence on sustainable development impacts that occur in life cycles of clothing: A report to DEFRA*, Environmental Resources Management Ltd, 2007.

the company's promotional and informational efforts and developing clear and complete ingredient labels for its products, much like those found on food items.[23]

Product efficiency

Historically, green cleaning products were often inferior to conventional products in terms of effectiveness/performance; for example, in 2008, grist.org blogger Sarah van Schagen tested six green laundry detergents (though Bio-Vert was not one of them) by soiling shirts with persistent stains. She stated, "It's a wash: none of the detergents fully removed all of the stains but they all produced otherwise-clean clothes."[24] Though she did not actually perform a comparison test between conventional and green detergents, the implication was that conventional detergents would have removed the stains in question.

For Savons Prolav's Bio-Vert brand, environmental friendliness and product efficiency were its primary differentiators. It invested heavily in research and development to continuously improve on existing product formulations and develop new ones. Grand-Maison proudly touted Bio-Vert's performance against national brand conventional detergents and had commissioned third-party comparison testing, which substantiated his claims that Bio-Vert worked as well as traditional cleaning products.[25] Additionally, Protégez-Vous, a Quebec-based consumer protection organization, compared several green laundry detergents and found Bio-Vert to be among the best of those tested, naming it a 'recommended' product because of its performance in removing stains and preserving colours.[26]

Qualifying 'green'

With increased consumer interest in environmental issues, the marketplace became flooded with a multitude of 'eco' or 'green' cleaning products. The wide variety of products and criteria for determining environmental characteristics or 'greenness' could be daunting; customers could easily become confused by the myriad of eco-friendly claims including recycled packaging, reduced energy and resource use, changing material compositions, etc. A 2009 review of 2,000 'green' products found that 98 per cent of them carried exaggerated or misleading claims based on the US Federal Trade Commission's guidelines for fair business

---

23 J. Lamarche, personal interview, October 22, 2010.
24 Sarah van Schagen, "It's a wash:A review of six green laundry detergents," in *Grist*, no date, www.grist.org/article/its-a-wash/, accessed November 5, 2010.
25 As shown through third party testing performed by Bureau Veritas and commissioned by Savon Prolav.
26 M-J. Boudreau, "TEST: Détergents pour laveuses à chargement frontal: Mission accomplie?" *Protégez-vous*, 2006.

practices.[27] Given the scale of the problem with green labelling, consumers felt largely left to their own devices to sort out which claims were most pertinent and which trade-offs they should make when deciding between products.

The Government of Canada attempted to address this problem through its 'EcoLogo' certification program. Launched in 1988, EcoLogo certification "provided customers—public, corporate and consumer—with assurance that the products and services bearing the logo meet stringent standards of environmental leadership."[28] The EcoLogo program compared products in the same category by developing "rigorous and scientifically relevant criteria reflecting the entire life cycle of the product"[29] and awarded the EcoLogo certification to products that met its standards and performed as well as their conventional counterparts. Only about 20 per cent of applications met these requirements and achieved certification. From this perspective, EcoLogo certification was one way Canadian consumers could choose quality green products; however, the cost of EcoLogo certification could be quite high and placed an undue burden on smaller firms (see Exhibit 7). As a result, there may have been many products which met EcoLogo criteria but could not afford to be certified. This offered an opportunity for firms such as Savons Prolav to further differentiate their products. For Savons Prolav, in particular, the cost of EcoLogo certification was worth the differentiated value and all 17 of Bio-Vert's products were EcoLogo certified.[30]

Pricing

Some of the raw materials used in Bio-Vert's products were up to three times as expensive as conventional equivalents and as a small manufacturer, Savons Prolav lacked the economies of scale of larger manufacturers to push these prices down. Despite this, Savons Prolav prided itself on pricing its products competitively with conventional products (see Exhibit 8). On a price-per-load basis, Bio-Vert laundry detergent ranked ninth, in the middle of the price range among 'green' products and less than 2 per cent more than the least expensive detergents.

Interestingly, economic trends were upending this price difference as the increasing prices of oil-based products put dual pressures on detergent manufacturers—increasing raw material and transportation costs. Many conventional formulations used petrochemical materials, yet price increases were difficult to pass on to consumers in this mature industry. Instead, manufacturers were reducing costs through product reformulations, often substituting conventional raw materials

27 "Greenwashing affects 98 per cent of products including toys, baby products and cosmetics," Terrachoice.com, 2009, http://www.terrachoice.com/images/Seven Sins of Green washing Release - April 15 2009 - US.pdf, accessed November 20, 2012.

28 Ecologo, no date, http://www.ecologo.org/en/index.asp, accessed November 6, 2010.

29 Ecologo, no date, http://www.ecologo.org/en/index.asp, accessed November 6, 2010.

30 Yan Grand-Maison, personal interview, October 12, 2010.

with 'greener' alternatives at lower cost.[31] The potential result was cheaper and greener re-formulations, thereby increasing green product competition.

The industry

Industry overview

The household cleaning products industry was highly competitive and mature, characterized by large international brands attempting to meet the traditional consumers' demands in the mass market and also address more niche areas such as eco-products.[32] As a niche within the cleaning products industry, the eco-friendly cleaning products market was growing rapidly, though still not entirely distinguished from conventional products. In the United States, large firms with international brands (e.g. The Proctor & Gamble Company, Unilever, Kimberly-Clark Corporation, Colgate-Palmolive Company, The Clorox Company, etc.) held 95.3 per cent of market share, leaving only 4.7 per cent for smaller brands.[33] Of the Canadian-based manufacturers, most were located in Ontario (85 per cent), with a secondary presence in Quebec (9 per cent).[34] Most of this Quebec presence was in the form of micro (less than five employees) and small (between five and 20 employees) manufacturing firms (see Exhibit 9).[35]

Industry strategies

Historically, price or product differentiation shaped the cleaning products market, with product differentiation being redefined over time as the industry evolved. Differentiating attributes such as scents, packaging and sanitizing had long been used. As consumers increasingly sought out environmentally friendly features, manufacturers incorporated these characteristics into their overall product differentiation.

31 Kate Phillips, Rebecca Coons, Alex Scott, Kerri Walsh, "Soaps & Detergents: Producers race to lower costs and go green." *Chemical Week*, 2008, www.chemweek.com/markets/specialty_chemicals/soap_and_detergents/10044.html, accessed April 19, 2011.

32 "ACI unveils cleaning product industry sustainability report," *American Cleaning Institute, For Better Living*, 2011, www.cleaninginstitute.org/aci_unveils_cleaning_product_industry_sustainability_report/, accessed October 25, 2011.

33 "Clorox," *Wikinvest*, no date, www.wikinvest.com/stock/Clorox_Company_(CLX), accessed October 25, 2011.Though no clear data exists for Canada on this point, it is likely similar to US-based information.

34 Karyne Boutin, Monique Tremblay, Marie-Lyne Turgeon, "Détergents pour lave-vaisselle et pour la lessive – Analyse économique," Développement durable, Environnement, et Parcs, Québec, 2007, http://www.mddep.gouv.qc.ca/eau/Projet-reglement/detergents/analyse_eco.pdf, accessed November 20, 2012.

35 "Gross domestic product by industry," *Statistics Canada*, 2006, Catalogue No.15-001-XPB.

However, at the very least, the cleaning products had to do what was expected of them: clean effectively.

Savons Prolav leveraged its green characteristics and continually innovated to reduce its products' environmental impact and reinforce its eco-friendly brand—a key part of which involved collaborating with other companies to develop new product formulations. Among its successful collaborations was a partnership with Innu-Science, a local biotechnology company that developed an eco-cleaning solution using enzymes and "grease-eating" bacteria, in 2007. The two organizations partnered to develop a new all-purpose cleaner which provided Innu-Science, already established in industrial cleaning markets, with an opening into the consumer market while providing Savons Prolav with a new all-purpose cleaning product with improved performance and strong environmental characteristics.[36]

Grand-Maison also began developing a partnership with the Inter-University Research Centre for the Life Cycle of Products, Processes and Services (CIRAIG), itself a partnership between École Polytechnique de Montréal, Université de Montréal and HEC Montréal. CIRAIG worked within the industry to provide academic expertise on issues of sustainable development such as environmental assessment, life-cycle analyses and general sustainability research.[37] Through this partnership with CIRAIG, Savons Prolav would be taking a first step towards adopting a 'cradle-to-cradle' approach to its business and products, which was intended to eventually encompass the company's entire operations. Despite the potentially major changes that this more encompassing approach would require of the company (e.g. with respect to logistics, material sourcing, packaging, end-consumer impact, etc.), Grand-Maison believed this type of partnership embodied Savons Prolav's core environmental values and would further differentiate the Bio-Vert brand.

Green marketing

Green consumer behaviours

With the emergence of green cleaning products, it was important to identify the values and motivations of North American consumers. Market research firm Mintel US reported that in 2009:[38]

---

36 Claude Turcotte, "Portrait–Innu-Science, quand le ménage se fait propre." *LeDevoir.com*, 2007, http://www.offres.ledevoir.com/economie/136546/portrait-innu-science-quand-le-menage-se-fait-propre, accessed October 11, 2010.

37 CIRAIG, no date, http://www.ciraig.org/, accessed November 20, 2012.

38 Barbara White-Sax, "'Green' goes mainstream, cleans up on retail shelves." *Drug Store News*, 2010, www.drugstorenews.com/article/%E2%80%98green%E2%80%99-goes-main stream-cleans-retail-shelves, accessed April 19, 2011.

- 40 per cent of consumers said they were more concerned about the environment than they were a year ago

- 70 per cent of consumers said they worry about chemicals in household cleaners

- 28 per cent of consumers cited allergies as a reason for using alternative cleaning products

Despite the growing interest in environmentally friendly products, consumers were nonetheless influenced by some or all of the factors of the 'value-action gap.' The value-action gap was defined as the gap or discrepancy between consumers' values and their subsequent purchase behaviours.[39] In other words, while many individuals considered themselves 'green' because they endeavoured to follow the 'reduce, reuse, recycle' strategy and/or minimize energy consumption, these actions did not necessarily translate into green purchasing behaviours. This gap could occur for a number of reasons, including:

1. **Self-interest:** Consumers were typically reluctant to purchase a product that did not align with their self-interests. When purchases satisfied self-interest, consumers felt better about themselves because the purchases enhanced their self-perception. If a buyer wishes to be perceived as an environmentally conscious individual, purchasing green products boosts the buyer's desired self-concept.

2. **Performance:** The purchased product had to match the performance of its conventional counterpart. While performance was often compared in the media and by consumer groups, consumers' personal experiences were the primary influences on opinions regarding performance and, subsequently, purchasing decisions. Consumers who held strong pro-environmental values tended to view a green product's performance more favourably and state that it was only "mildly difficult" for them to identify green products, versus "fairly difficult" for those less concerned with the environment.[40]

3. **Pricing:** Price premiums could also limit product purchases for moderately green consumers; furthermore, this tolerance threshold was demonstrably lower during difficult economic times.[41] Depending on the perceived value,

39 Anja Kollmuss, Julian Agyeman, "Mind the gap: Why do people act environmentally and what are the barriers to pro-environmental behaviour?" *Environmental Education Research*, 2002, pp.239-260.

40 Josephine Pickett-Baker, Ritsuko Ozaki, "Pro-environmental products: marketing influence on consumer purchase decision," *Journal of Consumer Marketing*, 2008, Vol. 25 Iss: 5, pp.281-293.

41 Haymarket Publishing Group, "Best business: Accreditations—green blindness," *Print-Week*, 2010.

price differences could direct potential green consumers to the conventional product offering.[42]

4. **Accessibility and Identification:** Brand awareness influenced purchase decisions. Established brands typically had loyal followings. Consumers newly interested in green products were more likely to opt for prominent brands because they already had a relationship with that brand.[43] These green product lines could offer higher-than-normal incremental growth to the parent brand even if their conventional and green products were marketed against each other, despite the cannibalistic nature of this behaviour.[44]

Consumer segments

Since 2000, the Natural Marketing Institute had identified five green consumer segments in North America (see Exhibit 10):[45]

- **LOHAS (Lifestyles of Health and Sustainability):** 19 per cent. LOHAS consumers were dedicated to personal and planetary health. They bought green products, supported advocacy programs and were active stewards of the environment. This segment doubled in size from 2002 to 2010.

- **Naturalites:** 14 per cent. These consumers were focused on natural/organic consumer packaged goods (CPGs) with a strong health focus in foods/beverages. They were not politically committed to the environmental movement nor were they driven to eco-friendly durable goods. This segment consisted of only 6 per cent of consumers in 2002.

- **Drifters:** 21 per cent. This segment had good environmental intentions but other factors (such as price) took primary influence in shaping their purchase decisions. This segment accounted for 31 per cent of consumers in 2002. Consumers in this central segment seemed to migrate towards more eco-friendly segments.

- **Conventionals:** 29 per cent. Conventionals made up the largest consumer segment. Although they did not have green attitudes, they did exhibit some environmentally aware behaviour, such as recycling and energy conservation. It appeared that many former "Unconcerned" consumers had migrated into this category, increasing its size from 19 per cent in 2002, to 29 per cent in 2010.

---

42 Centaur Publishing, "Where the green things are," *Precision Marketing*, 2008.

43 Josephine Pickett-Baker, Ritsuko Ozaki, "Pro-environmental products: marketing influence on consumer purchase decision," *Journal of Consumer Marketing*, 2008, Vol. 25 Iss: 5, pp.281-293.

44 Mitchell Adrian, Kenneth Dupre, "The environmental movement: A status report and implications for pricing," *S.A.M. Advanced Management Journal*, 1994, Vol. 59 Iss: 2. p.35.

45 "The LOHAS consumer trends database," Natural Marketing Institute, 2010, www.nmi solutions.com/lohasd_segment.html, accessed February 15, 2011.

- **Unconcerned:** 17 per cent. Environmental and social benefit were not priorities for this segment. These consumers demonstrated no concern for environmentally responsible behaviour. In 2010, this consumer segment was half its size as evaluated in 2002.

In light of this information, green companies might be tempted to market heavily towards the LOHAS segment; however, this seemingly accessible market segment was cautious of eco-friendly claims and suspicious of greenwashing.[46] Marketing to this segment was therefore mainly reserved for businesses that embodied these environmental values and whose processes fulfilled the most stringent sustainability criteria.[47] More broadly, there was a delicate balance between eco-friendliness, quality and price that had to be met for all segments. Additionally, while the LOHAS and Naturalites segments might willingly pay more for eco-products, the premium peaks could reach only 20 to 30 per cent of the conventional product's price.[48]

Savons Prolav believed that its clients knew that "Bio-Vert doesn't just talk green: it acts green" and that this was why they bought the company's products.[49] Most purchasing decisions for non-durable goods took an average of only 6.6 seconds as small expenditures did not warrant long mental deliberations among most consumers.[50] Savons Prolav therefore focused its advertising strategies on in-store promotions to increase unplanned consumer purchases. This included paying to place Bio-Vert's products at the ends of aisles, offering two-for-one promotions and developing in-store advertisements. Product displays could increase purchase probability by up to 40 per cent, and coupons helped direct consumers to certain products over others.[51] Promoting products' health benefits could further influence emotional buying and attachment to certain brands.[52] In addition, general media outlets, such as television advertisements, were simply too expensive for

46 Laurie Demeritt, "What makes a green consumer, *DJC*, 2005, www.djc.com/news/en/11170267.html, accessed November 7, 2010.

47 Jacquie Ottman, "Green Marketing Success Strategies from Sustainable Brands," *Jacquie Ottman's Green Marketing Blog*, 2009, www.greenmarketing.com/blog/comments/green-marketing-success-strategies-from-sustainable-brands-09/, accessed September 18, 2011.

48 Deborah Aarts, "Green consumers are skeptical," *Canadian Business Network*, 2010, http://www.profitguide.com/opportunity/green-consumers-are-skeptical-29960, accessed November 7, 2010.

49 Yan Grand-Maison, personal interview, October 12, 2010.

50 Philip Kotler, *Marketing Management*, 2009, Pearson.

51 Jeffrey Inman, Russell S. Winer, Rosellina Ferraro, "The interplay amongst category characteristics, customer characteristics, and customer activities on in-store decision making." *Journal of Marketing*, 2009, Vol. 73 Iss:. 5, pp.19-29.

52 Josephine Pickett-Baker, Ritsuko Ozaki, "Pro-environmental products: marketing influence on consumer purchase decision," *Journal of Consumer Marketing*, 2008, Vol. 25 Iss: 5, pp.281-293.

Savons Prolav and tended to have a very limited effect on consumer brand recall and purchase decisions.[53]

Quebec competitive landscape

By 2006, there were 22 laundry and dishwasher detergent manufacturers in Quebec, totalling $160 million in sales. Of these products, the three 'green' manufacturers were all located in the Montreal area: Bio-Vert (Savons Prolav), Nettoyants Lemieux and Attitude (BioSpectra).[54] Attitude was a direct competitor of Bio-Vert. It produced many of the same products as Bio-Vert, was EcoLogo-certified and used a marketing strategy similar to Bio-Vert's.[55] Attitude was sold across Canada and in select US locations, and was often partnered with its line of baby products. Nettoyants Lemieux was also EcoLogo-certified, though its products were sold exclusively in the company's own retail stores and select health stores. Nettoyants Lemieux also sold in bulk quantities, reducing single-use packaging by letting customers reuse their containers over time.[56]

In addition to these local manufacturers, many national conventional brands had introduced green products;[57] however, even by 2010, none of the conventional brands were EcoLogo-certified.[58] Some of the large international brands had introduced green versions of their well-known brands, such as Sunlight's Green Clean. Others created entirely new lines dedicated to the green market, such as Clorox's Green Works. For these reasons, Savons Prolav battled for market share with different competitors in different consumer segments (Exhibit 10).

A key industry development was the 2007 Environment Quality Act (EQA) in Quebec, which strictly limited the phosphate content of detergents as a result of the blue-green algae outbreak that adversely affected Quebec's waterways. Prior to this legislation, many detergents contained as much as 8.7 per cent phosphate content by weight. The EQA reduced this threshold to no more than to 0.5 per cent. When passed, the economic impact was considered to be negligible as

53 Cathy J. Cobb, Wayne D. Hoyer, "The influence of advertising at the moment of brand choice" *Journal of Advertising*, 1985, Vol 4 Iss: 4, p.5.

54 Karyne Boutin, Monique Tremblay, Marie-Lyne Turgeon, "Détergents pour lave-vaisselle et pour la lessive – Analyse économique," Développement durable, Environnement, et Parcs, Québec, 2007, www.mddep.gouv.qc.ca/eau/Projet-reglement/detergents/analyse_eco.pdf.

55 "La Bonne Attitude," BioSpectra Inc., no date, www.labonneattitude.com/fr/products/index/lessive#, accessed November 23, 2010.

56 "L'écologie dans le sang," Nettoyants Lemieux, 2010, www.produits-lemieux.com/index.php, accessed November 6, 2010.

57 Barbara White-Sax, "'Green goes' mainstream, cleans up on retail shelves." *Drug Store News*, 2010, www.drugstorenews.com/article/%E2%80%98green%E2%80%99-goes-mainstream-cleans-retail-shelves, accessed April 19, 2011

58 "Savons Prolav," Ecologo, no date, www.ecologo.org/en/participatingcompanies/details.asp?client_id=175&cat=2, accessed November 22, 2010.

many manufacturers were voluntarily committing to comply with this requirement before 2010.[59] The impact on green product companies, however, was less clear. In 2008, both Savons Prolav and Nettoyants Lemieux reported sharp sales increases: for example, in 2008, Bio-Vert's sales volume grew by over 500 per cent.[60] Nettoyants Lemieux, meanwhile, reported increases in net revenues of 43 per cent during the same period. Grand-Maison knew that rapid sales growth could be temporary, leading to a sharp peak in product demand before stabilizing. Furthermore, beyond this initial windfall, Grand-Maison was concerned that supermarkets would consolidate around a few key brands. He believed there would ultimately be only two small firms left to compete against the private labels and national brands. This competition was 'safe' because private labels were the supermarkets' own brands and national brands paid to obtain premium shelf space, something small firms simply could not afford. To ensure that Bio-Vert was one of the brands left standing, Savons Prolav needed to clarify its long-term strategy and operations.

Savons Prolav and the Bio-Vert brand

History of the company

Savons Prolav was founded in 1984 by Louiselle Mallette in Laval, Quebec, a suburb of Montreal. From its inception, Savons Prolav focused on manufacturing environmentally friendly alternatives to traditional household cleaning products.[61] Savons Prolav's strength was the efficiency of its products vis-à-vis conventional products. Mallette ran the company until 2002, at which time she handed over management of the company to her niece and nephew, Yan and Bianka Grand-Maison, though she retained a minority stake in the company for some time thereafter.

The Grand-Maisons grew up about 200 kilometres north of Quebec City, surrounded by the Canadian wilderness. This instilled in them a sincere respect for the environment from a young age. During their teenage years, the two spent summers working various jobs at Savons Prolav alongside their aunt, which strengthened their values of environmental stewardship.[62] Taking over the company was, therefore, a natural transition for them in 2002. They began managing the small company with plans to grow it while staying true to their core values: environmental

59 Karyne Boutin, Monique Tremblay, Marie-Lyne Turgeon, "Détergents pour lave-vaisselle et pour la lessive—Analyse économique," Développement durable, Environnement, et Parcs, Québec, 2007, www.mddep.gouv.qc.ca/eau/Projet-reglement/detergents/analyse_eco.pdf.

60 Yan Grand-Maison, personal interview, October 12, 2010.

61 "Journée de la terre - Bio-Vert fait des gestes concrets pour la planète!" *Canadian Newswire*, 2010, www.newswire.ca/en/releases/archive/April2010/20/c3877.html, accessed October 13, 2010.

62 J. Lamarche, personal interview, October 22, 2010.

awareness, sustainable decisions, meticulous hiring processes, uncompromising quality, honesty and, perhaps most importantly, valuing the company more than its mere financial worth.[63]

In 2005, Savons Prolav won a national award from the Canadian Council of Grocery Distributors for its breakthrough in detergents.[64] Inspired by European technology, it developed bleach caplets to replace traditional liquid bleach, thereby decreasing water consumption, packaging and transportation requirements of its bleach-based detergents. While the Grand-Maisons felt the breakthrough could potentially propel Savons Prolav into a national—or even international—playing field, they found themselves torn between their environmental values and their desire to grow the company. In the end, they decided to discontinue this award-winning product and all other products that used ingredients which they believed were environmentally harmful (such as bleach and phosphates). Previously, in 2002, Savons Prolav also acquired the Bio-Vert brand as a way to promote the distinctive environmental characteristics of its products. At the time, Savons Prolav paid less than $100,000 for the brand—a testament, Yan Grand-Maison stated, to the fact that environmental products were "not yet in fashion."

Building on this intensified environmental focus, Savons Prolav developed the Bio-Vert line of cleaning products. Initially, the line was sold only in local natural food stores; however, Bio-Vert gradually entered the mainstream market, eventually landing on the shelves of many of Canada's major pharmacies, grocery chains and 'big box' stores. From 2005 to 2008, Savons Prolav grew 20 to 35 per cent annually. Following the blue-green algae crisis and subsequent legislation in 2007, demand for Bio-Vert exploded by more than 500 per cent in 2008, and boosted market penetration in Quebec to 98 per cent.

This rapid growth caught the attention of others in the industry, and Savons Prolav received lucrative offers to expand into the US market. The company was approached by multiple distributors wanting to market Savons Prolav's products under their own brand names. Inevitably, however, the common 'catch' with these offers was the insistence on lowering Savons Prolav's price points —i.e., diluting the products' formulations to make them less expensive. Doing so would decrease both the products' efficiency and environmental characteristics, making them 'lighter green,' so to speak. For small businesses, such offers could be alluring and could often be a lifeline for a company's long-term survival. Again, this forced the Grand-Maisons to address the tensions of economic profit versus environmental value. While tempted, they had eventually declined such offers.

Savons Prolav's mission was to produce "the best ecological formula" possible by developing eco-friendly cleaners that were as efficient and competitively priced

63 Yan Grand-Maison, personal interview, October 12, 2010.
64 "Canadian grand prix new products awards winners 2004–2005," *Canadian Grocer*, 2005, www.bizlink.com/cangrocerfiles/PDFs/aug05/06_CGRO_GP_winners.pdf, accessed October 13, 2010.

as conventional products.[65] The company achieved this by continuing to strive for product efficiency and innovation. A large portion of Savons Prolav's net income was re-invested to improve its products.[66] The company officially defined its sustainability policy, formalizing its values in its pledge to 'act green.' It supported this pledge by focusing on five main areas: 1) operations and product development; 2) raising employee awareness and involvement; 3) suppliers; 4) communication and transparency; and 5) corporate social responsibility.[67]

Savons Prolav had a non-hierarchal, 'family business' feel. Many of the employees had worked for the company for several years, a loyalty due in part to the firm's tailored hiring process, which combined assessments based on pertinent skills and environmental values. While hiring environmentally minded employees had typically been more difficult in the past, it became easier as environmental issues became more of a public concern.[68]

Savons Prolav also actively engaged the local community through public awareness and fundraising campaigns run by local schools in the neighbourhoods around its headquarters. Some of the projects Savons Prolav supported included student scholarships, lake and river restorations and installing bicycle racks around the neighbourhood.[69] Yan Grand-Maison became vice-president of the Quebec Environment Foundation, a provincial-level non-profit organization aiming to "bring about and accelerate change in the attitudes and habits of Quebecers in terms of improving and protecting the environment."[70] Through his involvement, Grand-Maison worked actively to resolve the environmental issues affecting the local community. Both Yan and Bianka Grand-Maison supported these types of initiatives as a means of giving back to the community and as a way to educate potential customers.[71]

Consumer education was an ongoing challenge for Savons Prolav. Misinformation through faulty and/or incomplete media reports remained rampant and implicated Bio-Vert directly at times; for example, in February 2010, Radio-Canada, a government-funded news agency, reported that certain schools had discontinued the use of eco-friendly cleaning products due to skin rashes and respiratory issues. The report linked these health problems to enzyme-based cleaning agents

65 "Corporate philosophy & commitment," Savons Prolav, Inc, no date, www.bio-vert.com/en/engagement.php, accessed November 5, 2010.
66 J. Lamarche, personal interview, October 22, 2010.
67 "Sustainability policy," Savons Prolav, Inc, no date, www.bio-vert.com/en/developpement-durable.php, accessed November 20, 2010.
68 J. Lamarche, personal interview, October 22, 2010.
69 "Corporate sustainability report (CSR)," Savons Prolav, Inc., 2009, www.bio-vert.com/rapport-developpement-durable.php, accessed October 21, 2010.
70 "Mission et historique," Fondation Quebecoise en Environnement, no date, www.fqe.qc.ca/miss.php, accessed January, 7, 2011.
71 Yan Grand-Maison, personal interview, October 12, 2010.

in the eco-friendly cleaners.[72] Though this concerned industrial rather than household cleaning products, the story did not make this distinction. Some Bio-Vert household products used enzyme-based cleaning agents, although these were lacto-bacillus-based enzymes from the same family of bacteria found in dairy products.[73] Ultimately, Health Canada could not validate Radio-Canada's assertions; however, competitor Nettoyants Lemieux used the opportunity to aggressively market itself as a manufacturer of 'eco-technology,' using plant-based instead of enzyme-based cleaning agents (which indirectly implicated Bio-Vert) and publicly cited the Radio-Canada article.

While Savons Prolav had won several distinctions and awards (see Exhibit 11), the company was not content to simply stagnate once it reached these goals. In the short term, it explored alternative transportation modes to reduce the environmental footprint of shipments to Western Canada. Longer-term plans included exploring ways to develop an increased presence in Western Canada and expand into the United States without unduly increasing its environmental footprint. One strategy involved expanding its subcontracting of Bio-Vert formulas (much like Coca-Cola) in order to minimize transportation and distribution impacts.

2009: Decisions

Yan Grand-Maison glanced again at the multitude of laundry detergents on the grocery store shelves. His eyes settled on the store's house brand. Would it be so bad to take up a distribution offer to create formulations for a house brand of cleaning products? On the one hand, it would secure long-term demand, provide stability through the uncertainty facing this niche industry in the coming years and almost guarantee that the company would be around after the inevitable 'spring cleaning' of industry consolidation in the eco-cleaning products niche. On the other hand, Grand-Maison considered the family's sacrifices over the years to make Savons Prolav a successful and environmentally conscious company. What impact would Savons Prolav's partnerships with Innu-Science, CIRAIG and other organizations have on the company's future? As he started down the aisle again, Grand-Maison knew that he would have to raise these strategic options with his sister as soon as possible.

72 "Verts et potentiellement dangereux," Radio-Canada, 2010, www.radio-canada.ca/nouvelles/environnement/2010/02/25/003-verts-nettoyants-dangereux.shtml, accessed November 6, 2010.
73 J. Lamarche, personal interview, October 22, 2010.

EXHIBIT 1
Bio-Vert products

Laundry	Dishwashing	General Cleaning
Detergent	Dishwashing liquid	All-purpose cleaner
High-efficiency (HE) Detergent	Dishwasher gel	Bathroom cleaner
Fabric Softener	Dishwashing tabs	Glass cleaner

Source: Adapted from www.bio-vert.com/en/lessive.php.

EXHIBIT 2
Typical detergent ingredient list and purpose

Main Ingredients	Typical %	Purpose
Surfactants	50%	Most important; surface active agent for soil removal
Builders	15%	Support detergent action of washing, water softening, enhance surfactant properties
Bleaching Agents	7%	Chemically remove soil or stains using oxidative reactions
Other	**Typical %**	**Purpose**
Bleach Activators	n/a	Perform bleaching at lower temperatures (less than 60°C); biocidal effect improves hygiene of laundry
Enzymes	0–3%	Effective removal of stains with a protein, starch or fatty base
Foam Regulators	n/a	Provide foam-boosting characteristics—consumers equate foam with cleanliness
Corrosion Inhibitors	n/a	Prevent corrosion of mechanical parts of the machine
Optical Brighteners	n/a	Ensure the whitest whites
Dye Transfer Inhibitors	n/a	Keeps clothes looking newer longer
Fragrances	0–3%	Provide pleasant odor, mask unpleasant odors that arise from wash liquor
Dyes	< 1%	Improve aesthetic properties
Fillers/Formulation Aids	5–45%	Ensure a range of properties: flowability, good flushing, high solubility, no caking

Source: Adapted from Eduard Smulders & Eric Sung "Laundry detergents, 2. Ingredients and Products"; *Ullmann's Encyclopedia of Industrial Chemistry*, 2011, Wiley.

EXHIBIT 3
Selected conventional detergent ingredients, their health and/or environmental effects and typical replacements in green detergents

Type of Ingredient	Examples in regular detergents		Replacements in green detergents
	Name	Health and environmental effects	
Surfactants	LAS (linear alkylbenzenesulfonate)	Slow degradation; may cause irritation on sensitive skins	Plant or animal based surfactants, e.g. from coconut or palm or plant-based alcohol ethoxylate
	Nonylphenols (and ethoxylate derivatives)	Endocrine disruptor— can mimic estrogen and disrupt natural hormone balance (shown in aquatic life and rodents in labs)	
Builders	Sodium triphosphate	Causes eutrophication of lakes/rivers	Soda ash or soy; borax; citrates, sodium carbonate, Trilon M
	EDTA (ethylenediamine-tetraacetic acid)	Does not biodegrade— accumulates in oceans	
Bleaching Agents	Hypochlorites—sodium hypochlorite	Contains chlorine; can produce toxic by-products from the oxidation of organic matter; irritant for the skin	Sodium percarbonate (biodegradable)
Bleach Activators	Europe: TAED (Tetraacetyl-ethylenediamine)	Can be irritating to the skin, eyes and respiratory system	–
Optical Brighteners	Fluorescent whitening agents (FWA)	Slow to degrade, may harm aquatic life	Brighteners made from plant cellulose
Fragrances	Natural and synthetic (musks, phthalates)	Synthetic phthalates mimic hormones, possible human carcinogens	Natural essential oils derived from plants
Dyes	–	Do not biodegrade— accumulate in oceans	Not usually added

Source: Author generated, based on Henrik Grüttner, "Environmental assessment of laundry detergents— Bleaching agents," European Textiles Services Association, no date, www.eco-forum.dk/detergents/ index_files/Page775.htm, accessed November 17, 2010; "Linear alkylbenzene sulfonate," *OECD SIDS initial assessment report*, 2005, United Nations Environment Programme, www.chem.unep.ch/irptc/sids/ oecdsids/las.pdf, accessed November 17, 2010; Eduard Smulders & Eric Sung "Laundry detergents, 2. Ingredients and Products," *Ullmann's Encyclopedia of Industrial Chemistry*, 2011, Wiley; Josef Steber & Frederike Wiebel, "Laundry detergents, 4. Ecology and Toxicology," *Ullmann's Encyclopedia of Industrial Chemistry*, 2011, Wiley; Amy Weekley, "Optical brighteners: Are your clothes as clean as they appear?" Yahoo! Contributor Network, 2007, www.associatedcontent.com/article/259584/optical_brighteners_ are_your_clothes.html, accessed November 17, 2010; Environment Canada, "Priority substances list assessment report. Nonylphenol and its ethoxylates," *Canadian Environmental Protection Act*, April 2001; Torben Madsen, Helle Buchardt Boyd, Dorthe Nylén, Anne Rathmann Pedersen, Gitte I. Petersen,

Flemming Simonsen, "Environmental and health assessment of substances in household detergents and cosmetic detergent products," Danish Environmental Protection Agency, 2001 www2.mst.dk/udgiv/publications/2001/87-7944-596-9/pdf/87-7944-597-7.pdf, accessed March 18, 2011.

EXHIBIT 4
Desired properties of the builder component of laundry detergents and the comparative performance of trisodium phosphate

| | Performance of Trisodium Phosphate | | |
Desired property	Good	Adequate	Poor
Reduce water hardness		X	
Soil and stain removal	X		
Multiple wash cycle performance	X		
Handling properties	X		
Human toxicological safety assurance	X		
Environmental properties			X
Cost effectiveness	X		

Source: Adapted from Eduard Smulders & Eric Sung "Laundry detergents, 2. Ingredients and Products," *Ullmann's Encyclopedia of Industrial Chemistry*, 2011, Wiley.

EXHIBIT 5
Number of Quebec lakes and rivers with blue-green algae associated restrictions

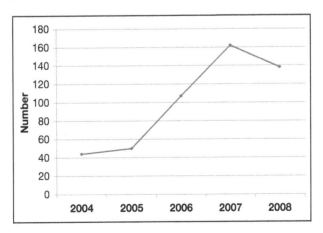

Source: Adapted from "Blue-green algae contamination a crisis: Quebec officials," CBC News, 2007, www.cbc.ca/health/story/2007/07/12/ot-algae-070712.html, accessed November 16, 2010; Eric Moreault, "Algues bleu-vert: le tiers des 119 lacs touches pour la première fois," LaPresse.ca, 2009, http://www.lapresse.ca/le-soleil/actualites/environnement/200910/25/01-914901-algues-bleu-vert-le-tiers-des-119-lacs-touches-pour-la-premiere-fois.php, accessed November 20, 2012.

EXHIBIT 6
Potential health effects of human exposure to blue-green algae

Type of contact	Effect
Direct, prolonged contact during aquatic activities	Itchy and irritated eyes and skin, nasal passages and throat
Ingestion of a small quantity of contaminated water	Usually minor gastro-intestinal symptoms (diarrhea, nausea, vomiting, etc.)
Ingestion of a large quantity of contaminated water	Long-term and chronic effects on the liver or nervous system

Source: Adapted from "Algues bleu-verts." Santé et Services Sociaux Québec. http://www.msss.gouv.qc.ca/sujets/santepub/environnement/index.php?algues_bleu-vert, accessed November 16, 2010.

EXHIBIT 7
Costs of EcoLogo Certification (per product)

Component	Cost
Initial Verification and Audit	Variable, typically $1,500–5,000
Verification of Additional Products	Variable, typically $250–2,100
Annual License Fees	0.5% of sales Min. $2,100 per category

Source: Adapted from http://www.ecologo.org/en/certified/cost/, accessed November 20, 2012.

EXHIBIT 8
Laundry detergent pricing comparison

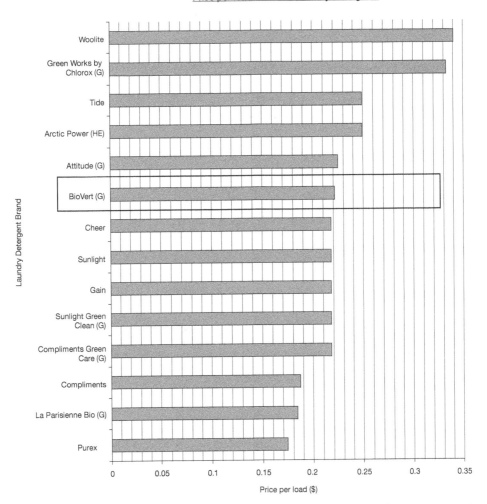

Price per load - Various Laundry Detergents

Source: Pricing data obtained from a Montreal, QC IGA on November 23, 2010; (G) green detergents.

EXHIBIT 9
Establishment size in 2008

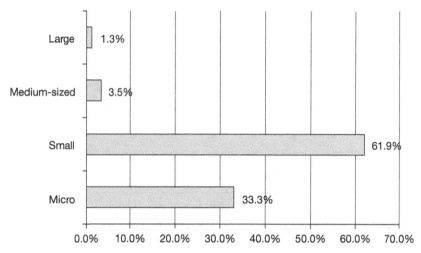

Source: Adapted from "Gross domestic product by industry," Statistics Canada, 2006, Catalogue No.15-001-XPB.

EXHIBIT 10
Marketing segments and competitors

Natural Marketing Institute segments	Bio-Vert competitors
LOHAS	Attitude, Nettoyants Lemieux, etc.
Naturalites	Healthy lifestyle cleaning products sold in major retail locations and green options from multinational producers: Tide Free, Sunlight Green Clean, Clorox Greenworks, etc.
Drifters	Green options and traditional cleaning products from multinational producers depending on price comparisons.
Conventionals	Traditional cleaning products from Procter & Gamble, Johnson and Johnson, Clorox, etc.
Unconcerned	Traditional low-cost cleaning products: big-box private labels.

Source: Author generated.

EXHIBIT 11
Awards and distinctions: Savons Prolav

2008	Walmart supplier of the month (March)—Walmart–Achat-Quebec Program
2008	Dunamis award from the Laval Chamber of Commerce in 2008 for 'Sustainable Development' category
2009	Ernst & Young 2009 Québec winner for Entrepreneur of the Year; 'Business to Consumers Products and Services' category
2009	Finalist for a Phénix—Quebec's highest environmental award
2009	2010 Montreal-East Chamber of Commerce Finalist

Source: Adapted from "Awards and Distinctions," Bio-Vert, no date, www.bio-vert.com/en/distinctions.php, accessed November 20, 2012.

CASE 5

TerraCycle
Outsmarting waste

Philippe Margery,[1] Stuart Read and Jan Lepoutre

In 2001 Tom Szaky, a Princeton freshman, founded TerraCycle in the hope of starting an eco-capitalist company built on waste—worm waste to be exact. Tom and his small team had little experience in building a business, but all possessed entrepreneurial spirit.

Eventually, Tom dropped out of Princeton to pursue his dream of eliminating waste. Surviving on the goodwill of family, friends—both old and new—and a tremendous amount of dedication, the team had to constantly keep developing new ideas to keep the business from bankruptcy. The company eventually moved into partnering with companies who would sponsor the collection of waste associated

1 Research Associate Philippe Margery of IMD prepared this case under the supervision of Professors Jan Lepoutre of Vlerick Leuven Gent Management School and Stuart Read of IMD as a basis for class discussion rather than to illustrate either effective or ineffective handling of a business situation. This case is based on widely available public sources, which are listed in Appendix A. This case won first prize in the Social Entrepreneurship track of the 2012 oikos Case Writing Competition. IMD-3-2311 v. 17.10.2012.

with their brands, and TerraCycle would transform that waste into affordable, high quality products.

In 2006 *Inc. Magazine* named TerraCycle "The coolest little start-up in America" and Tom "The no. 1 CEO under thirty." By 2011 Tom had successfully built TerraCycle into an icon for environmental sustainability that was projecting US$16 million in annual revenues. However, sustained profits continued to elude the company, and though Tom was committed to eliminating waste, he was beginning to question whether TerraCycle had the right business model to achieve the triple bottom line, which he clearly articulated in his approach to eco-capitalism:

> Every business should aspire to be good for people, good for the environment, and (last but definitely not least) good for profits.

Boy meets worm—the seed is planted

Born in Budapest, Hungary, in 1982, Tom and his parents, both physicians, fled Hungary as political refugees in 1986, eventually settling in Toronto when Tom was eight years old. From an early age, Tom had entrepreneurship in his blood, establishing ventures ranging from selling lemonade as a kid to founding a web design agency at the age of 14. Then after an inauspicious start trying to grow some special plants with his high school friends, Tom departed for New Jersey to attend Princeton University in 2001; his friends and their plants headed to McGill University in Montreal.

At Princeton, Tom met Jon Beyer, a computer science major. Their shared interest in entrepreneurship led them to the annual business plan competition sponsored by the Princeton Entrepreneurship Club. The grand prize was $5,000. All they needed was an idea to enter.

During his fall break at Princeton, Tom visited his friends in Montreal and was amazed to find their plants flourishing. His friend Pete had been feeding the plants worm poop, and in just four weeks the plants had produced a bumper crop. An ordinary compost bin filled with *Eisenia fetida*—commonly known as red wiggler worms—had quickly transformed table scraps and other organic waste[2] into a rich fertilizer for the plants. It was then that Tom's idea for the competition was born. The concept was simple. He would use worms to produce fertilizer from organic waste, make money and address a major environmental issue in the process. And if the project came to fruition, it could seed a new breed of eco-capitalism, where the product would be made entirely from waste. But how could Tom build a business on worm poop and garbage with no funds, few connections and little experience?

---

2 Organic waste is a type of waste, typically originating from plant or animal sources, which may be broken down by other living organisms. Source: <wiki.answers.com/Q/What_is_organic_waste#ixzz1b3wWF71H> (accessed 18 October 2011).

The Princeton Business Plan Competition

Back at Princeton, Tom and Jon worked on developing the idea for the business plan competition. All they had to do was show that a waste management business could make a profit.

Developing a viable business model

After doing some research, Tom and Jon realized the market was huge: Americans produced 12 to 14 billion tons of waste each year, 80% of which was organic, and paid roughly $1 trillion each year to dispose of it. On top of that, US consumers spent a total of $37.7 billion dollars on their lawns and gardens in 2001. Of that, fertilizers, other soils and mixtures for growing plants were estimated to account for over $6 billion and were growing at a rate of 5% annually. Nearly 60% of Americans bought some kind of fertilizer or plant food every year. Better still, organic fertilizers were expanding at double the rate of chemical fertilizers. The organic material in landfills produced vast amounts of methane gas, which contributed to ozone depletion and global warming. If Tom and Jon could feed that waste to worms and sell products made from worm poop, they could help save the planet. They envisaged that the waste materials would have a negative cost because they would be paid to haul away the garbage the worms would eat. This would mean that they could potentially start with raw material costs that could total as much as minus $1 trillion. They also learned that worm poop has all the characteristics of a top-quality fertilizer. It seemed to not only provide nutrients for the plants but also improve the quality of the soil.

Next they had to develop equipment that would allow them to scale up the household worm farm that Tom's friend had in his kitchen in Montreal. Jon eventually came up with the idea of putting the worms on a conveyor belt that would slowly turn away from the center of the device where the organic waste would be poured. The worms would work their way toward the center, leaving their castings (poop) behind them. The castings would eventually be deposited into a receptacle at the end of the conveyor belt. According to Tom, it was "... like a poop-producing treadmill!"[i]

The competitive landscape

Despite their fears that there would be a lot of competition taking advantage of this great opportunity, their research revealed that the existing worm-farming economy was in shambles. Greg Bradley of B&B Worm Farms had set up two years earlier and had earned $29 million through an illegal pyramid scheme in which over 2,900 clients bought worm-farming equipment. (Bradley was eventually found dead following a cocaine overdose in 2003.) This left Tom and Jon with no real direct competition and the expectation was low that new competition from the worm-farming community would emerge, as people burned during the previous round of investing were unlikely to invest more hard-earned money in the industry.

Other potential competitors were landfills and composting sites. However, because of the disastrous impact of landfills on the environment, an alternative would no doubt be welcome. Composting sites had a similar business model to Tom and Jon's. However, Tom and Jon's worms were able to process the waste much faster (in about 20% of the time) and the quality of the fertilizer was superior. Also, composting sites were spread over huge areas and emitted a foul smell, whereas worm farming was virtually odorless. All in all, the industry looked promising.

The Business Plan competition

Tom, Jon and a few others put together a detailed 100-page business plan for the worm project. It turned out that not everyone was enthused by worm poop, so the original team of eight eventually reduced to three—Tom, Jon and Noemi, an art student. They were confident they would win the contest.

After qualifying for the second and final round of the competition, which added to their confidence, Tom's team and the three other finalists had to deliver a formal presentation to the jury. Given their strong business plan, Tom and his team viewed the presentation as a formality. Much to their surprise, however, they ended up in fourth place—the only place in the final round for which there was no prize money. They soon realized that the judges had only skimmed their lengthy business plan and that their poor presentation had put the judges off reading it in more depth. It was a painful lesson. As Tom explained:

> Though we lost the Princeton business plan contest that cold day in March, we gained something more valuable: We understood the need for sizzle with the steak, a lesson we'd carry with us for the rest of our careers. We'd figured out what we'd done wrong, but was it too little too late?[ii]

The three were disappointed and deflated. Was it time to call it quits?

Taking the plunge

Though student life continued, neither Tom nor Jon could let go of the idea. The problem was they had no idea how to make it a reality, especially how to extract the worm castings from the container where the worms feasted on organic waste. Then one day Jon came across "Harry Windle's worm gin" while surfing the web. The machine seemed to do exactly what they wanted on an industrial scale. According to Tom:

> The second I spoke to Harry, I could tell he was a complete nut, but he was our kind of nut—a crazy inventor, a mad-scientist type whose business was making massive worm machines and compost screeners. Harry's system hinged on the same conveyor-belt principle that our idea had, only he took the concept to a whole new level—literally. Harry's worm gin boasted conveyors stacked on multiple levels and could accomplish what we'd imagined in a tenth of the space.[iii]

Tom and Jon had reached a moment of truth. Finding a solution that met their needs bolstered their enthusiasm for the idea, so they negotiated a $20,000 deal with Harry. The problem was neither of them had that kind of money. Tom and Jon's combined savings amounted to $5,000, which they sent to Harry as a down payment. Then Tom contacted an old high school friend who agreed to lend them another $5,000. Finally, Tom pushed the credit on the card his parents had given him to the limit. Within a month, they managed to reach the magic $20,000 they needed. Next they had to figure out where to get the waste to feed the worms once they had the worm gin. Eventually, after several meetings with various parties, they were able to get approval to remove the organic waste from Princeton's Wilcox Dining Hall every day during the coming summer and bring back the empty barrels each evening. The tedious process of obtaining Princeton's approval had a benefit; it allowed them to fine-tune their pitch. Finally, their steak was beginning to sizzle.

In mid-June Harry drove onto the Princeton campus with a brand new worm gin. TerraCycle, as they had decided to name the company, was born. But their problems were not over yet. They quickly realized that they needed to break the waste down so the worms could consume it easily. They were able to get their hands on a wood chipper, but by this time a few weeks of waste had accumulated. So the first day Tom and Noemi had to make several trips transporting the organic waste from the dining hall back to their base near Princeton University, where they shoveled it into the wood chipper, which ground it into a homogeneous sludge. Then they transferred the sludge into the worm gin where the worms were eagerly waiting. Unfortunately, the wood chipper kept getting clogged, so they had to regularly reach down into it to clear the obstacles. At around 2:30 in the morning, while manipulating the last barrel of foul-smelling, maggot-infested, rotting food, it fell over and the contents landed all over Noemi. She backed off in disgust, turned around, threw up and quit.

Cutting their losses

Jon left his summer job to help Tom shovel the rotting waste. As time wore on, the worms continued producing poop, but no one was interested in paying to have their waste removed or in buying the magic fertilizer. Tom and Jon had not budgeted for food and lodging and found themselves sleeping on the floor of their friends' dorm rooms and eating whatever they could get their hands on. The pair spent many sleepless nights worrying about the debts they had racked up with friends and family. Each evening they sent their business plan to every venture capitalist they could think of, and each time they were rejected, if they heard back at all. After many months of hard work, the money had run out and debt was accumulating, so Tom and Jon resigned themselves to cutting their losses and giving up on the worm project. They would sell the worm gin and use the proceeds to help pay back some of the loans they had received from family and friends.

They had one last commitment—a previously scheduled live interview on a local radio station—which felt like the ceremonial burial of TerraCycle before they went back to school in a month's time. They told their story on the program and left the station with a copy of the recording in hand.

An unexpected lifeline

As closure seemed imminent, an unexpected event offered a new opportunity. Tom received an email that he initially mistook for spam and almost deleted. It said, "I WANT TO INVEST. CALL ME."[iv] Suman Sinha, the sender, had heard their story on the local radio station that morning and wanted to see them. That night, Tom and Jon had dinner with Suman and left the restaurant with a check for $2,000.

The money gave them the time they needed to regroup. Priority one was to find a place to stay. They ended up renting a cheap basement space that had one central room and two small offices that would function as bedrooms. Showers would be taken at the gym. As for furnishings, Tom and Jon had gone "dumpster[3] diving" for chairs, desks and computers. It was all student waste they found in the trash on move-out day.

Tom and Jon fulfilled their promise to Princeton to dispose of the organic waste from the dining hall. But with summer coming to an end and school starting, they did not have time to continue production. Though they were still in business, they had to shut down the worm gin, box up the worms and store them in their office. After their summer experience, they realized that they would have to process several hundred tons of waste in order to turn a profit. This would require dozens of employees and worm gins, as well as millions of worms. And though worm poop was excellent fertilizer, to which everyone who tried it could attest, selling it had not gone to plan.

---

3 A dumpster is a large industrial trash container, sometimes called a skip outside the United States.

Survival mode

It soon became clear that the $2,000 investment was not going to last. They needed more money, and they needed it quickly. They came up with the idea of presenting a hairdresser friend from Los Angeles as a celebrity stylist to the Princeton community. They were able to fully book him for a weekend, which turned out to be lucrative enough to pay the rent. Inspired by the idea, they started to host art parties on most weekends during semester. One of the party regulars, a senior named Hilary Burt, convinced her father to invest $6,000 in TerraCycle. A lot of Princeton students who attended the parties also offered to volunteer at TerraCycle, which allowed the company to keep its nose just above water.

Though school was back in session, Tom could not stop thinking about how to build TerraCycle and make a difference to the environment in the process. Early in the fall, he asked a Canadian friend to join the company. Robin Tator, who had given Tom his first job ten years earlier, had a couple of ventures of his own, but one of them was a seasonal ice cream business, so he had some time and agreed to spend one week per month at TerraCycle in exchange for a share of the company.

Redefining the business

Tom and Jon's biggest challenge was figuring out what business they were in. So far no one outside the university was willing to pay them to haul organic waste away, so they decided to abandon the idea of being a waste-management company for the time being and focus on selling the vast amount of worm poop fertilizer they had accumulated. While they always planned to sell the fertilizer, they were quickly realizing that it was a necessity rather than just a nice additional source of revenue.

So off they went in jeans and t-shirts, trying to sell worm poop in plastic bags with black and white labels that said "Pure Worm Poop." As a cutting edge environmental company, fancy packaging and lots of flash just did not seem like their style. Yet their sales success was not forthcoming. Eventually, Robin, whose background was in marketing, came up with the idea of bottling the fertilizer in spray bottles. Liquid fertilizers also had a number of advantages over solid ones. And transforming the solid worm poop into a liquid would be relatively straightforward and would not require complex or expensive machinery. They put the liquefied worm poop—or tea as they called it—in a spray bottle with a label they had designed themselves with a new name: TerraCycle Plant Food. They now had a product to sell.

Treading water

As the fall wore on, Tom found himself spending more time figuring out where next month's rent was coming from than he was on his studies. So as the semester drew to a close, Tom decided to take a leave of absence from Princeton. Around the same time, Priscilla Hayes, who was responsible for solid-waste management in the county, introduced TerraCycle to the EcoComplex at Rutgers University. The Rutgers EcoComplex had a mission to "research and educate people about environmentally sound business practices." TerraCycle was a perfect fit, and it became the EcoComplex's first and only occupant when it set up its worm gin in the incubator.

Over the winter, Tom kept the company afloat by entering and winning several business contests including reentering the Princeton competition and walking away with first prize. He also recruited Bill Gillum, a highly experienced chemist with a PhD from MIT who was looking for a new challenge. Bill joined TerraCycle's team, which consisted of mostly Princeton interns, as director of operations, and spent his first six months shoveling poop.

Despite various injections of capital, TerraCycle found itself chronically short of cash. With only $500 in the bank, its existence was in peril. So Tom and Jon decided to participate in the mother of all business plan contests: the Carrot Capital Business Plan Challenge. The winner would take home $1 million.

Carrot Capital: the mother of all business plan contests

TerraCycle made it through the first round of the competition and on Saturday, April 26, 2003, Tom and Robin headed to New York City, where they found themselves adrift in a sea of white shirts and power suits. Each team had 20 minutes to present its case before a panel of judges. The day ended with a cocktail party for all involved at the Forbes building on Fifth Avenue. The judges and sponsors seemed to mingle with everyone—everyone except Tom and Robin. At one point, Robin called Tom aside and said:

> There's no point in staying here. We're out of it. They're not even looking at us. We've got better things to do. Let's go run a company.v

But lured by the promise of a free meal, they decided to stay for the awards dinner. As dinner progressed, the losers were called. When they did not hear their name, Tom and Robin became increasingly confused, until eventually, much to their surprise, they realized they had won.

The following Monday, the whole TerraCycle team—about thirty people—met with David Geliebter, Carrot's managing partner, in New York City where they opened the NASDAQ and were interviewed on some news shows including CNBC's Power Lunch. Over the following weeks, Carrot would work up a deal sheet about the specifics of the prize. When David and some investors arrived at the EcoComplex to discuss it, they took Tom aside and explained that they were not interested in the environmental benefits of producing and selling worm poop. They were more interested in the organic nature of the product because they saw a big opportunity in the fast-growing organic fertilizer and plant food market.

The following week Tom was invited to New York to meet with the Carrot Capital people alone. They got straight to the point. They did not want Bill or Robin or any of the other managers; they wanted Tom and they wanted to make him the "poster child" of organic fertilizers. They would bring in their own team to take over every aspect of the business. By telling his story, which he had become adept at doing, Tom could become rich and famous.

A turning point

Despite the promise of fame and fortune, Tom turned down the $1 million prize money from Carrot Capital. Needless to say, Carrot Capital was not pleased, and warned Tom that TerraCycle did not have a chance without them. But dropping the environmental angle, as Carrot Capital wanted to do, made no sense to Tom. The combination of environmental solutions and economic potential was the foundation of TerraCycle's business model. Plus Tom did not want Carrot Capital to oust his friends who had dedicated so much of their time and energy to the company.

The day after Tom turned down the Carrot Capital prize money, all of the TerraCycle people met in the basement of their Nassau Street office. Desperation was in the air. Though they had become experts at living on close to nothing, they could not go on that way for much longer. They needed to buy bottles to package the fertilizer solution, but the $500 they had available would not go far. They had to figure out a way forward. As Robin dropped into his chair, it nearly flipped over. Tom looked at him and said, "It's garbage, man." Indeed, garbage would prove to be the perfect solution to their problem.

When Jon suggested grabbing used bottles from people's recycling bins as a temporary measure, Tom picked up on it right away:

> That's a brilliant idea. We have a product that is made from garbage, that could in fact be considered garbage. Why not package it in garbage?[vi]

That same night, they decided to raid some recycling bins. It was originally meant to be a temporary solution, but the more time they spent chasing used plastic bottles, the more Tom was warming up to the idea as a permanent solution.[4] It was not what he had envisaged when starting TerraCycle, but it was perfectly aligned with the whole concept. Re-using something would definitely be more profitable than recycling something—and it would be better for the environment. As Tom explained:

> Waste is an entirely human concept. There is really no such thing in nature as waste. Everything is used; everything decomposes to become the building blocks of something else. More than that, the concept of waste is entirely a modern human idea. Basically, it didn't exist until the twentieth century with the invention of plastic and complex petrochemical materials. … The basic paradigm of eco-capitalism is that an object can have components that are waste and components that are valuable. The idea is to focus on what is "waste" and find a way to use it.[vii]

To their surprise, they found out that there were only four bottle sizes by volume—two liters, one liter, half a liter and twenty ounces—and they all took the same size caps. Even more surprising was that the bottles all had the same height and diameter, which meant they could be run through a high-speed bottling machine. Now all they needed were spray triggers for the bottles. After a little research, Robin discovered that there were enormous numbers of spray triggers available from companies that no longer had a need for them because of changes to their packaging. By redefining a waste stream as a resource stream, TerraCycle was moving beyond environmentally friendly capitalism. Waste was no longer something to write-off; instead, it was an asset.

What started as a desperate measure was turning into THE solution: selling a product that was entirely made up of waste. It was clearly a turning point for them—and all because they had turned down the Carrot Capital money.

Now the team needed a plan for acquiring more waste bottles. So far, the company had survived thanks to volunteers and goodwill, so Tom and gang figured they should ask people to collect bottles for TerraCycle. They came up with the idea of paying schools a minimal fee for each bottle they collected, and the company would pick up the bottles. As a result, the bottle brigade was born and it was a tremendous success. The kids understood that they could benefit the planet and they were excited about it. They also liked the idea of seeing the bottles they had collected appear on store shelves.

Despite all of this, TerraCycle still needed cash.

---

4 Each year Americans discarded more than 200 billion soda bottles, rather than recycle them. The environmental impact was enormous. Not only do soda bottles take thousands of years to degrade, it takes millions of gallons of oil to produce and ship them and they release poisons into the air when they are incinerated. They are so lightweight that recyclers are not paid much to handle them and recycling plastic bottles is also very costly as there is such a variety of different inputs in different bottles, which makes virgin plastic a more attractive option.

Lift off

Tom met the man who would become his biggest backer, Martin Stein, at a stock-holder meeting that he attended as a proxy as a favor to a friend. During the meet-ing, Martin was sitting beside Tom and asked Tom who he was and what he did. After hearing about TerraCycle and its financing problems, he asked Tom how much he needed. Tom, who was tired and not prepared to go into the numbers in depth, just said, "$500,000." Martin must have been impressed by Tom because he said, "I'm in. I'm your partner." Tom was skeptical, but the next day Martin called and went over to see the business—the office where Tom slept and worked. Not only did Martin provide the funding the company needed, he went on to become a strong supporter and a part of the company family. And unlike Carrot Capital, there were no strings attached.

Going big

TerraCycle had gone with a "start-small" model, which was a lot of work, and meant their sales would always be limited to a case here and a case there to local stores. They had tried trade shows but to no avail. So, they started knocking on the doors of big stores and received some small orders from Home Depot. It was not enough to feel they were finally "in business" but it meant they needed more space for production. TerraCycle Plant Food soon became the fastest-selling fertilizer on HomeDepot.com and Tom wanted to be ready when the real orders started coming in. The Home Depot order seemed to have opened a few doors and other big stores were finally starting to listen.

By the beginning of the summer of 2004, TerraCycle had 35 employees. Tom found a house to buy in a crime-infested neighborhood in New Jersey and an empty fac-tory not too far away. He felt he needed the house to provide accommodation for the many interns working at TerraCycle.

Luckily, the media had kept up their interest in Tom and TerraCycle. As a Cana-dian television crew for CBC was filming a segment on TerraCycle, Robin received a call from Walmart. It wanted to place a massive order for every store in Canada.

The Walmart order

Robin and Tom had been calling Walmart non-stop for quite some time and they were finally successful in getting a meeting with the buyer of garden supplies in Toronto. They were given 15 minutes. Tom and Robin knew from the first few sec-onds that the man in front of them would not do them any favors. They put three juicy tomatoes on the table. When the Walmart buyer asked what the tomatoes were for, Tom said:

> We wanted you to see what an amazing job our plant food can do on the vegetables. And the other reason is that, if you don't like what we have to offer you this morning, you can throw the tomatoes at us.[5]

It broke the ice and thirty minutes later they were still talking. The buyer from Walmart loved the concept—a product made from waste, packaged in waste, with a competitive price and good margins for the retailer. At the end of the meeting, the Walmart representative said:

> I thought I'd heard everything but I was wrong. How much do you think those tomatoes weigh? About two pounds?

Tom nodded. The man took three dollars out of his pocket, handed the money over and said:

> Thanks for the tomatoes. They look good.

When the order came, it was for 100,000 bottles, worth $250,000 to TerraCycle—four times bigger than their combined sales for all of 2004. But there was no way they could fulfill the order. The factory was not operational, they only had one worm gin, a single, malfunctioning bottling line and the few interns they had were due to leave for the Christmas holidays. The order was due to be shipped in mid-February—in two months' time. Furthermore, they needed bottles. As Tom explained:

> Once the reality hit it was gut-wrenching. When you are an entrepreneur, you just make decisions that seem right at the time. The scary thing is you are always making decisions without knowing the future. Should we have waited to go to them [Walmart] until we had all the inventory and machinery we might need? What if the order hadn't come in—we would have been broke and without the energy boost that comes from getting something like the Walmart order.[viii]

The brigades could not deliver sufficient bottles fast enough, so Robin visited every recycle center in the region, but they only had crushed bottles, which were of no use to TerraCycle. Fortunately, TerraCycle was located close to New York, a bottle-bill state where individuals were paid $0.05 for each bottle they returned—and those bottles were not crushed. Robin and Tom met with the director of a recycling center in New York and proposed buying the bottles before he had them crushed for the same price as he would sell them crushed. The director hesitated as new processes had to be put in place but in the end he agreed.

---

5   Szaky, Tom. *Revolution in a Bottle: How TerraCycle is Redefining Green Business.* New York: Penguin Group, 2009, p. 74.

At midnight on February 4, TerraCycle officially started production for the Walmart order. After twenty hours per day for 15 days straight, they delivered the order on time, proving that eco-capitalism can work on a large scale.

Publicity in Canada exploded after they shipped the Walmart order. CBC's hour-long documentary about TerraCycle, with Robin taking the Walmart call, was broadcast as they were finishing up the order. Suddenly, dozens of stores that had never returned their calls started to get in touch.

Another break came in 2006 when Inc. Magazine named Tom the "#1 CEO in America Under 30," as part of their coveted "30 under 30 Awards." The magazine also ran a cover story hailing TerraCycle as "The coolest little start-up in America."

Defining a new business model: sponsored waste

With worm poop fertilizer sales finally kicking in, Tom started to think about what they could do next.

> We had always been dumpster diving for our office furniture, but that was the first time we realized that greatly expanding our dumpster diving could fuel our production line. We had discovered that contemporary America is a vast dumpster of industrial products that manufacturers are constantly throwing away or recycling—even when they're in perfect condition. That opened the floodgates for TerraCycle.[ix]

With the amount of waste generated in America by consumers skyrocketing to 250 million tons per year—almost 1 ton per person per year—America's biggest export by weight was waste, and the majority of it was non-recyclable. In talking with his friend Seth, who operated a business producing organic juices for kids under the "Honest Tea" brand, Tom learned that environmentally aware companies would pay to have their branded waste handled. With a recyclable product, the onus is on consumers to do their part. However, with a non-recyclable product, the consumer does not have a choice. Seth had invested in a scheme whereby kids would return pouches to the company. However, Honest Tea represented only a tiny fraction of the juice pouch market. More than 90% of the pouches came from Capri Sun and Kool-Aid. Soon after his conversation with Seth, Tom received a call from Gary Hirshberg, CEO of Stonyfield Farm Yogurt, who had the same problem with yogurt cups.

Then, coincidentally, Tom discovered PREDA, the People's Recovery, Empowerment Development Assistance Foundation, founded in 1974 in the Philippines by Fr. Shay Cullen and Merle and Alex Hermoso. PREDA's original goal was to help teenagers from broken homes deal with problems of substance abuse. In September 2004 recovering teens from PREDA began producing, selling and shipping items made from waste juice pouches. This seemed like the perfect model for TerraCycle. Tom demonstrated a few ideas for products made from recycled drink pouches and

Seth loved the idea of sponsored waste. TerraCycle now needed to hire someone to administer a drink pouch brigade and Seth offered. TerraCycle would pay $0.02 for each pouch and would organize collection. The investment Seth made to protect his brand's eco-friendliness would turn waste into a valuable resource for TerraCycle—and the schools and organizations that would collect them would also benefit.

Tom wanted to start with one hundred brigades to test the model. They announced it on their website, and within twenty-four hours they had the candidates they wanted. A similar movement happened with the yogurt cups. Wishing to spend as little energy as possible upcycling a product on which a lot of energy had already been spent, the easiest product to produce for the yogurt cups was planting pots; which would also fit in perfectly with their Home Depot line of products. Gary loved the idea and joined in to sponsor a yogurt brigade.

Tom and his team kept developing ideas for waste drink pouch containers—pencil cases, lunch boxes, backpacks and many more—and started presenting them to retailers. The retailers were enthusiastic and some even thought the products had an Andy Warhol touch to them. By the spring of 2007 the number of brigades had grown from 1,500 to 4,000.

It was then that Walgreens, one of America's biggest retailers, placed a huge order with TerraCycle for juice-pouch pencil cases, an order for which they would need 10 million juice pouches. Even though the folks at TerraCycle had become used to Tom's increasing habit of selling without product, this order was way beyond their capacity. The brigades could not get enough juice pouches in time. Luckily, Robin found a solution in British Columbia, where juice pouches were recycled through deposit. When Robin called Encorp, the government agency that dealt with recycling these pouches, he asked what they did with them. "We store them," was the answer. Robin's heart skipped a beat. "And so how many would you have then?" he asked. "Well, about 20 million," was the response. In the end, TerraCycle and Encorp came to an agreement; TerraCycle could have them all.[x]

Just when Tom and Robin thought it was all sorted out, they discovered that almost all of the pouches were of brands owned by Kraft Foods, the biggest food company in America. Encorp would not release the juice pouches without Kraft's agreement. As Tom explained:

> Going up against Kraft Foods in a lawsuit was scary.[6] At this point, I had all the purchase orders from the stores in hand, so there was no backing out. I called Kraft.[xi]

---

6 TerraCycle had previous experience with a lawsuit from a large multinational firm, when Scotts, the garden products firm, sued TerraCycle over allegedly copying Scotts product. The lawsuit was eventually settled, but the cost to TerraCycle was very high.

Sponsored waste goes corporate: The Kraft Foods Partnership

In 2008 Tom contacted Kraft Foods just as the food giant was looking for ways to help divert packaging that could not be recycled from going to landfills. Although sustainability was not new to Kraft Foods, there had been an increased sense of focus in the years leading up to Tom's telephone call. Kraft had worked hard on building sustainability into its business strategy and on changing its corporate culture. TerraCycle's business model was in line with Kraft's ambition to rethink how packaging was used and how it could reduce its environmental impact. A core team devoted to sustainability provided strategic direction from the very center of the company. It helped provide focus, direction and leadership but, ultimately, it was up to the business leaders of each of the company's categories to decide on and execute specific projects that impacted their business. Tom had first approached Kraft with a specific need in mind: upcycling waste, and more specifically Capri Sun pouches across the United States. TerraCycle was receiving a significant number of them from the drink-pouch brigade sponsored by Honest Tea and was making pencil holders out of them. However, even though the empty pouches were waste, Kraft Foods still owned the brand.

Tom's enquiry to the Capri Sun team was directed to the corporate sustainability team within Kraft. When they met Tom, Kraft's corporate sustainability team liked what they saw in the eager, young entrepreneur. He seemed confident, aspirational, customer oriented, creative, somewhat experienced (for a 27-year-old) and projected a strong can-do attitude. As Jeff Chahley, senior director of sustainability at Kraft Foods commented:

> We were working hard to optimize end-of-life solutions and find ways to encourage the right behaviors such as recycling. One way we found to do so was to partner with innovative companies like TerraCycle, which had solutions for non-recyclable packaging and rewarded consumers for sending it to them rather than putting it in the trash.

TerraCycle's size made starting a partnership with it somewhat of a risk for Kraft, but the potential for success was there. Kraft felt that TerraCycle had a unique business model that educated people and rewarded them for doing the right thing. Also, TerraCycle already had experience working with retailers such as Home Depot through its fertilizer product. The corporate sustainability team could see TerraCycle playing a key role in its packaging endof-life strategy, and recommended that the Capri Sun team take a chance on sponsoring the young company's work. Jeff commented:

> We weren't afraid to take a chance on a smaller partner or an upstart with the right know-how, because the results can be huge.

So, once senior management was convinced of the program and its merits, approval to proceed was obtained and Capri Sun struck a deal with TerraCycle, making Kraft Foods TerraCycle's most important branded waste partner and TerraCycle a key element in Kraft's sustainability program.

It was not long before Capri Sun was benefiting from positive PR. Seeing the success Capri Sun was enjoying with the program, including positive feedback from consumers and the grassroots involvement that TerraCycle promoted, other Kraft Foods brands decided to get involved.

Though the Kraft partnership gave legitimacy to TerraCycle and the environmental industry as a whole, it also resulted in a lot of trash for TerraCycle. While it was able to turn some of the materials into backpacks, tote bags and pencil cases, orders for these upcycled products were not enough to turn a profit. Garbage was piling up in TerraCycle's warehouses, and so were its losses, which totaled $4.5 million on sales of $6.6 million in 2008. Being "the hottest little start-up in America" was no longer enough; the time had come to show that eco-capitalism could turn a profit.

By 2009 the partnership with Kraft had started to produce significant volume. Capri Sun, for example, had more than 35,000 locations where millions of pouches had been collected and over $250,000 had been donated to schools and other charities. The Kraft initiative, including the cross into Canada with Kraft in 2009 and subsequent partnerships with Mars and Kimberley-Clark, had been largely enabled by the success of TerraCycle's earlier partnerships with smaller companies, such as Honest Tea and Stonyfield Farm yogurts. The sponsorship of collection programs of these larger companies was TerraCycle's biggest source of revenue.

By 2011 several Kraft Foods brands were involved in collection brigades for drink pouches (sponsored by Capri Sun, Kool-Aid and Del Monte), cookie wrappers (sponsored by Nabisco Cookies), cheese packaging (sponsored by Kraft Cheeses), lunch kits (sponsored by Oscar Mayer Lunchables), Tassimo packaging, Kenco eco refill bags, Tang pouches and gum packaging (sponsored by Trident). TerraCycle was in multiple countries by this time and had grown its range of partners to include some of Kraft's peer companies like Frito Lay (Pepsi), Stonyfield Farm, Mars, Wrigley and many others.

With more than 120,000 locations around the world with around 2 million people in total collecting post-consumer waste, Kraft was the key partner and largest sponsor for launching the TerraCycle program in most new markets. It supported them in Argentina, Brazil, Canada, Ireland, Mexico, Sweden, Norway, Denmark, the UK and the United States with plans to launch in more markets in 2012. Together with TerraCycle, Kraft developed a scorecard to track progress that included countries, brigades, number of locations, units of waste diverted through consumers' actions, tons of waste diverted from factories, PR hits and impressions, and so on. Working with TerraCycle had enabled the company to divert more than 130 million household packages and 3,800 tons of manufacturing waste away from landfills or incineration.

Following the initial successes of the partnership, TerraCycle was also bringing new ideas to Kraft's marketing teams in the various regions in which the two companies had partnerships. The relationship with TerraCycle had evolved from "waste-centric" to "growth-centric"—from managing Kraft's non-recyclable waste to working with Kraft as a marketing partner. And it rapidly became clear to Kraft that the biggest impact of working with TerraCycle came from the holistic investigation of the supply chain that the partnership demanded. For packaging, this meant optimizing product design, using the right source materials and figuring out up front what to do with it after consumers were done with it. It was also about the source ingredients and the impacts all the way up the supply chain.

The Kenco coffee brand in the UK became one of Kraft's biggest success stories. Kenco coffee beans were already 100% sourced from Rainforest Alliance Certified™ farms. TerraCycle helped Kraft design the packaging and work with consumers to collect used eco refill bags to be upcycled into new consumer products. As a result, this was the first offering in the Kraft product line to meet its 2015 sustainability objectives. For both firms the successful results raised new questions. The initial TerraCycle agreement had just covered the upcycling of existing packaging, yet the relationship was already extending far beyond.

A choice between profits and growth?

TerraCycle was changing the way a large number of people were thinking about waste. But the hard work of the collection brigades and the creativity of the TerraCycle team had not been enough to turn the company into a profitable business. TerraCycle's strategy had been about growth—aggressive growth. But as Tom explained:

> Until 2008, the more we grew the more money we lost. ... There is an explicit expectation of aggressive revenue growth. ... It hasn't always synched with that other very important line on our profit-and-loss statement: the profit.[xii]

The first year TerraCycle produced a profit was 2010, and it was a modest profit at that. The company executives constantly struggled with whether they should favor revenue growth over profits or if they should de-emphasize revenue growth in favor of profit growth. Different investors preferred different approaches. Some favored a short-term earlier exit while others preferred a long-term payoff. An IPO (initial public offering) was not something Tom was considering, stating he preferred to remain private. Instead, he was in it for the long term and growth was his priority.

Where's the cash?

TerraCycle continued to explore alternative product and distribution strategies that might pave the path to profit. For example, it arranged an agreement with DwellSmart to offer products online that were not initial sell-outs with retail partners such as Walmart. It also added an important industrial revenue stream—plastic pellets made out of low-quality plastic waste that was not suitable for upcycling. The pellets were then sold to extrusion molding manufacturers who turned them into products. Ironically, one of the products these companies produced was large plastic trash bins.

At the same time, a Brazilian investment group bought a minority interest in TerraCycle's Brazilian subsidiary. The new investor injected capital and resources, which allowed the Brazilian business to grow at a much faster rate and the proceeds of the sale brought liquidity back to investors in the parent company. Tom remarked on these developments:

> This approach, should we choose to roll it out more broadly, might be a way for a relatively small company to develop strong local partnerships to turbo charge activities in foreign operations, while also creating cash to let earlier investors in the parent company exit. That would allow the company to remain private, independent and focused on growth. So far, it seems like both our short-term and long-term investors like this approach.[xiii]

Tom had successfully built TerraCycle into an icon for environmental sustainability that had attracted investors en masse. It had established itself as a leader in innovation based on its entrepreneurial culture and mindset. However, this same innovation had resulted in a diverse set of activities and products and, beyond the fact that they were all built on waste, the synergies between each were not always clear. The company was struggling in its efforts to produce so many products that it knew nothing about, and none of the products had achieved the scale necessary to be deeply successful consumer products. Investors, suppliers and customers were questioning if TerraCycle knew what business it was really in. While Tom believed the company should hold strong to its core—eliminating waste—he was beginning to question whether TerraCycle had the right business model to consistently achieve a necessary and important element of his triple bottom line—profits.

EXHIBIT 1
Financial figures

2011	
3-year growth	329%
Projected revenue	US$16 million
Employees	80
Employee growth	40
2010	
Revenue	US$13.2 million
Employees	60
2009	
Revenue	US$6.6 million
Employees	50
Founded in 2001	

Source: "Inc. 500." *Inc. Magazine*, 2011.

Appendix A

Public sources

Feldman, Loren. "Garbage mogul makes millions from trash: With a brilliant business model built around recycling, TerraCycle will either go big or go broke." *CNN Money*, 25 March 2009. <http://money.cnn.com/2009/03/24/smallbusiness/trash_talker_TerraCycle.fsb/index.htm> (accessed 26 October 2011).

"Inc. 500." *Inc. Magazine*, 2011. <www.inc.com/inc5000/profile/TerraCycle> (accessed 26 October 2011).

"Kraft Foods & TerraCycle, Inc. Partner on World's First Sponsored Waste Programs." *Small Business Trends*, 18 August 2008. <smallbiztrends.com/2008/08/kraft-foodsTerraCycle-inc-partner-on-worlds-first-sponsored-waste-programs.html> (accessed 26 October 2011).

"Princeton to Poop." *Forbes Driven* <video.forbes.com/fvn/driven/princeton-dropout-sell spoop-makes-millions> (accessed 18 October 2011).

"Start-up seeks profits in mounds of garbage." *The Wall Street Journal*, 3 May 2010. <online.wsj.com/article/SB10001424052748703572504575214431306540058.html> (accessed 26 October 2011).

Strauss, Robert. "But the Employees Really are Spineless." *The New York Times*, 10 April 2005. <query.nytimes.com/gst/fullpage.html?res=9F06E0DF173EF933A25757C0A963 9C8B63> (accessed 18 October 2011).

Szaky, Tom. *Revolution in a Bottle: How TerraCycle is Redefining Green Business.* New York: Penguin Group, 2009.

Szaky, Tom. "TerraCycle crosses the border into Canada, together with Kraft Canada." *Green Package*, 9 November 2009. <www.greenerpackage.com/experts/tom_szaky/blog/terra cycle_crosses_border_canada_together_kraft_canada> (accessed 27 October 2011.).

Szaky, Tom. "How many business models can one company have?" *The New York Times*, 20 April 2011. <boss.blogs.nytimes.com/2011/04/20/how-many-business-models-can-onecompany-have/> (accessed 26 October 2011).

Szaky, Tom. "Choosing between profits and growth." *The New York Times*, 25 August 2011. <boss.blogs.nytimes.com/2011/08/25/choosing-between-profits-and-growth/> (accessed 26 October 2011).

TerraCycle website. <www.terracycle.net/en-US/histories.html> (accessed 18 October 2011).

"TerraCycle helping Canadian schools, non-profits reduce waste." *Solid Waste and Recycling*, 17 January 2011. <www.solidwastemag.com/news/terracycle-helpingcanadian-schools-non-profits-reduce-waste/1000399650//> (accessed 26 October 2011).

"TerraCycle: The Beginning, Part 1." *Venture* www.youtube.com/watch?v=UvWNlH_\4gRg (accessed 18 October 2011).

"TerraCycle: The Beginning, Part 2." *Venture* <www.youtube.com/watch?v=VUyUdgNKoQ&f eature=related> (accessed 18 October 2011).

"The coolest little start-up in America." *Rediff Business*, 23 June 2006. <in.rediff.com/money/2006/jun/23inc.htm> (accessed 17 October 2011).

References

i Szaky, Tom. *Revolution in a Bottle: How TerraCycle is Redefining Green Business.* New York: Portfolio, Penguin Group, 2009, p. 19.

ii Szaky, *Revolution in a Bottle*, p. 21.

iii Szaky, *Revolution in a Bottle*, p. 22.

iv Szaky, *Revolution in a Bottle*, p. 26.

v Szaky, *Revolution in a Bottle*, p. 41.

vi   Szaky, *Revolution in a Bottle*, p. 45.

vii   Szaky, *Revolution in a Bottle*.

viii   Szaky, *Revolution in a Bottle*, p. 78.

ix   Szaky, *Revolution in a Bottle*, p. 102.

x   Szaky, *Revolution in a Bottle*.

xi   Szaky, *Revolution in a Bottle*, p. 126.

xii   Szaky, Tom. "Choosing between profits and growth." *The New York Times*, 25 August 2011. <boss.blogs.nytimes.com/2011/08/25/choosing-between-profits-and-growth/> (accessed 26 October 2011).

xiii   Szaky, "Choosing between profits and growth."

CASE 6

Tropical Salvage's growth strategy
From recession to expansion[1]

R. Scott Marshall, Lisa Peifer and Erin Ferrigno

> [Tropical Salvage] demonstrates that business can adjust its values and
> practices to become a part of the solution to social and environmental
> challenges, while remaining responsible to the financial bottom line.
>
> *Tim O'Brien, Founder and President*

Tim O'Brien, founder of Tropical Salvage, was preparing for another warehouse
clearance sale of his unique, handcrafted hardwood furniture. It had been an
enormously challenging year and it was important to reduce inventory before the
next container arrived from Indonesia. The market for fine furniture had begun to
decline steadily in early 2008 following the stock market crash of the prior September. The company survived a difficult period, but not without suffering a decline in
sales. O'Brien had spent ten years building a sustainable business model based on
environmental stewardship, worker empowerment and unique, high quality product. As the economy recovered, O'Brien believed Tropical Salvage needed to pursue
an aggressive expansion strategy.

Although the warehouse clearance sale was occupying O'Brien's mind, he was
excited about the prospect of implementing a bold growth strategy for the coming

---

years. The two most significant strategies for growth focused on diversifying product offerings beyond hardwood furniture and opening branded retail stores in the
United States. Many fundamental business challenges, including brand awareness,
financing and operational efficiency, had to be overcome to make these strategies
effective. However, O'Brien was confident that the highly vertically integrated structure, unique product designs, cost-competitive sourcing and deeply engrained social
mission of Tropical Salvage provided the leverage to overcome these challenges.

As O'Brien considered how best to expand, he prepared to mark down the
remaining inventory from his last shipment. Are his growth plans overly ambitious
while the economy is so uncertain? Does it make sense to extend his product line
beyond the hardwood furniture for which Tropical Salvage is known and has experience manufacturing? Is it financially sound to expand into branded retail at this
time? Perhaps most importantly, are the trends in 'conscientious' consumerism
significant enough to support the growth of a values-driven, sustainability inspired
business like Tropical Salvage?

Introduction to Tropical Salvage

Headquartered in Portland, Oregon, Tropical Salvage is a private manufacturer of
distinctive handcrafted furniture made from salvaged, or rediscovered, hardwoods.
O'Brien established the company in 1998 to utilize underemployed, yet highly
skilled Javanese woodworkers and a nearly inexhaustible supply of salvageable
(non-virgin) tropical timber from around Indonesia. Combining these resources
provided O'Brien with the capability to create unique furniture products whose
sale can profitably advance positive social and environmental change.

Tropical Salvage has become largely vertically integrated. The company operates timber salvaging operations and designs and builds furniture in Indonesia and
markets and wholesales the furniture in North America. In addition to selling its
products to wholesale customers, Tropical Salvage invites consumers to purchase
goods directly from its Portland shipping and receiving warehouse. Despite the
business challenges of bootstrapping a young company and operating in Indonesia, for over ten years Tropical Salvage has steadily added to its production capacity
and may now be poised for expansion.

Indonesia: Systemic connections of economy, communities and the forest

Indonesia has extremely high levels of biodiversity. It is home to about 10 percent of
the world's flowering plant species, 12 percent of the world's mammals, 16 percent
of the world's reptile and amphibian species, 17 percent of the world's birds, and

at least 25 percent of all of the world's fish species.[2] On the islands of Borneo and Sumatra are the last remaining Sumatran tigers, orangutans, pygmy elephants and Sumatran rhinos and are a key source of freshwater to Borneo and Sumatra's 56 million people. It is not possible to overstate the extent to which the long term viability of Indonesians, the archipelago's flora and fauna and the country's economy are systemically linked and delicately balanced.

It has been conservatively estimated that at least 20 million people depend on Indonesia's forests for their livelihoods.[3] Wood-based industries' contributions to Indonesia's GNP rank second to petroleum, generating approximately US$7 billion in formal revenues and perhaps another US$1 billion in informal revenues associated with illegal logging and unreported exports.[4]

Logging in Indonesia's forests played a significant part in boosting the country's economic status from the late 1960s until the Asian Financial Crisis in 1997. Commercial and illegal logging practices during President Suharto's "New Order" drove Indonesia's economy but severely diminished a substantial portion of its tropical forests, placing the country's environment and economy in jeopardy. Although a number of regulations mandated government control of Indonesia's forests during Suharto's presidency, it was not until more recently that forest conservation became seriously regarded. Illegal logging practices have decreased as a result of this frame of mind, but they are still responsible for much of Indonesia's forest loss and violent crime rate.

In addition to logging jobs with commercial firms, residents rely on the forests for fuel, construction materials, water supply, soil nutrients for farm systems, and shelter and shade for crops and animals. Non-Timber Forest Products (NTFPs) such as game, medicines, fruits, and nuts have deep cultural significance and other NTFPs, such as rattan, charcoal, resin, and seeds are traded locally and internationally.[5] Indonesians rely on income and benefits from over ninety other NTFPs.

Indonesia's widespread deforestation has led to massive environmental, social and economic disruption. The intense deforestation rates that have occurred over the years pose a significant threat to the country's economy and its residents' livelihoods. Most employees in the wood products industry will face unemployment if the area can no longer sustain commercial forestry. Forest loss is also diminishing the area's biodiversity; aside from the direct endangerment of native trees

2 Case, M., Ardiansyah, F. and Spector, E. 2007. *Climate Change in Indonesia: Implications for Humans and Nature.* World Wildlife Fund.

3 Sunderlin, W.D., Resosudarmo, I. A. P. 1996. *Rates and Causes of Deforestation in Indonesia. Towards a resolution of the ambiguities.* CIFOR Occasional Paper No. 9. Bogor, Indonesia: CIFOR.

4 CIFOR. 2004. *Generating Economic Growth, Rural Livelihoods, and Environmental Benefits from Indonesia's Forests: A Summary of Issues and Policy Options.* Report prepared for the World Bank. Bogor, Indonesia: CIFOR.

5 The World Bank. (December 2006). *Sustaining Economic Growth, Rural Livelihoods, and Environmental Benefits: Strategic Options for Forest Assistance in Indonesia.* Jakarta: World Bank Office.

and plants, wild orangutans, sun bears, and clouded leopards are only a few of the species that face extinction in the next ten to twenty years.[6] Of course, the afore-mentioned NTFPs are also threatened by forest loss; without forest products, Indo-nesians would experience increased poverty and health risks. Because of these systemic connections, the effects of forest loss are becoming more severe and com-pound the difficult economic and social conditions in Indonesia. Unfortunately, in the minds of most Indonesians, the immediate benefit of income from logging still outweighs its negative long-term effects.

The town of Jepara,[7] on the north coast of Central Java, is well known globally for its handcrafted hardwood furniture and woodworking. Over 15,000 furniture work-shops, showrooms, log parks, sawmills, warehouses and ironmongers are located in Jepara, making it a localized network, or "industrial cluster".[8] The industry's suc-cess garnered political support to accommodate the growing volume of furniture exports. For instance, roads were paved and are maintained in order for container trucks to move wood and furniture in and out of the area from other significant parts of the island. At its height, Jepara's hardwood furniture industry employed about 170,000 workers[9] and firms competed fiercely for both inputs and markets.

There are a number of companies and organizations responding in numerous ways to Indonesia's deforestation. Home Depot, for example, cut its purchases of Indonesian lumber by more than three-quarters since 2000. Many companies, including IKEA, require that their hardwood supplies be harvested from Forest Stewardship Council (FSC) certified forests. As O'Brien sees it, FSC-certification is a step in the right direction but still ultimately results in trees being cut down. So, Tropical Salvage is addressing deforestation concerns through its own unique busi-ness model. In time, it seems likely that other large companies will follow suit and discontinue the purchase of illegally obtained wood.

Tropical Salvage: The inspiration and start-up

Having lived in and visited Indonesia over the course of nine years, O'Brien was familiar with the archipelago and felt personally attached to its culture when he became inspired to start Tropical Salvage. During a week of trekking in 1998,

6 Clifford, M.L., Tashiro, H., Natarajan, A. The race to save a rainforest. (2003). Business-Week Issue 3859, pp. 125-26.

7 Jepara's sprawling population is nearly 1,000,000; the wide majority of people in Jepara are Javanese.

8 An industrial cluster consists of production, processing and distribution enterprises along the manufacturing and marking chain. (*Atlas of Wooden Furniture Industry in Jepara, Indonesia*)

9 Roda, Jean-Marc, Philippe Cadene, Philippe Guizol, Levania Santoso & Achmad Uzair Fauzan. (2007). *Atlas of Wooden Furniture Industry in Jepara, Indonesia*. CIRAD & CIFOR, Jakarta: Harapan Prima.

O'Brien encountered stunning biodiversity juxtaposed with wasteful exploitation of natural resources and underutilization of craft traditions. O'Brien saw that the impressive array of wildlife and fantastically diverse population of trees was, quite unfortunately, offset by vast areas of recently clear-cut primary, or old-growth, forest. More than once he came upon areas that had been among the most biologically diverse locations on earth, reduced to an eerie, silent ruin of power-saw litter. For O'Brien, the experience was ominous and affecting.

As his travels continued through cities on the islands of Java, Bali, Lombok and Sumbawa, O'Brien noticed old wooden structures being replaced by more secure structures built from concrete and rebar. In many instances no plan existed to re-use the old beams, boards and poles. Old, hand-hewn wood derived from mature, wild-grained, tropical hardwood trees was fueling simple cooking fires. The idea for Tropical Salvage struck—salvaging wood from deconstructed buildings can be a significant source of raw material for hardwood furniture production.

As the wheels for his new business venture turned in his head, O'Brien began to view Indonesia a little differently. Travel in population centers made him acutely aware that the high deforestation rates have devastating effects, not only on the environment, but also on the social and economic climate. Depletion of the forests was not only leaving wildlife homeless, but was also putting millions of Indonesians out of work. O'Brien started Tropical Salvage based on a conviction that "a reasonable and promising market-oriented strategy can contribute to positive change in a part of the world beset by extraordinary challenges."

The Tropical Salvage business model

O'Brien knew that earning and maintaining the respect of Indonesians, especially in Java, would be important to the success of his business model. One day by chance, he was fortunate to meet Agus Rafiqkoh, a likeminded, well-connected and trustworthy businessman. After many lengthy conversations, the two of them set out to actualize Tropical Salvage.

Rafiqkoh, Partner and the Director of Indonesian Operations, had worked in Jepara's wood furniture production industry for eight years prior to meeting O'Brien. He now plays a number of critical roles in Tropical Salvage's Indonesia operations: hiring employees, designing new pieces, directing production, and locating and coordinating wood salvage projects. He is skilled in networking and admits to approaching most new interactions with the business in the forefront of his mind. Brought together by rather random circumstances, O'Brien and Rafiqkoh have developed a strong partnership and friendship, based on shared philosophies, trust and commitment. It is this relationship in particular that serves to anchor Tropical Salvage and has permitted it to overcome the many obstacles faced since its inception.

Both social and environmental mission objectives were implemented at the onset of business in 1999 with eight employees working in a two thousand square foot rented space. O'Brien was excited about the market back then, but was also uninformed about it. After a number of setbacks, he still marvels in the company's utter existence. Today, the company's operations in Indonesia have grown into a salvaging operation and production facility that employs 85 people, including wood salvagers, millers, kiln operators, artisan furniture-makers and carvers, and finishers, some of whom quite likely used to be employed in the illegal logging industry. Tropical Salvage employees are compensated with benefits and wages 20 percent higher than the local industry average and the company has been instrumental in developing the Jepara Forest Conservancy, which protects land for reforestation, economic opportunity and educational purposes.

Sourcing

Tropical Salvage uses only salvaged, or rediscovered, wood to build its line of furniture. So far the company has worked with wood from around 55 different species of trees including teak, acacia, jackfruit, and ingas. O'Brien claims to be a pioneer in using ingas for constructing hardwood furniture and much of what the company finds and uses is this particular specie. Although, and perhaps because, they carry the heaviest weight with consumers, primary forest teak trees have possibly the saddest story of depletion. Today these fast growing hardwoods are grown on plantations and tend to be cut after just ten years. This is half the time it takes for teak to fully mature. Because mature teak has become increasingly rare, much of the teak used by Tropical Salvage comes in the form of old objects used for outdoor purposes, such as boats.

Fortunately for Tropical Salvage, the company's business model has not yet required it to compete for raw materials. Most of the wood the salvaging crews retrieve is without value in Indonesia. The beauty is that, through years of experimentation, Tropical Salvage has determined how to give new life to the wood so that it becomes valuable again, in the form of furniture. One piece of Tropical Salvage furniture might consist of several species of wood aged from thirty to thousands of years. O'Brien and many of Tropical Salvage's customers feel that the effects of nails, seasoning cracks, bore holes, wild-growth grain, and mineral deposits in the finished products are a wonderful testament to the wood's historical richness.

The company estimates that the supply of salvageable wood in Indonesia is inexhaustible for meeting its own demand. Tropical Salvage has already discovered and surveyed multiple wood salvage sites in Sumatra, Kalimantan and Sulawesi. When it discovers salvageable wood, the company pays for short-term 'rent' of the land immediately surrounding the site. If the salvaging process compromises crops or other NTFPs, it will pay the landowner to replace them after the process is completed. Well known as the authority on wood salvaging in Jepara, the company is often contacted by government officials when salvageable wood is discovered.

However, as other producers adopt salvaging methods, Tropical Salvage may face competition for rights to salvage in certain areas.

Using hard labor, basic winch systems and limited heavy machinery, the company applies five principle wood salvage strategies on the island of Java. It reclaims wood from demolition sites where old buildings, houses or bridges have been razed or deconstructed. Old fishing boats and truck roofs are also used. It salvages old, wild growth trees from rivers and lakes (Appendix 1), as well as those that have fallen off logging barges or were felled by floods and landslides during the rainy season. The company also uses diseased or unproductive plantation coffee, cacao, and fruit trees. And finally, unique to the company, since 2003 it has mined entombed trees from beneath the ground (Appendix 2).

Manufacturing

After the wood is salvaged it is transported to a storage yard in Jepara and cut into boards. Currently, Tropical Salvage contracts primary milling of the wood it salvages. This makes sense in a very soft market where wood processing facilities are operating at a fraction of capacity. From here it moves to the production facility where it is treated for insects and placed in a kiln for drying. Discovering the optimum adjustments for the kilns in order to dry the numerous species is an ongoing challenge, but has gotten much easier with years of experience. The unique expertise that Tropical Salvage has developed in drying a vast array of species serves the company well and provides it with a competency that competitors find difficult to imitate. From the kiln, millers, artisan furniture-makers, carvers, and finishers construct the furniture that makes up Tropical Salvage's product offerings, including dining tables, chairs, benches, drawers, armoires, cabinets, buffets, shelves, desks, beds, side tables, media stands, coffee tables, and console tables.

Warehouse employees receive specification guidelines from Rafiqkoh in order to assemble and finish the furniture; each piece passes through many hands to complete the process. The greatest challenge during the manufacturing process is determining how to put together the different species and grain patterns to create attractive finished products. Rafiqkoh also handles quality assurance, making sure each piece is built to Western standards. The product catalog includes roughly 150 different models, but the company also builds one-of-a-kind custom pieces and furnishings built to commercial specifications. O'Brien and Rafiqkoh keep the catalog fresh by introducing at least one new design with each container shipment, about four times a year.

By offering steady employment, Tropical Salvage positively affects an area distressed by high rates of poverty, underemployment and unemployment.[10] In addition, the company offers benefits such as paid vacations and health care. Tropical Salvage is committed to its employees and respects their rights to fair wages, health,

10 According to a local source, Jepara is experiencing 25–30% unemployment.

and safe work environments. The company became a member of the Fair Trade Federation in 2003; all of its products are Fair Trade certified, a result of which being that wages are 20 percent above the local standard.

Distribution

Containers are loaded with finished Tropical Salvage products (Appendix 3) in Jepara and shipped to North America. These containers take anywhere from 25 to 40 days to arrive and come directly to the main warehouse in Portland, Oregon, or to Ten Thousand Villages Canada's receiving warehouse and distribution center. From these receiving locations, the products are dispersed to each Ten Thousand Villages store location in Canada and wholesale retailers in the United States.

Tropical Salvage has only a few employees in its Portland, Oregon, headquarters, which is home to a receiving warehouse and small showroom that manages wholesale sales and distribution and some retail transactions. Independent contractors are occasionally brought in to assist with unloading containers or to make local deliveries.

Customers in Portland have the option to come to Tropical Salvage's warehouse location to buy products directly at standard retail prices. As a furniture manufacturer, Tropical Salvage is able to offer products at wholesale prices to its retail partners, but can also gain higher margins by selling at regular retail prices in its own warehouse location.

ECOpdx, also located in Portland, Oregon, is the company's largest local wholesale customer. Tropical Salvage has a number of other wholesale customers including: Small Planet Trading in Hood River, Oregon and Kizuri in Spokane, Washington. The Banyan Tree in Portland sells Tropical Salvage furniture to customers on consignment.

Beyond the local market, Ten Thousand Villages Canada is a key retail partner for Tropical Salvage. Ten Thousand Villages Canada has truly embraced the Tropical Salvage business model and its products. In fact, the Fair Trade retailer took the initiative to create a hard-copy "Tropical Salvage" catalog for its customers. This strong retail partner regularly stocks a number of furniture pieces and has arranged to receive direct container shipments of specifically selected pieces. In addition to the local partners and Ten Thousand Villages Canada, Tropical Salvage caters to other retailers across the United States for occasional wholesale orders.

Partnerships

Tropical Salvage initiated its business model without deliberate attention to partnerships outside of its supply chain and manufacturing operations. In the refinement and actualization of its sustainability-inspired mission, Tropical Salvage found NGO partnerships to be a critical resource. NGO partnerships bring expertise and credibility that have, according to O'Brien, permitted Tropical Salvage "to hasten development and expansion of the model."

Since 2007, Tropical Salvage has been a leader in the creation of a conservation, education and reforestation project in Kunir, a village community in Jepara experiencing the widespread effects of overdependence on unsustainably harvested teak forests. The Jepara Forest Conservancy (JFC) shows how ecological restoration integrates with and positively influences cultural, social and economic conditions. For instance, with the help of Tropical Salvage, Kunir has recently adopted a number of Etawah goats, which are highly valued and produce exceptionally nutritious milk. Not only will this provide nutrients directly to the community, it will eventually result in improved economic conditions. JFC's restoration efforts have also had a positive effect on the area's native wildlife; its work is crucial in saving the Lutung monkey species.

Tropical Salvage collaborates with the Institute for Culture and Ecology (IFCAE) to maintain the JFC. IFCAE, a 501(c)(3) nonprofit organization, seeks to improve human and environmental conditions through applied research, education, and community improvement projects. Through its cross-sector partnership with IFCAE and the creation of the JFC, Tropical Salvage is able to fully realize its social mission objectives. The JFC provides a recreational botanical park for the community, educational facilities for school children and community members, and a model for alternative, economically sustainable land uses for local landholders. O'Brien firmly states that, "such collaborations are very important to Tropical Salvage's current and future business model," partially because Tropical Salvage does not have in-house expertise to overcome many of the challenges that arise in developing its mission. And, both O'Brien and Rafiqkoh do not consider the partnership with IFCAE and the creation of the JFC as optional; rather these efforts are at the core of the market-based strategy that seeks to reverse the destruction of Indonesian forests and the communities that depend on them.

The hardwood furniture industry

Hardwood furniture is a sizable global industry, requiring intense labor and natural resources (Appendix 4). Between 1995 and 2000, trade in furniture grew by 36.5 percent, faster than world trade as a whole (26.5 percent), and, also in that time, became the largest low-tech sector.[11] Indonesia ranks fifth among the world's 15 major furniture exporters (Appendix 5). Sixty-two percent of all furniture exports are wooden, which includes both solid wood and flat-pack, or ready-to-assemble, furniture made by both craft-based firms and large-volume producers.

---

11 United Nations Industrial Development Organization. 2003. *The Global Wood Furniture Value Chain: What Prospects for Upgrading by Developing Countries?*

The United States is not a major exporter of hardwood furniture. In fact, in the last ten years the United States has become a major importer. In 2000, US hardwood furniture manufacturing was a $13 billion industry employing over 135,000 individuals.[12] In 2006 the industry had shrunk to US$8.6 billion in revenue and 63,066 employees.[13] These numbers reveal the significant decline in the US industry over a relatively short period of time. Between 1997 and 2005 US demand for furniture grew by 27 percent,[14] but the market share was captured by imports whose outsourced labor and production costs are much lower than those in the United States. For example, China's household furniture imports to the United States increased 78 percent between 2003 and 2007,[15] and rose a total of 525 percent between 1998 and 2005.[16] Currently, nearly 70 percent of hardwood furniture purchases in the United States are imported products; about half of those are manufactured in China. Amidst this global competition, hardwood furniture has remained the largest sector of the US-manufactured furniture industry.

The growth in demand for furniture occurred while the US real estate market flourished from 2001 to 2006, due to favorable mortgage interest rates. Furniture sales are closely related to the state of the real estate market, which includes new and resale housing sales as well as home remodeling. The real estate market's sharp downturn in 2008, correlating with the US financial crisis, resulted in a decrease in sales for numerous industries, including hardwood furniture. The effects of this downturn are noticeable throughout Jepara; a city that, before the recession, had been teeming with foreign business people buying furniture. Many warehouses and showrooms in Jepara now stand empty as a result of this decreased demand.

Another important trend in the furniture industry is consumers' shift from considering furniture a lifetime or even generation-to-generation investment to deeming it disposable and easily interchangeable. Often sold by big-box retailers and warehouse stores because it requires less inventory space, ready-to-assemble (RTA) composite wood furniture has proven to be the answer to consumer demand. A report by Mintel/Simmons NCS revealed that people in older age groups bought less RTA furniture. But older people buy less furniture and younger, more mobile, people buy more furniture in general and embrace RTA furniture; stand-alone furniture stores selling high quality, fully-assembled furniture have faced increased competitive pressures. This shift was likely brought on by increased frequency in

12 The Gale Group, Inc. 2010. Industry Report: Wood Household Furniture, Except Upholstered, NAICS 337122.

13 US Census Bureau, 2007. http://factfinder.census.gov/servlet/IBQTable?_bm=y&-ds_name=EC0700A1&-NAICS2007=337122&-ib_type=NAICS2007&-_industry=337122&-_lang=en.

14 Wood Digest. Datamonitor Industry Market Research. 2000. *US Wooden Household Furniture.*

15 Kaiser, Emily (2008). "Furniture demand falls, ripples felt worldwide". Reuters, http://www.reuters.com/article/idUSN2537252220080725.

16 Industry Report: Nonupholstered Wood Household Furniture Manufacturing. Business & Company Resource Center.

relocation and less immediate disposable income. Because RTA furniture sells on average for less than half the price of comparable assembled furniture, price is a major driving factor in the increased demand for RTA items.

Although RTA furniture has increased in popularity, some providers of solid hardwood furniture continue to successfully compete in the furniture industry. The wood furniture industry is structured as a buyer-driven value chain with few scale- or technology-entry barriers in production. The consequence of this structure is that lead or governing firms that set prices, delivery schedules and quality standards are located at the apex of the chain; that is, among the buyers. The top two furniture retailers in the United States,[17] WalMart, Inc. and Ashley Furniture, both carry solid wood pieces. In addition to distributing its products to a range of specialty and department stores, Ashley Furniture sells its products in over two hundred branded retail stores called Ashley Furniture HomeStores. Williams-Sonoma is third in total sales and focuses exclusively on high quality, premium furniture. It owns Pottery Barn and Ethan Allen. Both Williams-Sonoma subsidiaries have built their reputations on consistent high quality, distinctive product and store designs and standalone branded retail stores. The next tier of competitors includes Cost Plus World Market and Pier 1 Imports, both of which sell mid- to low-end furniture.

There are only a few, smaller competitors that offer hardwood furniture with explicit social and environmental missions. The Wooden Duck in San Francisco uses reclaimed timber from pre-1920 structures to manufacture and sell household and office furnishing. The Wooden Duck's sales are primarily in San Francisco and the surrounding area. Environment Furniture is headquartered in Los Angeles and has showrooms in New York, Atlanta and Orange County. It salvages wood from Brazil as well as from forests certified by the Forest Stewardship Council and the Sustainable Forest Initiative. It offers uniquely designed, premium products for the home.

These two companies, as well as Tropical Salvage, are well-positioned to take advantage of a more recent trend impacting the tropical wood and hardwood furniture industry. The trend entails regulatory and non-regulatory initiatives to limit imports from non-sustainably managed tropical forests and promote sales from sustainably managed tropical forests. The Lacey Act,[18] the Rainforest Alliance's SmartWood program, the Sustainable Furnishings Council, and The Prince's Rainforest Project were all launched between 2007 and 2009. By restricting importation of illegally harvested tropical timber—whether raw logs or in finished product—and by encouraging consumers to buy sustainability-based certified furniture, these developments seem to provide ample opportunity for socially minded businesses in this industry to expand. In fact, with growing consumer awareness of environmental issues, eco-friendly furniture is no longer a niche market. It is increasingly common for wood products to be manufactured with Forest Stewardship Council-certified wood and environmentally friendly finishes. Recycled materials are also

---

17 Mintel Reports. Home Furniture—US. 2008. (Data from 2006).
18 The Lacey Act, part of the Farm Bill of 2008, combats trafficking of illegally acquired or off-limits wildlife, fish and plants, including tropical hardwoods.

gaining popularity. Although less common in the industry and not well recognized as an issue by the marketplace, there is significant opportunity for furniture companies to focus on social issues, such as labor conditions and wages. All facets of sustainability will gain importance over the coming years as both governments and consumers demand greater transparency of environmental and social impacts.

O'Brien knows that his craft-based company must produce affordable, high-quality furniture products to effectively compete. His unique business model—combining low raw material and production costs with a clear and compelling social mission—helps mitigate some of the current industry trends and competitive risks faced by other companies. Tropical Salvage's profit margins remain high because the company controls the majority of its value chain. Furthermore, Tropical Salvage has a clear sustainability–oriented brand, which provides an authentically differentiated position in the marketplace.

Challenges to the business model

> The road to the vision has been a lot more fun and a lot more difficult than I expected it to be. Both the risks and rewards have been a thrill and have brought true happiness. (Tim O'Brien)

Although O'Brien is confident in his expansion plans for Tropical Salvage, the company has had, and continues to have, its share of challenges. In the beginning, O'Brien needed to learn the Indonesian culture and language. It was important for him to be able to communicate his philosophies and vision first-hand. Furthermore, because the company's wood salvaging techniques were groundbreaking in the region Tropical Salvage had to work to determine proper and effective kiln times for the 55 different woods to be utilized. Today O'Brien's knowledge of the language and culture, his partnership with Rafiqkoh, and the company's salvaging and dry-kilning techniques are considered to be the company's key competitive advantages.

Operations

Distance contributes greatly to the challenge of quality control. North American consumers expect unique designs and exceptional quality in high-end hardwood furniture and O'Brien is not able to oversee warehouse operations year-round. Rafiqkoh has developed good insight into North American consumers and is charged with managing the furniture designs and quality standards. One of the most recent issues the company has encountered involves the presence of boring insects in certain pieces of recently fallen wood. Tropical Salvage lost some sales as a consequence and had to add a permethrin treatment for the wood at the production facility.

Expanding salvage operations presents another challenge for Tropical Salvage. The expense of setting up operations at a new site on the island of Kalimantan has been much higher than originally anticipated; mechanized systems are necessary to recover the wood and it is more difficult to move the wood across the Java Sea to the Jepara warehouse. There is an abundance of quality salvageable wood in Kalimantan's rivers and O'Brien is confident that the volume of wood recoverable from this new site will more than compensate for the additional expense. However, as Tropical Salvage continues to seek out additional sources of salvageable wood around the Indonesian archipelago, it will need to ensure efficient salvage and transport processes to maintain the margins that are key to its expansion efforts.

Inventory

Tropical Salvage also must deal with unreliable shipping schedules. Due to traffic in Indonesian and US ports or extreme weather, a container can be delayed by several weeks. Such delays have been costly, particularly when working with commercial clients facing deadlines of their own.

Tropical Salvage also lacks a formal computer-based system to track and control its incoming and outgoing inventory. While the current informal approach has been sufficient for the small warehouse in Portland and its retail partnerships, this is a challenge that will become more evident with the introduction of one or more branded retail locations. O'Brien understands that he will need to be able to accurately evaluate a store's sales turnover and support the retail staff's forecasting and inventory management processes. Further, tracking inventory will help O'Brien understand the customers in a given location and place appropriate orders for the future.

Marketing

Increased demand for its furniture is necessary in order for Tropical Salvage to expand its operations and social and environmental missions. While untapped prospects and channels of distribution remain, determining the most effective ways to market the product line and mission is essential. O'Brien considers this his greatest challenge.

Tropical Salvage serves three core audiences: B2C retailers, commercial businesses, and consumers. Each audience requires a unique message. Creating the appropriate marketing approach for each group will involve learning about their needs and values. For example, commercial business prospects include both restaurants and offices. Determining the messages that resonate and which materials will get noticed for these two segments of the commercial business market is critical.

While the demand for sustainably sourced furniture increases, the majority of Americans remain unaware of the effects of illegal logging and deforestation. Because Tropical Salvage produces high-quality furniture while at the same time promoting social and environmental sustainability, the marketing must blend and balance two notions that perhaps consumers have yet to associate. Images are exceptional tools for telling a story and are an asset to Tropical Salvage, whose business model allows direct access to sourcing and restoration sites. By emotionally connecting consumers to its products through images of Tropical Salvage's work in Indonesia, the company may be able to offer a persuasive marketing message. But to what extent should Tropical Salvage take responsibility for educating its audiences on the effects of illegal logging and deforestation? And could too much emphasis on the mission deter certain prospective customers?

Although the hardwood furniture market is fairly saturated, O'Brien believes there is an opportunity to continue to supply the Lifestyles of Health and Sustainability (LOHAS) market segment (Appendix 6). LOHAS consumers are passionate, environmentally and socially responsible and tend to be early adopters who can be used as predictors of upcoming trends. They are also influential over friends and family, are more brand loyal than other consumers especially to companies whose values match their own, and most importantly, are willing to put their money behind their beliefs and values.[19] It is roughly estimated that a third of Portland's population practices a LOHAS perspective; O'Brien knows that most of his customers in the Portland warehouse are LOHAS consumers. These consumers share many of Tropical Salvage's values, focusing on health and fitness, the environment, personal development, sustainable living, and social justice.[20] These consumers are educated and informed, and many have traveled abroad to less developed destinations which increased their awareness of social, environmental, and health-related issues on a global scale. About one in every four adults in the United States, roughly 41 million, falls into this market segment; this US$209 billion market is shaping future consumer trends. O'Brien can incorporate his existing knowledge of the target customer into the marketing message; however, he still needs to determine how to reach this target market with his value proposition.

The business expansion plan of 2010

It is obvious to O'Brien that expansion is necessary in order to sustain Tropical Salvage's growing business. In response, he has devised an extensive expansion plan to move toward branded retail stores, and has numerous other ideas and new products in mind.

O'Brien sees forward vertical integration of the company into branded retail stores as the first step toward growth. In remaining loyal to his retail partner, ECOpdx, O'Brien will seek retail space outside of Portland. Seattle is an obvious choice for the first market that Tropical Salvage will enter with a branded store.

---

19 French, S. and Rogers, G. "Understanding the LOHAS Consumer: The Rise of Ethical Consumerism: A Strategic Market Research Update from The Natural Marketing Institute (NMI)." Available from http://www.lohas.com/Lohas-Consumer.

20 http://www.lohas.com/.

Because of its proximity to Portland, O'Brien can be as involved as is necessary to find a location, hire a team to maintain the store, and create a strong storefront. Further, he will be able to supply a Seattle location through his existing Portland warehouse and a third-party trucking company. Appendix 7 provides the estimated annual operating expenses for the Seattle-based store, including on-going and one-time expenditures. Although the new store represents a significant financial commitment for Tropical Salvage, the financial projections (shown in Appendix 8) suggest that this expansion plan could be quite successful.

Fortunately, Tropical Salvage has not acquired any debt during the recession, but O'Brien needs to decide how to proceed with the financial outlay required of opening a retail store. Venture capital financing or a small business loan seems to be the most appropriate options, but O'Brien has not yet settled on one over the other.

It may make sense to incorporate some of O'Brien's other expansion ideas into his branded retail store strategy. Some new products that he would like to introduce include: sustainably sourced bamboo and rattan, coffee, tea, spices, and textiles (including pillows and cushions). Offering a more diverse product line may, in fact, be necessary for a successful retail location. The diversity of sustainability-oriented products will draw more people into Tropical Salvage storefronts to increase opportunities to sell higher-end—and often higher margin—furniture. Tropical Salvage could acquire these products through its relationship with JFC, further benefiting the residents of Kunir and fulfilling the company's mission.

The future of Tropical Salvage

As O'Brien prepared signs for the warehouse clearance sale, he thought about different ways to arrange his furniture in a retail store. He believed that strong displays would draw more customers and increase demand so that he could expand his sourcing operations and employ more people. He was also confident that he could introduce new merchandise to complement Tropical Salvage's furniture, which would greatly benefit the small communities in Indonesia working with the company.

O'Brien still questioned the best financing option for his expansion plan however. Does it make sense to appeal to investors or continue down his financially independent path? Further, is he in a secure enough position to take on expansion while the economy's future is so unclear? He worried that if his expansion efforts failed, Tropical Salvage's social mission could be compromised. He also wondered whether he should consider the Rainforest Alliance's SmartWood certification in order to increase visibility to consumers in the LOHAS market. This question was part of the larger challenge of how to effectively communicate the value of Tropical Salvage to its target customers. What marketing efforts would best serve his plans? O'Brien had a lot of thinking and work to do before he would be able to jump into branded retail stores successfully.

APPENDIX 1
Wood salvaging

River salvage site in Bundu (Java, Indonesia)

APPENDIX 2
Tropical Salvage wood salvaging methods

Deconstruction wood	Indonesia is replacing a number of its buildings and structures with concrete and rebar; deconstruction wood is very common. Teak was used in many of the deconstruction projects Tropical Salvage comes across. Old doors and shutters from deconstruction are often used in Tropical Salvage's armoires and wine cabinets.
River and lake salvage	Years of severe weather and volcanic activity in Indonesia have knocked down a number of trees that have been swept into rivers. Low water levels in the dry season make it easy to find these trees; the wood is pulled out of rivers and lakes, cut into two-meter lengths and brought to the sawmill.
Flood and landslide salvage	Trees and houses fallen victim to landslides are a result of illegal logging. Deforestation eliminates the soil's protective canopy, increasing the likelihood of landslides during Indonesia's rainy season.
Plantation "waste"	Coffee and cacao trees are not typically used in furniture, but Tropical Salvage has learned to use them in their furniture designs. These woods are traditionally burned when they are culled from a plantation.
Entombed wood	Entombed wood exists as a result of volcanic eruptions hundreds of years ago. These trees became entombed in bogs and aged below ground, deep enough so that oxygen has not decomposed them. The rainy season erodes the soil around the bogs and brings the entombed wood closer to the surface. While the logs are entombed, they absorb minerals from the soil to add density to the wood; the woods are very hard and very heavy. Tropical Salvage can sometimes make tabletops with a single plank of wood that still holds the shape of the tree's trunk.

APPENDIX 3
Tropical Salvage finished products

Tropical Salvage patio furniture

Mimpi Manis Day Bed

Higher Cause Storage

APPENDIX 4
Wood furniture industry value chain

Value chain in the wood furniture industry

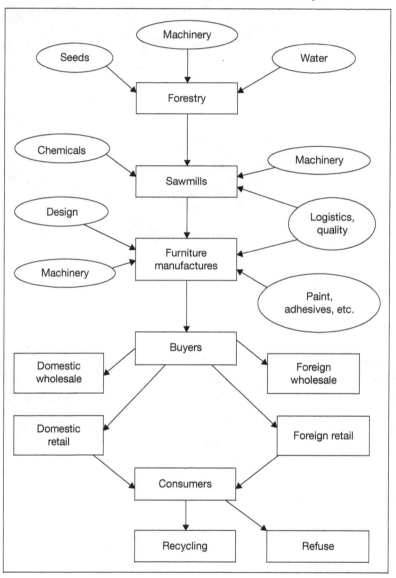

Source: United Nations Industrial Development Organization, *Global Wood Furniture Value Chain: What Prospects for Upgrading by Developing Countries*, Sectoral Studies Series.

APPENDIX 5
Top 15 furniture exporters (2000; US$ million)

Country	Gross exports 2000	Net exports 1995	Net exports 2000	Net exports percentage change 1995-2000
Italy	8,359	7,595	7,395	–3
China	4,582	1,671	4,412	164
Canada	5,179	685	2,044	198
Poland	2,191	1,180	1,815	54
Indonesia	1,518	819	1,498	83
Malaysia	1,596	826	1,491	80
Denmark	1,900	1,687	1,209	–28
Mexico	3,315	468	1,173	151
Thailand	949	712	909	28
Spain	1,453	523	531	2
Slovenia	586	409	461	13
Czech Rep	780	148	445	201
Romania	445	472	377	–20
Sweden	1,298	510	338	–34
Brazil	496	212	333	57
Total of rest	22,742			
Total	57,388			

Notes: Standard International Trade Classification SITC821, Furniture and stuffed furnishings and includes wood, metal and plastic items.

Source: ITC (www.intracen.org).

APPENDIX 6
LOHAS market

LOHAS (Lifestyles of Health and Sustainability) populations are the ideal target customers for Tropical Salvage. A market analysis of the top six potential markets is below:

Market Analysis		2009	2010	2011	2012	2013	
Potential Customers	Growth						CAGR
Portland	3%	247,405	254,827	262,472	270,346	278,456	3.00%
Seattle	3%	384,741	396,283	408,171	420,416	433,028	3.00%
San Francisco	3%	473,369	487,570	502,197	517,263	532,781	3.00%
Boston	2%	351,000	358,020	365,180	372,484	379,934	2.00%
Chicago	2%	419,000	427,380	435,928	444,647	453,540	2.00%
Minneapolis	3%	424,807	437,551	450,678	464,198	478,124	3.00%
Total	2.67%	2,300,322	2,361,631	2,424,626	2,489,354	2,555,863	2.67%

APPENDIX 7
Estimated annual operating expenses for Seattle store

Category	Expense (US$)
On-Going Expenses	
Wages and salaries	$110,000
Lease	$80,000
Utilities (phone, broadband)	$12,000
Marketing	$50,000
State/local license and permits	$3,000
Container furniture shipments (5 shipments, 40' containers	$100,000
Computer and organizational/inventory software	$6,000
Information kiosk in storefront	$5,000
Miscellaneous supplies	$2,000
Travel	$5,000
Furniture maintenance tools	$3,000
Subtotal	$376,000
One-Time Expenses	
Delivery truck (used)	$8,000
Signage	$10,000
Expansion of production capacity in Indonesia	$20,000
Lighting system in storefront	$10,000
Subtotal	$48,000
Total	$425,000

Source: Tropical Salvage Growth Plan, August 2010.

APPENDIX 8
Tropical Salvage condensed financial data

Consolidated Income Statement Data	FY 2009	FY 2010	FY 2011	FY 2012	FY 2013	FY 2014
Sales	$470,000	$478,813	$863,480	$1,674,450	$2,881,364	$4,529,157
Gross Margin	$204,000	$282,682	$583,266	$1,212,062	$2,113,682	$3,435,952
Gross Margin %	43.40%	59.04%	67.55%	72.39%	73.36%	75.86%
Total Operating Expenses	$250,000	$288,420	$520,000	$903,000	$1,304,450	$1,719,900
Profit Before Interest and Taxes	($46,000)	($5,378)	$43,266	$289,062	$774,232	$1,716,052
Other Income	$77,212	$0	$0	$0	$0	$0
Retail Door Build Out & Remodel	$0	$0	$20,000	$20,000	$35,000	$0
Net Profit (Loss)	**$31,212**	**($10,258)**	**$27,123**	**$200,762**	**$541,962**	**$1,201,237**
Consolidated Balance Sheet Data	FY 2009	FY 2010	FY 2011	FY 2012	FY 2013	FY 2014
Current Assets						
Cash	$28,593	($10,598)	($16,933)	$52,207	$473,381	$1,652,700
Accounts Receivable	$5,000	$5,608	$10,113	$19,610	$33,745	$53,043
Inventory	$14,400	$48,859	$133,639	$257,027	$429,349	$524,416
Total Current Assets	$47,993	$43,868	$126,819	$328,844	$936,476	$2,230,159
Total Long-term Assets	$4,837	$3,517	$8,517	$6,517	$4,517	(16,483)
Total Assets	**$52,830**	**$47,835**	**$135,336**	**$335,361**	**$940,993**	**$2,213,676**

Accounts Payable	$5,000	$9,813	$50,641	$95,102	$158,772	$230,218
Total Current Liabilities	$5,000	$9,813	$50,641	$95,102	$158,772	$230,218
Long-term Liabilities	$45,197	$45,197	$45,197	($1)	($1)	($1)
Total Liabilities	**$50,197**	**$55,010**	**$95,838**	**$95,101**	**$158,771**	**$230,217**
Paid-in Capital	$0	$0	$20,000	$20,000	$20,000	$20,000
Retained Earnings	($28,579)	$2,633	($7,625)	$19,498	$220,259	$762,222
Earnings	$31,212	($10,258)	$27,123	$200,762	$541,962	$1,201,237
Total Capital	**$2,633**	**($7,625)**	**$39,498**	**$240,259**	**$782,222**	**$1,983,458**
Total Liabilities and Capital	**$52,830**	**$47,385**	**$135,336**	**$335,361**	**$940,993**	**$2,213,676**

Source: Tropical Salvage Growth Plan, August 2010.

CASE 7

Husk Power Systems
Lighting up the Indian rural lives

Manish Agarwal and D. Satish

I can guarantee that the pleasure and happiness you will get when you see a village light up every evening is literally "priceless". No amount of Wall Street bonuses or Hedge Fund's profit sharing can bring you that level of satisfaction, happiness, and of course recognition (Manoj Sinha, Co-founder, Husk Power Systems, in September 2011).[1]

In June 2011, Husk Power Systems (HPS), a social enterprise based in Bihar, Eastern India, won the prestigious Ashden Award for Sustainable Energy,[2] considered as the "Green Oscar". The international award carried prize money of £120,000.[3] On this occasion, Gyanesh Pandey,[4] Co-Founder and Chief Executive Officer (CEO) of HPS, said, "Winning the Ashden awards is a big achievement for Husk Power Systems. Almost a third of India's population has no access to electricity and the role of energy

---

1 "SOCAP11 Social Entrepreneur Spotlight: Manoj Sinha, Husk Power Systems (India)," http://socialcapitalmarkets.net, September 3, 2011.
2 Started in 2001, Ashden Awards for Sustainable Energy are the internationally recognized annual awards in the field of green energy.
3 £ = British pounds sterling. As of September 2012, US$1 was approximately equal to £0.6279.
4 Gyanesh Pandey is a native of Bihar. He did his B.Tech in Electrical Engineering from Benaras Hindu University before moving to the US for his Master's degree in Electric Power and Power Electronics Engineering from Rensselaer Polytechnic Institute. He worked in the Power Management Semiconductor industry before HPS.

is vital in catalyzing the economic development in India."[5] Jacqueline Novogratz, CEO, Acumen Fund[6] said, "Companies like HPS are working to impact positively not only the environment, but to ensure that someday everyone, including the poorest of the poor in rural India, will have access to clean and affordable electricity."[7]

Even as of 2012, electricity and electrification remained a major problem in India, especially in rural hinterlands. Around 125,000[8] villages in the country do not have any kind of electricity connection. This situation was worse in Bihar, the third most populous state in the country. In Bihar, per capita consumption of electricity was just 117.48 per kilowatt-hour (kWh)[9] in 2009–10 whereas the average per capita consumption in India as a whole was 570.9 kWh.[10,11] Due to lack of electricity 89.3% (94.5% in rural areas and 39.9%[12] in urban areas) of the households in Bihar use kerosene[13] to light up their houses after sunset. Raghunath Prasad Chauhan, a farmer in Tamkuha, Bihar, describing the situation, said, "It was dark and because of that there were so many problems. There used to be a lot of thefts and snakes and dogs would bite. There was problem to go out in night. My children could not study at night."[14] Slow economic development, political corruption, and red tape were the root causes for absence of electrification in Bihar according to analysts.

However, things changed after HPS set up its first power plant in Tamkuha, Bihar, on August 15, 2007. HPS was the brainchild of Pandey and his friend Ratnesh Yadav.[15] Later, Pandey's friend Manoj Sinha[16] and Sinha's friend Charles W. (Chip)

5 Pranava K. Chaudhary, "Husk Wins Intl Award for Clean Energy," http://articles.times ofindia.indiatimes.com, June 18, 2011.

6 Acumen Fund is a non-profit global venture fund started in April 1, 2001.

7 "Acumen Fund to Invest $375,000 in Bihar based Husk Power System," www.siliconindia .com, March 24, 2010.

8 Pranava K. Chaudhary, "Husk Wins Intl Award for Clean Energy," http://articles.times ofindia.indiatimes.com, June 18, 2011.

9 "Per Capita Power Consumption," http://pib.nic.in, May 18, 2012.

10 "Data—Electric Power Consumption (kWh Per Capita)," http://data.worldbank.org.

11 On the other hand, in the UK and the US average per capita consumption in 2008 was 6,067 kWh and 13,647 kWh respectively.

12 "Households using Kerosene for Lighting," Chapter III in Town and Planning Organization, *Households with Elecricity Connection in India 2011*, www.tcpomud.gov.in.

13 Kerosene is a thin liquid blue fuel. It is mostly used by households for lighting and heating purposes.

14 "Bringing Sustainable Light to Communities off the Grid," www.youtube.com, July 21, 2010.

15 Ratnesh Yadav is the co-founder of HPS. He is a native of Bihar. He has a Bachelor of Arts degree from Delhi University. He has experience in bio-diesel (Jatropha plantation), fisheries, and floriculture. He founded a nonprofit organization—Samta Samriddhi Foundation — before he founded HPS with Pandey and the others.

16 Manoj Sinha is a co-founder of HPS. He did his B.Tech in Electronics Engineering with honors from Benaras Hindu University in 1999. He did his MS in Electrical and Computer Engineering at the University of Massachusetts, Amherst. He also has a Master's in Business Administration (MBA) from Darden Graduate School of Business associated with the University of Virginia.

Ransler IV[17] joined them. The plant generated power using rice husk,[18] which was abundantly available in Bihar.

As of September 2011, HPS had made an impact on the lives of almost 250,000 people in the rural and remote areas of India. Moreover, HPS had plans to become a global provider of off-grid electrification and to reach out to millions of people in the underdeveloped countries. But such expansion requires quick availability of funds and deep and clear understanding with local knowledge.

Also, experts stated that the HPS model was the cheapest in the world as it was able to generate and distribute electricity for capital expenditure less than US$1 per watt.[19] However, some experts expressed doubts over HPS's ability to generate cheap electricity in the long run due to rising input costs.

Electricity crisis in India

As of September 30, 2012, India had the fifth largest[20] power generation capacity in the world with installed capacity of 207,876.04[21] megawatt (MW). However, the per capita electricity power consumption in India was just 570.9 kWh, significantly lower than the global consumption of 2,806.9 kWh in 2009.[22] According to experts, around 400 million people, living primarily in rural areas, did not have access to power. It was necessary to add 160,000 MW of capacity by 2018 to satisfy the needs of the second fastest growing economy in the world.

Experts stated that almost all the cities in the country including the megacities experienced at least 360 hours of power cut per year. Tier II and Tier III cities had almost 1,000 hours of power cut per year. The situation was worse in the small towns and villages. Many of them were not electrified and those which did have electricity got on an average only 2,500 hours of electricity per year. The variation in the consumption of power differed across the country. Dadra & Nagar Haveli, a Union Territory, had the highest per capita power consumption at 11,708.59 kWh in 2009–10 (11,567.67 kWh in 2005–06) whereas Bihar had the lowest at 117.48 kWh (85.86 kWh in 2005–06) in the same period.[23,24]

---

17 Charles W. (Chip) Ransler IV is a co-founder of HPS. He holds a bachelor's degree and an MBA degree from the University of Virginia and Darden Graduate School of Business Administration associated with the University of Virginia, respectively.

18 Rice husk or rice hull is the yellowish-colored outermost layer of paddy grain. It is separated from rice when rice is milled in a rice mill.

19 "Rural Electrification using Biomass," www.oasyssouthasia.info, February 2, 2011.

20 After the USA, Japan, China, and Russia.

21 "Highlights of Power Sector," www.cea.nic.in, September, 2012.

22 "Data—Electric Power Consumption (kWh Per Capita)," http://data.worldbank.org.

23 "Per Capita Power Consumption," http://pib.nic.in, May 18, 2012.

24 "Per Capita Power Consumption—Rajyasabha," http://pib.nic.in, August 20, 2007.

According to the official website of energy department of the Bihar government, out of 45,103 villages in the state, only 18,217 villages[25] (40.38% of total villages) in the state were electrified. The state electricity board had only 2.18 million consumers (out of around 100 million population in the state) across eight transmission circles in the state in March 2009.[26]

It was this shortage and unavailability of power which eventually became a driver for entrepreneurs like Pandey and Yadav, to develop a sustainable business model around this need.

Idea behind Husk Power Systems

Pandey and Yadav, childhood friends, had faced the problem of non-availability of electricity as both hailed from rural Bihar. Even after they moved to different cities—Pandey was in Los Angeles, US, and Yadav was in New Delhi, India—the electricity problem that they faced during their growing up years in Bihar remained a point of discussion between them. They wanted to supply electricity to the rural areas at a low price as the conventional electricity system was unable to deliver power to everybody especially in remote and undeveloped areas, and to people in the bottom of the pyramid segment who earned less than US$2 per day.

The duo came to the conclusion that there was a need for a cheap, village-based non-conventional system to produce and supply electricity in place of the power grid system, which required huge investment and a trained manpower. They realized that only a non-conventional system would be able to produce electricity at the least possible cost without much capital investment and without educated and skilled workers. Pandey said, "The conventional technologies and grids had failed to deliver for the pervasive energy starvation in the country and I wanted to find an environmental-friendly non-conventional source and low cost of energy."[27]

Initially they tried installing solar-power lights and generating electricity through jatropha seeds.[28] However, very soon they realized that these would not work out when the goal was to serve a large rural population which mostly lived below the poverty line. In their search for an alternative, they met with Krishna Murari, a salesman of a gasifier system.[29] Murari told them about a decades-old biomass gasification system that rice millers powered their mills with, which used rice husk

---

25 "Important Indicators," http://energy.bih.nic.in.

26 "Bihar, November 2010," www.ibef.org, November, 2010.

27 "Rice Husk Power to Light up Villages," www.hindu.com, July 26, 2010.

28 Jatropha is a species of flowering plant belonging to the spurge family. The jatropha seed contains oil which can be processed to produce high quality biodiesel fuel.

29 The gasifier system is a system in which the husk burns in a controlled manner to generate gases (smoke). These gases are further filtered and fed into an engine that drives an alternator to generate electricity. The process of generating gas from the gasifier system is known as gasification.

as input. Pandey and Yadav learned that the millers used diesel engines to power their mills but did not use 100% diesel to run these engines. They used the duel-fuel mode of operation in which they used only 30–35% of the actual required diesel in conjunction with the Producer Gas[30] generated by the gasification system to run the engines. This helped the millers save around 50–60% on diesel costs.

The duo thought that the gasifier system could be used for electrification of rural and remotes areas as rice husk was easily available in these areas. As per an esti-mate, Bihar alone produced 1.8 billion kg[31] of rice husk every year. Experts, how-ever, pointed out that having to use 30–35% diesel would make it unviable for rural people because it would increase the cost of the electricity produced. Pandey and Yadav learned that using only rice husk as a fuel to produce electricity was not via-ble, as it produced gas with high tar content.

Here, Pandey's educational background and experience in the power manage-ment semiconductor industry helped. He did not see much of a problem in using the gasifier system with single fuel. According to him, a dirty (polluted) gas could clog up the engine but if the engine was cleaned before it became clogged, then such a problem would not arise. His reasoning convinced S.K. Singh, Scientist, Ministry of New and Renewable Energy[32] (MNRE), Government of India. Though Pandey and Yadav did not have any experience in biomass gasification, they took it up as a challenge with Singh's assistance in the form of accepting the idea eligible for government subsidy.

They developed their gasifier at a local workshop, arranged for a cheap CNG engine from a small dealer, and customized it to produce electricity. Though there were some initial hiccups, they succeeded in producing electricity from the gasifier system using rice husk under the single-fuel mode. At last, on August 15, 2007, on the occasion of India's 60th Independence Day, the commercial operation of the HPS started at Tamkuha a remote village in the Dhanaha region of West Champaran district in Bihar, with electricity generated using HPS's proprietary, cost-effective technology. On the occasion, Rambalak Yadav, a local teacher, commented, "After sixty independent[33] years, we have found freedom from darkness."[34]

However, just having the right technology was not enough to ensure a successful business model. Neither Pandey nor Yadav had the experience to know how to go further and to expand and run a business, nor had they studied business manage-ment. It was at this juncture that Pandey's friend Sinha stepped in to help. At that time, Sinha was studying business at Darden Graduate School of Business associ-ated with the University of Virginia in the US. Sinha and his friend Ransler put their experience to good use and presented their business plan for the project at vari-

---

30 Producer Gas is a low-grade fuel gas. It has different gases including nitrogen, methane, carbon monoxide, hydrogen etc.

31 "An Electric Idea," http://articles.timesofindia.indiatimes.com, July 20, 2012.

32 Before October 2006, the Ministry of New and Renewable Energy was known as the Min-istry of Non-Conventional Energy Sources.

33 India got independence on August 15, 1947, from the British.

34 "Husk Power System—Background," www.huskpowersystems.com.

ous business plan competitions and forums (Refer to Exhibit I for various awards and recognition for HPS) in 2008. Their idea was highly appreciated and they won several of those competitions.

This success attracted recognition and the much needed funds (they won US$96,000 in prize money from various competitions) and also attracted investors (Refer to Table 7.1 for various investors in HPS). The prize money helped HPS to expand and it started three more power plants in the same year.

In 2009, HPS won the Global Business Plan competition and received an investment of US$250,000 from Draper Fisher Jurvetson[35] (DFJ) and Cisco TelePresence[36] (Refer to Table 7.1). By the end of December 2009, HPS had installed 19 power plants. By August 2010, the number of installed plants had increased to 50. As of mid-2011, the company had 80 installed power plants in operation (Refer to Exhibit II for time line of HPS growth).

Table 7.1 **Investors in Husk Power Systems**

Source: "Investors," www.huskpowersystems.com; "Acumen Fund to invest $375,000 in Bihar based Husk Power System," www.siliconindia.com, March 24, 2010; Terrence Murray, "Cornerstone Conversation: Manoj Sinha, Co-Founder, Husk Power Systems," www.greenenergyreporter.com, June 2, 2010.

Investors	Investment of
Acumen Funds	US$ 375,000
Bamboo Finance (Oasis Capital)	US$ 375,000
Draper Fisher Jurvetson (DFJ) and Cisco	US$ 250,000
International Finance Corporation (IFC), Member of the World Bank Group	US$ 1.5 million
LGT Venture Philanthropy	US$ 300,000
Royal Dutch Shell Foundation	US$ 75,000
Ministry of New and Renewable Energy (MNRE), Govt. of India	N.A.
US Government's Overseas Private Investment Corp (OPIC)	US$ 750,000

These plants provided around eight to ten hours[37] of electricity in the evenings to around 25,000 households and covered around 200 thousand people in more than 300 villages and hamlets. HPS had trained and provided employment to more than 300 rural people. The company was growing by two to three plants per week and this was expected to further increase to five plants per week in 2012. According to analysts, since its inception, HPS had shown enormous growth thanks to the huge demand for reliable and cheap electricity in rural areas and the abundance of raw material (rice husk). An efficient management team, government support, the business model built around the 3Rs—Reliable, Renewable and Rural—along with

35 Draper Fisher Jurvetson (DFJ) was a California, US-based venture capital firm.
36 Cisco TelePresence is a product of Cisco Systems, Inc. which was launched in October 2006. It helps in face to face collaboration.
37 Pranava K. Chaudhary, "Pandey of HPS Gets Real Heroes Award," http://articles.times ofindia.indiatimes.com, August 20, 2011.

the passion of the founders also played a major role in the growth of the company (Refer to Exhibit III for management team of HPS).

Operating Husk Power Systems

A typical husk power plant required around 5,000–6,000 sq. ft[38] of land to be set up. According to Pandey, "Each plant takes about 3 months to get started. This can go up to 5 months depending on how many houses need to be connected. We have hired local people and trained them to run these plants. We have also set up an HPS University curriculum to train these workers."[39]

The main part of the power plant was the biomass gasifier, which was around 10 to 12 feet high. A husk loader fed the rice husk into the biomass gasifier from the top. The biomass gasifier generated producer gas. The producer gas was then transferred to coolers which cooled the gas with the help of water and sent it to the filters to be cleaned. The producer gas passed through a total of three–four filters which cleaned the tar and dust from the gas. The gas finally reached an engine that drove an alternator to generate electricity (Refer to Figure 7.1 to understand the basic model of electricity generation and distribution by HPS plant). The generated electricity was then sent to a mini distribution grid which distributed power to customers within a range of 2 to 3 kilometers (km) with the help of low-voltage insulated wiring. The mini distribution grid could not supply beyond 2–3 km due to a drop in voltage after this range. After burning, the husk was converted into waste black ash, which was nothing but a kind of solid waste. A husk plant also needed 150 cubic feet of water, which is around 4,200 liter, and needed to be changed every two weeks.

Figure 7.1 **Basic model of electricity generation and distribution by HPS plant**
Compiled by the author from various sources.

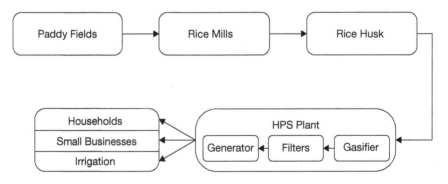

38 Grace Boyle, "How to Make Electricity from Rice Husk," http://blogs.independent.co.uk, December 10, 2010.
39 "He is Lighting up Villages With Rice Husk!" www.rediff.com, July 6, 2010.

Developing a sustainable business model

The objective of HPS was to provide a comparatively cheaper, eco-friendly, reliable power system for the poor living in the rural and remote areas of Bihar (initially), while making sufficient profit to ensure that the business model could function smoothly in the long run. Pandey said, "Our goal is to have our model help to deliver rural electrification to India's villages and eventually to rural areas around the world."[40]

To achieve its objectives, HPS carried out a detailed study before setting up the husk power plant. It first tried to understand the types of electricity, existing source of energy, and the per kWh cost to the target customers. After understanding the target customers and their energy needs, HPS did a feasibility study of the potential for using a husk power plant in the target area. It tried to understand the target locality's access to biomass and the total energy need of the target locality, the availability of rice mills in nearby areas, the size and operation period of the rice mills, what the different uses of rice husk in the target locality were, and the use of diesel generators, specifically for providing electricity, cost of diesel, and the cost of electricity provided by diesel generators per kWh (Refer to Exhibit IV for detailed questionnaire used to assess the feasibility of HPS plants).

HPS followed two business models. The first was the Build, Own, Operate, Maintain (BOOM) model while the second was the Build, Transfer, Maintain (BTM) model. If the BOOM model was used, then a detailed study was conducted by HPS. Otherwise, the interested parties conducted the study.

BOOM was the primary model that HPS had followed since inception. The company later adopted the BTM model to fuel its expansion plans, especially into other territories. Under the BOOM model, HPS developed, operated, maintained, and owned the power plant. Under this model, the major source of revenue was electricity sales, followed by the sale of rice husk ash (RHA).[41] In addition, HPS also earned revenue by selling the products of partner corporations. Carbon credit created another stream of revenue for the company as the husk plant reduced the use of kerosene and diesel.

Under the BOOM model, HPS generated revenue by selling electricity to households and business customers. Household customers paid Rs 80[42] per month in advance and they got electricity for 6–8 hours a day, which was sufficient to light up two 15 W Compact Fluorescent Lamps (CFL) and to recharge their mobile phones. While explaining the pricing of HPS, Yadav said, "The baseline price is Rs. 80 per month for two CFLs + mobile charging (approx. 50 W) per month. Users get

---

40 "Acumen Fund to Invest $375,000 in Bihar Based Husk Power System," www.siliconindia .com, March 24, 2010.

41 It is sold to cement companies and others.

42 Rs = Indian rupees. As of September 2012, US$1 was approximately equal to Rs55.57.

discount if they purchase more than 100 W. The idea is to slash the cost of the alternative [kerosene lamps etc.] by at least half."[43]

Business customers used more electricity—around 60–75 W—and had to pay around Rs 145–164 per month in advance. Customers with different electric appliances had to take additional electricity if they wanted to run their appliances. They could do so by paying Rs 40 per month for every additional 15W of power. Industry experts stated that HPS was providing the cheapest lighting that was reliable, safe, and environment friendly compared to other available sources like candles, kerosene lamps, and Light Emitting Diode (LED) lanterns which fulfilled only lighting needs.

Under the BTM model, HPS built and transferred the plant to partnering agencies in exchange for a lump sum amount.[44] These partnering agencies were independent owners and operators of the plant. They were liable for all costs and entitled to all the revenue of the plant. After transferring the plant, HPS generated revenue for itself providing fee-based maintenance and repair of the plant. HPS also generated revenue by assisting the independent owner in product channeling (channelization), selling of by-products, and in obtaining carbon credit in exchange for a certain percentage of additional revenue generated. In the BTM model, HPS also helped the partnering agencies in getting an MNRE subsidy.

On the capital expenditure side, Pandey said, "Each plant costs less than Rs. 15 lakh (Rs. 1.5 million) for generation as well as for the distribution grid, and generates about 32 kilowatts of electricity."[45] The major running costs of HPS came from what it spent on rice husk followed by workers' salaries. According to a company source, a plant required around 300 kg of husk to produce 32 kilowatt of energy, sufficient to supply about 6 hours of electricity per day to around 500 households. Husk was available at the rate of Rs 1–2 per kg. Where the second major cost — salaries—was concerned, each plant required four employees: one operator, one husk loader, one collector, and one electrician. The average cost of four employees was Rs 12,000 per month. However, HPS reduced the number of employees to three or two with the help of process and technology improvement, which would help the HPS to reduce costs and to increase the salary of employees to some extent. Other costs were maintenance and repair, management overheads, and land rent.

According to the International Finance Corporation,[46] typically, it took two to three months for a plant to reach operational profitability, and three to four years to recoup capital expenditures, depending on whether (and how much) government

---

43 "Rice Husk Power to Light up Villages," www.hindu.com, July 26, 2010.
44 According to HPS source, a minimum investment required by the interested parties (independent owner and operator) was Rs 10 million which was sufficient to developed 6+ plants.
45 "He is Lighting Up Villages With Rice Husk!" www.rediff.com, July 6, 2010.
46 The International Finance Corporation is a member of the World Bank group. It provides financing and advisory services to private social ventures and projects in developing countries.

subsidy was received.[47] According to experts, HPS was able to manage a short pay-back period[48] mainly due its ability to maintain an above normal net profit margin. The ability to keep non-payment and other losses under 5%, where national average was around 30%, was another reason for the better margin.

A very conservative estimate showed that HPS was able to run its power plants at 35% to 51% net margins[49] (Refer to Exhibit V for approx. revenue and cost of husk power plant). While commenting on profitability and breakeven point, Pandey said, "This is definitely a very profitable business. We are working on a margin of 46 per cent at the unit level, which is considerably good. We will start generating profits by the end of this year (2010)."[50] Large net margins and a short payback period helped HPS to generate the funds needed for expansion without any major difficulties.

Social and environmental impact

Each HPS plant served around 400 households and helped save on approximately 42,000 liters of kerosene and 18,000 liters of diesel per year which was used to generate electricity. This contributed to reduced home pollution, and improved the lives as well as health of the villagers, especially the women and children who used to huddle around the kerosene lamps after sunset to work and study. According to a company source, it had already saved 9,244,800 liters of kerosene by August 2012 (Refer to Exhibit VI for social and environmental impact of HPS).

With HPS plants, the villages had a far better lighting system in the form of CFL lamps which gave out bright white light, which helped children to study and helped women to do their household work better without having to face the problems associated with using kerosene lamps and diesel generators. As Chauhan said, "We did not have electricity before the power plant. It has helped a lot toward people's happiness, and the local economy. I want my children to study and find a good job somewhere. I want my son to be an engineer. Since the electricity came, my children can study even after the sun goes down. It is also good for business. I used to live in darkness and now I live in a world full of light. It makes me feel very happy

---

47 "Husk Power Systems," www.ifc.org, 2011.
48 A period in which cost of the investment is recovered is known as "pay-back period." It is calculated by dividing the cost of project by annual cash flows.
49 A net margin is the ratio between net profit and revenue. Entrepreneurs always try to increase net margin as a higher net margin is better than a lower one. If any company has 10% net margin than it means that it earned net profit of Rs 10 on every Rs 100 sale.
50 "He is Lighting up Villages With Rice Husk!" www.rediff.com, July 6, 2010.

from the bottom of my heart. What other big power plants could not do, this one did. It has gone from dark to light."[51]

HPS helped to generate direct as well as indirect employment for the local youth of the villages. In addition, it brought about a lot of tangible savings to the households and businesses. Earlier, each household spent around Rs 150 per month on kerosene. This went down to Rs 80–100 per month, a saving of at least 33%. Besides, kerosene lamps met fulfilled the lighting needs of the people. Now, they could charge their mobile phones, run other electrical appliances. Earlier, the villagers had to travel around 10 to 15 kilometers and spend up to Rs 20 to charge their mobiles. As Garak Yadav, a liquor store owner, said, "I used to pay 5 rupees each day to have my mobile phone charged, now I can just charge it in my shop."[52] According to a company source, by August 2010, HPS had saved US$1.25 million in cash for all the households served by it.[53] This figure went up continuously with each new husk power plant coming into existence.

In the same way, HPS saved money for farmers as irrigation costs reduced by 45%.[54] Various other businesses also benefited. Anush Kumar, a businessman running a hostel for schoolboys in Sariswa, had a grid connection through which he got electricity only once or twice a month. He therefore had to pay Rs 1,700 to run a diesel generator to get three hours of electricity between 6 p.m. and 9 p.m. However, after taking electricity connection from HPS, he got electricity from 6 p.m. to 1 a.m. and that too, for a monthly payment of only Rs. 1,200. According to experts, it was not only existing businesses that benefited from the cheap and reliable power connection and extended business hours. Some new business such as a photocopier shop also profited from it.

Lighting also reduced the fear of snakes and dog bites and small crimes. Sinha said, "Poisonous snakes typically kill up to two villagers every year. But we have been told that in villages where our plants operate, the death-toll is down to zero. We don't have a clear explanation, although we suspect that snakes fear the white light from the electric light bulbs."[55]

HPS not only lighted up the lives of the villagers, it also lighted up the lives of the village children by providing them with education support. HPS helped around 250 students as part of its corporate social responsibility through the Samta Samriddhi Foundation. It took care of the educational expenses of these students. Haresh Kumar Yadav, a 14-year-old, was one such student. The boy used to work in the fields in the evenings to earn enough to pay his school fees and studied under

51 "Bringing Sustainable Light to Communities off the Grid," www.youtube.com/watch?feature=player_embedded&v=6MpTmckocYQ.

52 "Case Study Summary Husk Power Systems India," www.ashdenawards.org, April, 2011.

53 "Home," www.huskpowersystems.com/index.php.

54 "2008 Dell Social Innovation Challenge Winner: Husk Power Systems," http://content.dell.com.

55 Terrence Murray, "Cornerstone Conversation: Manoj Sinha, Co-Founder, Husk Power Systems," www.greenenergyreporter.com, June 2, 2010.

the yellow light of a kerosene lamp in the night till he was 11 years old. However, HPS changed his life completely. He said in delight, "I can study late into the night (under the white CFL light) and the (Husk) power plant pays my school fees of Rs. 50 a month."[56] HPS planned to train local primary school teachers and set up an internet facility and a radio station to improve the quality of education.

HPS also worked toward women empowerment. It developed a method to produce incense sticks using a char[57] and a binder. This not only opened up a new revenue stream for the company but also provided a source of income to the women. An article in the *Economics Times*[58] described the simple model that HPS used. HPS brought the bamboo sticks and the women made them into incense sticks using the char and the binder. The company bought the incense sticks and added extras like color, perfume, and packaging.[59] HPS trained around 200 women in incense stick making in 2010. These women were able to earn around Rs. 60 per day. HPS also developed a machine to make incense sticks which increased production (output of sticks) and improved the quality of the sticks. On the incense stick maker, Rajini said, "We've been trying out the new way to make agarbattis (incense stick) and it seems to be working out. I am earning Rs. 60 to Rs. 80 per day."[60]

Challenges in the way

Social entrepreneurs are responsible not only to their shareholders but also to the government (which provides a subsidy) as well as to society (which is impacted positively or negatively by the act of the social entrepreneur). Commenting on the challenges faced by this project, Pandey said, "The biggest challenge always is to get the right people for the right job. Besides, convincing villagers about the need to bring about a change in their lives was tough. We need a continuous supply of machines and manpower to effectively implant our plans."[61]

Early on, when HPS started buying rice husk for their power plant, rice millers began to realize that there was money to be made from the husk. They started hoarding the husk, which consequently became dearer. To tackle this challenge, HPS came up with a unique solution. It set up its own rice mill and offered to dehusk farmers' rice free of cost in exchange for keeping the rice husk. As a result, the other rice millers who had been charging a price for the dehusking soon went

---

56 Ahona Ghosh, "The New Colours of Venture Capital," http://business.outlookindia.com, March 6, 2010.
57 Char is the burned husk and by-product of gasification process.
58 *The Economics Times* is one of the leading business newspapers in India.
59 Pranava K. Chaudhary, "Incense Sticks Empower Women, Courtesy HPS," http://articles .timesofindia.indiatimes.com, September 25, 2011.
60 Preeti Mehra, "Whiff of a New Livelihood," www.thehindu.com, February 28, 2012.
61 "He is Lighting up Villages With Rice Husk!" www.rediff.com, July 6, 2010.

out of business. However, running a rice mill had never been HPS's objective. In the end, it entered into a contract with the rice millers. Under the contract, HPS gave a guarantee to the rice millers that it would buy rice husk from them for six to eight years at an affordable price. In return, it would stop the free dehusking.

In the early days, HPS also faced regulatory hurdles. Under the Indian Electricity Act, 2003, anyone generating and distributing electricity in rural areas did not require a license. According to the act, "A person intends to generate and distribute electricity in a rural area to be notified by the State Government, such person shall not require any licence for such generation and distribution of electricity."[62] However, when HPS had 25 power plants, an official of the MNRE pointed out that state government had not defined what constituted the rural areas. In such a situation, HPS would have had to close down all its plants. However, a clause of the Electricity Rules, 2005, saved the day for HPS. Pandey said, "We would have had to shut down, but we found the clause of a 2005 ruling that all areas governed by panchayats[63] are rural areas. Some luck, some good people have helped us."[64]

According to analysts, financing would have been another big challenge for HPS if it had not won business plan competitions in the early stage as banks and other financial institutions would have hesitated to fund the project, especially in a state like Bihar which did not attract many businesses or industries. According to experts, getting the right mix of capital was a challenge for any business including social enterprises like HPS. It also needed the right kind of capital mix. Sinha said, "One major challenge was to tap the right mix of capital from sources that enabled it to stay true to its mission of bringing renewable and affordable electricity to people in underserved villages in India, while also allowing it to make the necessary investment."[65]

Getting suitable human resources was another challenge for HPS. It was really tough to find the right kind of educated and trained persons in the villages where literacy rates were negligible and those who were literate had migrated to other places in search of better opportunities. HPS planned to scale up its business by starting five power plants per week. Each plant needed three to four persons. At this rate, HPS would require around 2,340 trained persons over the following three years (Refer to Table 7.2 for man power required by HPS). There was no government or private infrastructure which could train the rural people in the required skills. Understanding this challenge, HPS started the "Husk Power University" in Bihar, the first of its kind, to train people in the various skills required for rural

62 "The Electricity Act, 2003," http://powermin.gov.in, June 2, 2003.

63 A panchayat is a group of five wise and elder persons. Panchayats settled disputes between individuals and villages.

64 Usha Rai, "Bihar's Husk Power," www.thehindubusinessline.com.

65 "SOCAP11 Social Entrepreneur Spotlight: Manoj Sinha, Husk Power Systems (India)," http://socialcapitalmarkets.net, September 3, 2011.

electrification. Sinha said, "A power company does not have a core business to open a university, but it is essential for us to do it."[66]

Table 7.2 **Estimation of human resource requirement by Husk Power Systems**
Source: Prepared by the author.

(in numbers)	Scenario I (four employees per plant)				Scenario II (three employees per plant)			
Plant per week (A)	2	3	4	5	2	3	4	5
Employees required per plant (B)	4	4	4	4	3	3	3	3
Employees required per week (C) = (A) × (B)	8	12	16	20	6	9	12	15
Employees required per year (in 52 weeks) (D) = (C) × 52 weeks	416	624	832	1,040	312	468	624	780
Employees required over next three years (E) = (D) × 3 years	1,248	1,872	2,496	3,120	936	1,404	1,872	2,340

According to experts, communication between members of the management was one of the challenges for HPS. In villages and remote areas, mobile phones and the internet did not work due to a poor network. HPS developed its own technology to overcome this challenge. This technology was a combination of SMS and Wi-Fi technology and it helped the management team to monitor power plants even without being physically present at each plant each time.

Electricity theft in distribution is a major problem in India. HPS had also faced such a problem. However, it had developed a smart metering solution for a total landed cost of under US$9/meter (arguably the world's cheapest smart meter) with the help of IDEO.[67] This solution would help HPS expand and keep the total default and/or stealing rate under 5% (as compared to a national average of approximately 30%).

On the other hand, reducing costs and bringing in efficiency would be an ongoing challenge for HPS. In May 2012, HPS received a grant of €90,000[68] from Alstom Foundation under the Dry Gasifier project. The grant money was used to upgrade existing power plants by reducing the water usage by as much as 80% and significantly reducing operational cost.[69]

---

66 Stephanie Hanson, "Energy for the Masses: Husk Power Helps Fuel India," www.ecomagination.com, January 9, 2012.
67 IDEO is an innovative product design company.
68 € = Euro. As of September 2012, US$1 was approximately equal to € 0.7915.
69 Debjoy Sengupta, "Alstom Grants Euros 90K to Husk Power Systems Project for a Green Project," http://economictimes.indiatimes.com, May 22, 2012.

HPS faced challenges from other social enterprises such as SELCO Solar Pvt. Ltd,[70] D.Light,[71] and Mera Gao Micro-Grid Power.[72] National Thermal Power Corporation[73] (NTPC), a public sector enterprise, also played a significant role in the off-grid industry. But according to experts, the off-grid market was huge and could accommodate even more players.

The road ahead

HPS was looking forward to massive expansion based on its award-winning business model and the huge demand for off-grid electricity in its home country as well as in different parts of the world. The company planned to expand its business into other states in India like Maharashtra, West Bengal, Uttar Pradesh, and Tamil Nadu. Outside India, it planned to expand into Bangladesh, Cambodia, Ethiopia, Indonesia, Nepal, Tanzania, and Uganda. Pandey said, "We plan to have 2,014 plants by 2014. Besides, electrifying other villages across India, we also plan to make a foray into countries like Nepal, Indonesia, Cambodia, and Ethiopia in the near future."[74]

HPS planned to expand its reach to 6,500 villages by the year 2014. This would create 7,000 local jobs. The expansion would also help to save 750,000 tons of CO_2 and US$50 million[75] in cash for more than 5 million people by 2014. But, HPS ability to achieve its massive expansion in India and other parts of the world would depend upon its ability to successfully attract new funding. The company still had to prove that its operating model would work effectively in other developing and underdeveloped nation as it worked in India in order to attract large funding. [76]

Familiarity and local knowledge also played an important role in the success of HPS. The founders of HPS were well versed with Bihar as they grew up there.

---

70 SELCO Solar Pvt. Ltd is a Bangalore based social enterprise established in 1995. It provides energy solutions and after sale services to underserved households and businesses by using solar photovoltaic modules. It also provides financing facilities for purchasing solar lighting and thermal systems.

71 d.light was founded in 2007 by Sam Goldman, Ned Tozun, and Sandeep Singhal. It provides lighting and energy solutions to underserved households and businesses especially in India and Africa. The company's vision is to replace every kerosene lantern with clean, safe, and bright light.

72 Mera Gao Micro-Grid Power (MGP) is a for-profit company of the VDI Group (Value Development Initiatives Group). It started working in August 2010 to cater to the energy needs of off-grid rural areas.

73 The National Thermal Power Corporation (NTPC) was the largest power generator company in India.

74 "He is Lighting Up Villages With Rice Husk!" www.rediff.com, July 6, 2010.

75 "Husk Power Systems Win Int'l Sustainable Energy Award," www.business-standard.com, June 17, 2011.

76 Stephanie Hanson, "Energy for the Masses: Husk Power Helps Fuel India," www.ecomagination.com, January 9, 2012.

Whether they can operate successfully in the countries where they are planning to expand would remain a challenge as they were not familiar with the local context. [77]

Funding would only come if the investors were clear about the cash flow and the source of revenue. This happens only when there is a demand for the product. There exists a persistent misconception that people at the bottom of the pyramid are not willing to pay for electricity. It would take quite a bit for convincing the investors on this. On the success of HPS, Simon Desjardins, Program Manager at the Shell Foundation[78] said, "Bihar is the poorest of the poorest states in India. These are the bottom of the bottom of the pyramid consumers. These consumers are not only willing but desperately able to pay for this service."[79]

The company was confident about the funding for such a massive expansion program. Sinha said, "We've seen a tremendous shift in investor expectations and understanding. People are more willing to invest in social enterprises now."[80] Vandana Gombar, Analyst, Bloomberg New Energy Finance, was equally positive. She said, "Once the wider investment community sees the opportunity, you're going to see more private equity funding."

A confident HPS planned to expand its scope keeping in mind the needs and wants in the rural market and play an important role in the development of the country. Pandey said, "In India, our vision will be rural development with focus on education, healthcare, power, and women's empowerment. In the coming years, we will implement programs to address the most critical needs of rural people."[81]

77 Stephanie Hanson, "Energy for the Masses: Husk Power Helps Fuel India," www.ecomagi nation.com, January 9, 2012.
78 Shell Foundation was started by Royal Dutch Shell in 1997.
79 Stephanie Hanson, "Energy for the Masses: Husk Power Helps Fuel India," www.ecomagi nation.com, January 9, 2012.
80 Ben Edwards, "Rice Husks Follow Solar to Power Indian Towns off Utility Grid," www.bloomberg.com, July 26, 2011.
81 "He is Lighting up Villages With Rice Husk!" www.rediff.com, July 6, 2010.

EXHIBIT I
Awards and recognition for Husk Power Systems

When	Where	Award Details	Position in Competition	Prize Money
April 7, 2008	US	Darden's Annual Business Plan Competition, University of Virginia	Winner	US$10,000
April, 2008	US	Global Social Venture Competition, University of California, Berkeley	Finalist	NA
May, 2008	US	Social Innovation Competition, University of Texas	Winner	US$ 50,000
May, 2008	US	People's Choice Award at Social Innovation Competition, University of Texas	Winner	US$ 1,000
May, 2008	US	Dell Social Innovation Competition for "Most Compelling Idea to Change the World"	NA	NA
May 12, 2008	US	Ignite Clean Energy competition, Massachusetts Institute of Technology	2nd Prize winner	US$35,000
December, 2008	US	FastCompany recognized HPS as one of the Top-10 Social Enterprises of 2008	NA	NA
June 29, 2009	US	Draper Fisher Jurvetson (DFJ) and Cisco's Global Business Plan Competition.	Winner	NA
May, 2010	India	Sankalp's Emerging Enterprise Award under the category of Technology for Development	Winner	NA
July, 2010	US	In Changemakers Competition—Leveraging Business For Social Change: Building The Field Of Social Business	Finalist	NA
September, 2010	US	The Tech Museum under the category of BD Biosciences Economic Development Award	NA	NA
September, 2010	UK	Finalist in the BBC World Challenge	Finalist	NA
June, 2011	UK	International Ashden Award for Sustainable Energy	Winner	£120,000
August, 2011	India	Real Heroes award to Gyanesh Pandey under the category of Social Welfare	Winner	NA

Source: "News & Updates," www.huskpowersystems.com.

EXHIBIT II
Time line of Husk Power Systems growth

Month	Year	Number of Power Plant
August	2007	First Plant
December	2008	3
December	2009	19
August	2010	50
December	2012	500*
December	2014	2014*

* Number of planned power plant.

Source: Adapted from www.huskpowersystems.com.

EXHIBIT III
Management team at Husk Power Systems

HPS Team	HPS Board of Directors
Gyanesh Pandey, Co-Founder, CEO/CTO	Raj Kundra
Ratnesh Yadav, Co-Founder and COO	Eric Berkowitz
Manoj Sinha, Co-Founder	Charles W. (Chip) Ransler IV
S.B. Mishra, Director, Human Resources	Gyanesh Pandey
Rama Siva, Senior Director, Training & Technical Aggregation	Ratnesh Yadav
Satish Prasad, Accounts Officer	Manoj Sinha
Alok Bhushan, Director - Operations & Projects	

Source: http://www.huskpowersystems.com.

EXHIBIT IV
Questions to assess the feasibility of HPS power plants to serve the villages

Understanding the customers and their lighting needs:

1. What kind of electricity uses do your target customers engage in? Is electricity mainly used for lighting purposes and for running small businesses?

2. What does a community/village or small town look like structurally speaking? Are these communities comprised of people living in a radius of 4-5 miles?

3. What do households and businesses use for lighting and running small machines? How much does a household spend on electricity on a monthly basis?

4. What would be the estimated household income on a monthly basis? What are some of the income generators and jobs available in such communities?

5. What is the current energy source for lighting, irrigation, and other such applications for electricity?

6. How much do domestic uses of electricity cost on a per kWh (kilowatt hour) basis? Please include all the costs, that is, taxes, transmission costs, and any other charges that government or local agencies may levy.

Feasibility study of the potential of using Husk Power Systems' plants:

Ques. 1: Do communities have plentiful access to biomass such as rice husk, corn cob, wood chips, etc? How much rice is produced in these areas?

Ques. 2: Do communities engage in local farming? How far does one need to go to procure rice husk? What are some of the current uses of rice husk?

Ques. 3: Are diesel generators widely used as a source of electricity? What is the cost of diesel per liter or per gallon?

Ques. 4: In the case of electricity provided by a diesel generator set, what is the total cost of electricity on a per kWh basis?

Ques. 5: How much would such communities typically need electricity for addressing their daily energy needs? Is that less than 100kW?

Ques. 6: Are there rice mills close to the communities? What is the size of a typical rice mill — that is, how many tons of rice do they mill on a monthly basis? Do these rice mills operate throughout the year?

Financial considerations:

Ques. 1: Are you considering investing money for forming partnership with Husk Power Systems? What is the minimum and/or maximum amount you are considering?

Ques. 2: What kind of interest rates do local banks charge for commercial long term loans?

Source: http://huskpowersystems.com.

EXHIBIT V
Approximate monthly revenue and cost for 35kW Husk power plant

Particulars		Amount (Scenario I)	Amount (Scenario I)
Revenue:			
Monthly revenue from electricity sales		Rs 50,000	Rs 50,000
Monthly revenue from 2 ton of char/month (approx.) (Rs 15,000 – Rs 45,000)		Rs 15,000 (minimum)	Rs 45,000 (maximum)
Revenue from Product Fulfillment/channeling		Not Available	Not Available
Revenue from CDM		Not Available	Not Available
Total Revenue		Rs 65,000 (approx.)	Rs 95,000 (approx.)
Cost:			
Land Rent	Rs 5,000 (approx.)		
Maintenance and repair	Rs 10,000 (approx.)		
Management Overhead	Rs 5,000 (approx.)		
Salary (4 persons) (Rs 3,000 approx. × 4)	Rs 12,000 (approx.)		
Approx. 10 Ton of feedstock (at Rs 1.50 per Kg approx.)	Rs 15,000 (approx.)		
Total Cost		Rs 47,000 (approx.)	Rs 47,000 (approx.)
Net Profit		Rs 18,000	Rs 8,000
Net Margin		28%	51%

Source: Compiled by the author from various sources.

EXHIBIT VI
Social and environmental impact Husk power plant

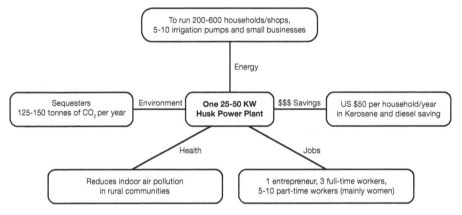

Source: Adapted from www.huskpowersystems.com.

References and additional readings

1 "Highlights of Power Sector," www.cea.nic.in, September, 2012.
2 "An Electric Idea," http://articles.timesofindia.indiatimes.com, July 20, 2012.
3 "Per Capita Power Consumption," http://pib.nic.in, May 18, 2012.
4 Stephanie Hanson, "Energy for the Masses: Husk Power Helps Fuel India," www.ecomagination.com, January 9, 2012.
5 Pranava K Chaudhary, "Incense Sticks Empower Women, Courtesy HPS," http://articles.timesofindia.indiatimes.com, September 25, 2011.
6 "SOCAP11 Social Entrepreneur Spotlight: Manoj Sinha, Husk Power Systems (India)," http://socialcapitalmarkets.net, September 3, 2011.
7 Pranava K Chaudhary, "Pandey of HPS Gets Real Heroes Award," http://articles.times ofindia.indiatimes.com, August 20, 2011.
8 Ben Edwards, "Rice Husks Follow Solar to Power Indian Towns off Utility Grid," www.bloomberg.com, July 26, 2011.
9 Pranava K Chaudhary, "Husk Wins Intl Award for Clean Energy," http://articles.times ofindia.indiatimes.com, June 18, 2011.
10 "Husk Power Systems Win Int'l Sustainable Energy Award," www.business-standard .com, June 17, 2011.
11 "Case Study Summary Husk Power Systems India," www.ashdenawards.org, April, 2011.
12 "Rural Electrification using Biomass," www.oasyssouthasia.info, February 2, 2011.
13 "Husk Power Systems," www.ifc.org, 2011.
14 Grace Boyle, "How to Make Electricity from Rice Husk," http://blogs.independent .co.uk, December 10, 2010.

15 "Bihar, November 2010," www.ibef.org, November, 2010.

16 "Rice Husk Power to Light up Villages," www.hindu.com, July 26, 2010.

17 "Bringing Sustainable Light to Communities off the Grid," www.youtube.com, July 21, 2010.

18 "He is Lighting up Villages With Rice Husk!," www.rediff.com, July 6, 2010.

19 Terrence Murray, "Cornerstone Conversation: Manoj Sinha, Co-Founder, Husk Power Systems," www.greenenergyreporter.com, June 2, 2010.

20 "Acumen Fund to Invest $375,000 in Bihar based Husk Power System," www.silicon india.com, March 24, 2010.

21 Ahona Ghosh, "The New Colours of Venture Capital," http://business.outlookindia .com, March 6, 2010.

22 Preeti Mehra, "Whiff of a New Livelihood," www.thehindu.com, February 28, 2012.

23 Usha Rai, "Bihar's Husk Power," www.thehindubusinessline.com.

24 "SOCAP11 Social Entrepreneur Spotlight: Manoj Sinha, Husk Power Systems (India)," http://socialcapitalmarkets.net, September 3, 2011.

25 Debjoy Sengupta, "Alstom grants Euros 90K to Husk Power Systems Project for a green project," http://economictimes.indiatimes.com, May 22, 2012.

26 "He is Lighting Up Villages With Rice Husk!" www.rediff.com, July 6, 2010.

27 "Per Capita Power Consumption—Rajyasabha," http://pib.nic.in, August 20, 2007.

28 "The Electricity Act, 2003," http://powermin.gov.in, June 2, 2003.

29 "Data—Electric Power Consumption (kWh Per Capita)," http://data.worldbank.org.

30 "Households Using Kerosene for Lighting," Chapter III in Town and Planning Organization, *Households with Elecricity Connection in India 2011* www.tcpomud.gov.in.

31 "Data—Electric Power Consumption (kWh Per Capita)," http://data.worldbank.org.

32 "Important Indicators," http://energy.bih.nic.in.

33 "2008 Dell Social Innovation Challenge Winner: Husk Power Systems," http://content .dell.com.

34 "Home," www.huskpowersystems.com.

35 "Husk Power System—Background," www.huskpowersystems.com.

CASE 8

Better Place

Shifting paradigms in the automotive industry[1]

Dror Etzion and Jeroen Struben

In February 2010, Better Place opened its first demonstration center in
Israel, constructed inside a refurbished industrial oil storage tank, with
a 1.5 km test track allowing visitors to drive an electric car. The demonstration center showcased Better Place's ambitious plan to challenge the
status quo in a complex and rigid industry. Its opening was the latest
milestone in the company's three-year history, during which it had established partnerships with Israel's national electric utility, venture capital
firms, battery companies, car manufacturers, corporate clients and the
Israeli government to launch a nationwide network of electric vehicles. In
addition, Better Place had announced partnerships with firms and governments in Denmark, the United States, Canada, Australia and Japan
and had engaged in conversations with 25 other governments around the

1 This case won first prize in the Social Entrepreneurship track of the 2011 oikos Case
Writing Competition.

Copyright © 2011 by the Authors and licensed under the Creative Commons
Attribution-NoDerivs 3.0 Unported License. To view a copy of this license, visit http://
creativecommons.org/licenses/by-nd/3.0/

This case is accompanied by a teaching note, available to faculty only. Please send
requests to freecase@oikosinternational.org.

world. Along the way, Better Place raised $200 million in its first round of venture capital funding in 2007, and $350 million in a second round in 2010, based on a valuation estimated at $1.25 billion, making it the second largest startup in history. The company's mission was nothing short of audacious—to reduce and eventually eliminate the automobile industry's dependence on oil.

A brief history of the automobile industry

Prior to the emergence of motorized personal vehicles, very few people traversed long distances on a regular basis. For shorter distances, besides walking, horse-drawn carriages had long been the dominant mode of transportation. But around the middle of the 18th century, population, especially in city centers, increased sharply. As a result, the use of horses in cities became problematic due to increased street congestion and accumulation of startling amounts of manure in the streets. With animal waste leeching into waterways, health and sanitation problems surfaced, leading to increasing alarm about the future of transportation.

As these concerns mounted, steam engine technology, originally developed for industrial applications, was gradually adapted to personal vehicles, thereby revolutionizing the transportation sector. Although early steamers were too heavy to be used as personal vehicles, ongoing development, mostly in the agricultural sector, eventually led to the development of technology that would enable the steam vehicle to function as a mode of personal transport. Nicolas Joseph Cugnot was the first to apply steam engine technology to a self-propelled mechanical vehicle, in 1769. Water was heated by combusting a source of fuel, mainly coal or wood, expanding the water to create steam, thus propelling the vehicle. It took roughly 20 minutes to start the vehicle because of the time required to heat the engine, and the water tank needed refilling roughly every 50 kilometers.

Yet, in the 1870s, when steam-powered personal transport became technologically feasible, demand for travel was limited, because roads were unpaved and social networks were—in large part—local. In fact, demand for personal vehicles took off only after a short-lived bicycle craze and the emergence of trams, first drawn by horses, then self-propelled. Such modes of transport had encouraged people to relocate to suburban areas, thereby generating demand for convenient personal transportation. As personal vehicles became increasingly popular, they spawned unprecedented opportunities for mobility, fundamentally altering the way people perceived time and distance. The automobile era, which characterizes society to this day, had begun.

With demand for steam cars increasing steadily, propulsion technologies attracted entrepreneurial attention. Thomas Davenport and Robert Davidson are credited with inventing the first practical application of the electric vehicle as early as 1842. The use of electric vehicles (EVs) expanded in the second half of the 19th century, as they outperformed the steam-powered automobile on several dimensions, including ease of use, cleanliness and near-silent operation. Many inventors made contributions to electric vehicles through improvements in motor technology, battery technology and electricity storage. Early EVs used non-rechargeable batteries, and the energy stored within them was released as electrical current used to propel the car. Typical EVs reached an average speed of 15–30 kilometers an hour and could travel approximately 65 kilometers per charge. Despite being more expensive than steam vehicles, at the end of the 19th century automotive manufacturers sold more electric cars than other types of vehicles, primarily to the upper class. However, EV production, peaking in 1912, began declining with the ascendance of the internal combustion engine (ICE) vehicle in the early 20th century. By 1935, electric car production had declined to virtually zero.

The emergence of the ICE can be traced back to 1876, when Nicolaus Otto invented and built the four-stroke engine which is still used in petrol-fueled cars today. These engines used a mixture of liquid fuel and air, ignited by a spark plug. Gottlieb Daimler, later co-founder of Daimler Motoren Gesellschaft, the maker of Mercedes vehicles, contributed to the evolution of the industry with the development of a small, light, fast engine.[2] Its timing was opportune, reaching the market just as familiarity with personal vehicles began to grow, driving rules and regulations coalesced, and the paved road network in and around cities began taking shape. Further, the electric starter, developed around 1910—ironically, based on electric vehicle technology—had rendered the awkward crank-start obsolete, eliminating one of the main disadvantages of the ICE vehicle. Additional factors, unrelated to intrinsic vehicle performance, helped the ICE win the race to mass adoption, including the production and availability of an energy dense fuel. Moreover, a particularly vocal consumer group, young male drivers, preferred the ICE, whereas EVs were preferred primarily by women. As more people became aware of ICE technology, their preferences shifted from silence and air quality—which characterized the EV—to price, speed and range. Henry Ford's invention of the assembly line, coupled with his eventual decision to embrace the ICE, fueled its meteoric rise. The assembly line process produced a new car every 15 minutes, dramatically reducing labor costs per produced vehicle, making them available for $850. Consequently, by 1915 there were 1 million ICE vehicles on the road and the number was rising steadily. ICE vehicles became the first global car, produced and driven throughout North America and Europe.[3]

The development of extensive highway infrastructure, the improvement of fuel efficiency and the rapid evolution and expansion towards a network of 150,000 gas stations in the United States alone, also contributed to the ubiquity of the ICE.[4] Detroit, Michigan, emerged as the hub of the automotive industry, headquartering

2 History of the Automobile.
3 Auto Atlantic, 2008.
4 Electrification Coalition, 2009.

the big three car manufacturers and many of their suppliers. General Motors (GM), Chrysler and Ford became model companies for the industry while France-based Citroen introduced the ICE prototype to Europe. These companies and others demonstrated that mass-producing vehicles could be a lucrative business while improving the quality of life of people around the world. Major car manufacturers and suppliers appeared and created millions of jobs in Japan, China, Germany, South Korea, Canada and 14 other countries around the world. The ICE led to dramatic economic growth in the fuel extraction, refinement and distribution industries as well.[5]

For many years, consumers and producers alike remained unaware of the associated health, environmental and political issues that would arise from the dominance and ubiquity of the ICE. Lead was one of the first additives in gasoline and was used to increase the level of octane, which allowed gasoline to burn in a more controlled manner. It was first used by GM in the 1920s and the health effects on humans, including lead poisoning and heart disease, were not recognized until the 1960s when Clair Cameron Patterson, an American geochemist, published his research on the increasing levels of lead found in the environment due to its combustion in automobiles.[6] In response to Patterson's findings, governments began pressuring manufacturers and, subsequently, oil companies to eliminate the use of lead in gasoline. Its complete phase-out culminated in 1986. Additionally, governments pressured manufacturers to install catalytic converters to reduce the emission of hydrocarbons and carbon monoxide and, later, nitrogen oxide, all potent greenhouse gases.[7] The US government required that, by 1975, all cars manufactured in the United States would have a catalytic converter installed, but even today this policy is not enforced globally.[8]

As of 2010, there were nearly 750 million vehicles on the planet, roughly 600 million of which were passenger vehicles.[9] Together they were responsible for 25 percent of global greenhouse gas emissions,[10] half of global oil and rubber consumption, 25 percent of glass consumption, 23 percent of zinc and 15 percent of steel production.[11] Oil imports placed a significant burden on many countries' balances of trade. For example, the US trade deficit on oil imports reached $388 billion in 2008, representing over half the country's deficit.[12] With growing populations and personal transportation unlikely to decline significantly in the short or medium terms, the economic and environmental sustainability of an ICE-dominated transportation sector had become increasingly dubious.

5 OICA, 2008.
6 Kitman, 2000.
7 McCarthy, 2009.
8 McCarthy, 2007.
9 Worldwatch Institute, 2008.
10 Moriarty, 2007
11 Orsato, 2009.
12 Electrification Coalition, 2009.

The Better Place model

In 2005, Shai Agassi took part in a Young Global Leaders seminar for young innovators, where the question, "What would you do to make the world a better place by 2020?" was posed. At the time, Agassi was President of the Products and Technology Group at SAP AG, a multinational software development company based in Germany, and heir-apparent to the company's CEO position. Before that, the Israeli high-tech entrepreneur had established and led a software start-up, which he sold to SAP when he was 33 for $400 million. In the months after the gauntlet was thrown in the Young Global Leaders seminar, the challenge of making the world a better place remained implanted firmly in Agassi's mind. By 2007, Agassi quit his job at SAP and had founded the Better Place Company with headquarters in Palo Alto, California and an R&D center in Israel.

Agassi's vision for Better Place was to create linkages between car companies, battery companies, utilities and consumers in a manner that would enable EVs to attain widespread adoption. Agassi believed that the only way to make consumers adopt EVs on a massive scale was by overcoming the most significant hurdle that beset the EV paradigm—limited mobility. While others believed that widespread adoption would not occur until dramatic improvements in battery capacity would enable electric cars to traverse more than the 100 miles currently possible, Agassi sought to develop a comprehensive EV-based solution, suitable for all driving profiles and implementable with existing, off-the shelf technology. Agassi's fundamental insight was that "the solution to electric cars lay not in re-engineering the battery but in re-engineering the car."[13]

In essence, the Better Place model could be summed up simply: "We buy batteries and electricity, and we sell miles."[14] It was based on the concept that the battery and the automobile would be sold separately. Not having to include the battery in the vehicle purchase positioned the EV, price-wise, on par with an ICE vehicle, with its price projected to be roughly $20,000.[15] At the time of purchase, the buyer would sign up for a service plan with Better Place—or a competing Electric Recharge Grid Operator (ERGO)—which would provide electric car services that including the energy required for the car's propulsion. With each car sold, the ERGO—not the buyer—would purchase a battery, estimated at roughly $12,000. In addition, and unrelated to the ERGO, drivers would pay vehicle maintenance and insurance costs (as with standard ICE cars). Maintenance costs for the EV powertrain, having very few moving parts, were expected to be much lower than for ICE vehicles.

13 Thomspon, 2009.
14 Goodman.
15 Levinson, 2009.

Service plans

As envisioned by Better Place, drivers would sign up for a service plan with an ERGO in which "electricity will be sold in miles as opposed to kilowatt hours."[16] ERGOs would be able to provide a menu of service plans to their consumers, analogous to those offered by mobile telephony operators. Better Place predicted that its clients would be offered three tiers of service plans—all-you-can-drive, fixed monthly fee, and pay-as-you-go.

The all-you-can-drive plan was designed for heavy users, such as taxi-drivers. Better Place market research found that the top 25 percent of drivers consumed 66 percent of gasoline in the US, and believed this ratio to be broadly true in other target countries.[17] Frequent drivers would thus be best suited to a program with a fixed monthly fee based on a locked-in price (meaning they would not pay more if energy prices spiked), for a roughly 4-year contract. Similar to cell phone companies, drivers who chose to sign up for the top tier service plan, estimated to be $500 per month, would likely obtain a rebate from Better Place, potentially offsetting the entire capital cost of the car.[18]

For medium-range drivers that were able to predict their yearly driving range, Better Place created the fixed monthly fee plan, which allocated the driver a pre-determined amount of miles. For example, a driver would be able choose a plan that offered her 12,000 miles for the entire year for a fixed monthly price of roughly $350 per month.

The third tier to be offered by Better Place was the pay-as-you-go plan, for less frequent drivers. The major advantage of this plan was that drivers would be able to purchase miles in smaller quantities, similar to calling cards. However, the drawback was that, unlike the other two plans, these drivers would be exposed to fluctuating electricity prices.

Software and infrastructure

In order for Better Place's model to work, the company would be required to build and maintain the recharging infrastructure for the EVs. The infrastructure for recharging would be composed of two main components—charge spots and switching stations. Resembling a short post with an electric socket, charging spots would enable drivers to recharge their cars at convenient locations, whenever the car was stationary for some duration, such as at work, while shopping or at a restaurant. Charge spots, with an estimated installation cost of $1,000, would be abundantly placed in key locations—train stations, malls, offices, grocery stores,

16 Sandalow, 2009.
17 Agassi, 2009.
18 Agassi, 2009.

parking lots and even along sidewalks. Moreover, for a fee of $250–$300, drivers would also have the option to install a charge spot at home.[19]

A full recharge of an EV battery with existing technology required several hours of connectivity to a charge spot, thereby significantly constraining mobility. To address this problem, the ERGO infrastructure offered a complementary component— switching stations. Switching stations would be analogous to conventional gas stations, and would serve cars traversing longer distances. Inside these switching stations, robotic arms would automatically replace depleted batteries with fully charged ones. Cars would be moved along a conveyor belt to swap their batteries in less time than it took to refuel an ICE vehicle at a gas station. Every switching lane would have the capacity to swap 12 batteries per hour. Behind the scenes, each battery switching lane would be equipped with ten battery chargers, potentially yielding 20 available batteries per hour, given that it would take roughly thirty minutes to charge each battery.[20] A switching station was forecast to be much more costly than a traditional fuel station, on the order of $1M fixed cost, and, on top of that, would require cost-effective management and stocking of expensive batteries.

In the United States, 90 percent of car trips are less than 30 miles,[21] and the average number of miles driven is usually around 12,000 per year.[22] As a result, Better Place believed that its customers would rely on charge spots for the bulk of their energy needs, using switching stations much less frequently. In the early stages, Better Place expected to build 2.1 charge spots per subscriber.[23] Agassi believed that switching stations, intended primarily to support long range driving, needed to be placed roughly 25 miles apart on major thoroughfares.[24] Since a multitude of charge spots substantially reduced demand at switching stations, Better Place believed that one switching station would be able to support 3,000 cars, and planned to install no more than 100 switching stations in each of its primary launch locations. By comparison, there were roughly 1,100 gas stations in Israel,[25] 2,000 in Denmark,[26] and 2,100 in the San Francisco Bay Area in the United States.[27]

Finally, cars would be equipped with computers that would track the time to depletion, the distance the car could drive with remaining power, and the location of switching stations. Additionally, information about driving behavior would be transmitted to ERGOs, enabling them to place cars in priority sequence for charging when demand for electricity was high. Driving patterns would also be analyzed

19 Pogue, 2009.
20 Roth & Gohla-Neudecker, 2009.
21 Electrification Coalition, 2009.
22 Kanellos, 2010.
23 Kanellos, 2010.
24 Agassi, 2009.
25 Haaretz, 2010.
26 Datamonitor, 2010.
27 Kanellos, 2010. To put this into perspective, there are roughly 25 million cars and 10,000 service stations in California. On average, a gasoline station services roughly 350 vehicles per day, at 10–20% utilization.

so that, for example, drivers who were typically parked at the office for 8 hours a day would only receive their charge when electricity demand was low, and energy prices were relatively inexpensive.

Renewable energy

One major criticism of EVs was that, in regions with low levels of renewable energy production, the production of greenhouse gas emissions was merely transferred from the car engine to large energy production facilities that converted carbon-intensive feedstocks such as coal into electricity. For Better Place to really make the world a better place, the company could not simply transfer emissions from car tail-pipes to conventional electricity production facilities—the energy source needed to be renewable. Albeit renewable energy production had not passed the 10 percent threshold in most countries, Better Place committed itself to "buying only clean electrons that come from renewable sources."[28] Better Place believed that it would be able to cost-effectively purchase electricity from renewable sources at wholesale prices in the markets in which it operated. In fact, Better Place believed that when renewable energy production had scaled up to meet the increased demand emanating from the transportation sector, the cost to drive an electric vehicle would be equal to or less than driving a gasoline-powered ICE. In the United States, the average cost per mile for electricity was $0.06–$0.08 (albeit most electricity was generated by coal-fired plants[29]), compared to $0.10–$0.12 per mile for gasoline. In Denmark gasoline cost as much as $7 to $8 a gallon, or roughly $0.20 per mile.[30]

Peering into the future, EVs could offer additional value as a way to capture and store renewable energy. One of the greatest barriers with renewable energy was that wind and solar energy are intermittent; therefore, to fully capture these sources, utility companies needed large batteries to store excess energy for use when production was low (night-time and windless periods). Denmark, for example, already produced 20 percent of its energy from renewable sources but was required to export electrons when production exceeded demand, due to lack of adequate storage capacity.[31] Since the typical vehicle is parked for 90 percent of the day, it constituted a potentially ideal source of renewable energy storage for utility companies. By partnering with an ERGO, a utility would not be required to jettison excess production, because capacity could be stored in car batteries, assuming car owners were given an incentive to provide storage services. And indeed, "smart grid technology", which utilities had started developing, would allow drivers to buy energy from the grid when their car required recharging and sell to the grid when the battery was full.[32]

28 Pogue, 2009.
29 See Exhibit 3.
30 Pogue, 2009 (see Exhibit 7 for a list of more countries).
31 Coherent Energy and Environmental System Analysis, 2010.
32 EPRI, 2008.

Even though the stars appeared to be in alignment for Agassi and his revolutionary model to take hold, industry stakeholders including governments and auto manufacturers were pursuing other initiatives to reconceptualize transportation.

Personal transportation: an industry in turmoil

Governments the world over had developed a mix of incentives and deterrents to reduce the use of personal vehicles, and thereby curb both oil consumption and emissions. These strategies included congestion pricing, highway tolls, parking tolls, car pooling lanes on highways and tax rebates on environmentally preferable vehicle options. The investment and development of sidewalk infrastructure and bike pathways in major cities also influenced public behavior, by providing convenient means of transportation that were not based on motorized vehicles. The development of public transportation, such as buses, trains and subways as well as intermodal transportation (which combined two or more transportation modes) further reduced the use of personal vehicles.

The automotive industry itself responded to the greenhouse gas challenge primarily through development of new technology. Many car manufacturers introduced efficiency improvements and alternative fuel capabilities, all targeted at reducing greenhouse gases and oil dependency. Other investments centered on new propulsion systems, some compatible with the ICE and others requiring entirely new power trains and infrastructure.

In fact, variants of the internal combustion engine had been around nearly as long as the ICE had existed. The diesel engine was invented in 1897 by Rudolph Diesel, and differed from the petrol-fueled engine because it used a different process to ignite the fuel. It did not require a spark plug, but instead used compression to combust the fuel and propel the car. Although diesel engines produced a persistent knocking sound which drivers found problematic, diesel engines were 20 to 40 percent more fuel-efficient than petrol-fueled ICEs. Diesel fuel was less flammable and had lubricating properties that allowed diesel engines to last longer than regular gas engines. However, the diesel engine did not gain attention until governments set emission abatement requirements and consumers lost confidence in big oil companies during the oil embargo crises of the 1970s. Governments favored diesel engines because they burned much cleaner than gasoline and reduced dependence on foreign oil. Moreover, they produced lower levels of carbon dioxide, carbon monoxide and hydrocarbons. By 1981 diesel engine cars accounted for 10 percent of GMs sales and made up more than half of Mercedes-Benz, Peugeot and Isuzu's sales.[33] Yet, diesel engines still produced greenhouse gases and soot, which contributed directly to air pollution.

33 The History of Diesel.

Other ICEs could operate on liquid fuels other than petrol. A notable example was the Ford Model T, which could run on gasoline, kerosene, or ethanol. More generally, "flex-fuel" vehicles could handle blends from two fuels, whereas "bi-fuel" vehicles could run on two different fuels. Specifically, flex-fuel vehicles could utilize combinations of gasoline or diesel with alcohol derived from a plant base, such as corn, sugar cane or cellulose from sources such as grass, wood and old crops. Methanol, which is alcohol derived from sources such as biomass, natural gas or coal, had also been investigated as an alternative, but ethanol attracted greater attention, partially due to the availability of inexpensive corn.

Flex fuels were measured in ethanol or methanol content. Ethanol blends could range from 5 percent to 100 percent (E5–E100). Ethanol vehicles burned cleaner than pure gasoline vehicles and could provide both better performance and longer life. Since part of the volume of these fuels originated in plant-based carbon, the net greenhouse gases released through combustion could potentially be lower than that of pure petrol-based fuels. As the share of ethanol in the blend increased, the energy density decreased; on the other hand cars burned the fuel more efficiently, the net result being slightly increased energy use on a per-mile basis. A price point at 20–30 percent less than petrol made ethanol economically viable. In Brazil, for example, the widespread availability of arable land and the prominence of agribusiness made ethanol and flex-fuel vehicles particularly attractive, and they comprised over half the country's fleet. Importantly, the use of these fuels did not require a massive shift in fuel supply infrastructure. Moreover, as expertise in ethanol production increased, production costs declined. However, widespread adoption of alcohol-based fuels did face several hurdles. Critics pointed out that, in many instances, ethanol required more energy to produce than it generated, when agricultural inputs such as fertilizer and machinery were factored in. Other critics questioned the appropriateness of growing food for fuel, which put upward pressure on the price of food, thereby affecting distribution and affordability.

Compressed natural gas (CNG) had been used as a fuel source since the 1930s and was pursued as another alternative to the ICE. In 2008 there were 9.7 million CNG vehicles worldwide.[34] These vehicles were concentrated primarily in Pakistan, Argentina, Brazil, Iran and India. Typically, CNG for vehicles cost 30 to 60 percent less than gasoline fueled cars.[35] The fuel stock was composed primarily of methane, derived generally from drilling.[36] A refining process allowed for removal of toxic substances from CNG, but the main component, methane, was a potent greenhouse gas. CNG was delivered to the engine from large tanks found in car trunks. Fuel availability, however, necessitated a dedicated infrastructure, incompatible with pipelines, storage facilities and fuel stations designed for petrol.

Perhaps the most significant advance in recent years was the rise in popularity of hybrid electric vehicles (HEV). HEVs were equipped with both an internal

---

34 Green Car Congress.
35 Gas Fueling Technology, 2006.
36 Natural Gas Org., 2004.

combustion engine and an electric motor to propel the car. The cars were equipped with a regenerative breaking mechanism, which captured energy released when the car braked, thus replenishing the car's battery. The Toyota Prius was the world's best-selling HEV with sales in 40 countries. According to the US Environmental Protection Agency, it was the most fuel-efficient car in the United States, offering roughly 45 miles per gallon. It was also rated one of the cleanest by the California Air Resource Board. The car retailed for roughly $21,000, and average refueling costs were approximately $900/year (at $2.80 per gallon).[37]

Plug-in hybrid electric vehicles (PHEV) also used a combination of an ICE and electric motor, but in addition could be recharged using energy from the electrical grid. The cost of the battery was added to the cost of the standard car model.[38] PHEVs boasted a fuel economy similar to HEVs, but could also drive 40 miles running on pure electricity. Some made the argument that cost savings in fuel, of up to 75%, were not sufficient to recoup the higher initial price of the car.[39]

Hydrogen fuel cell vehicles (HFCVs) had long been pursued as a particularly compelling alternative. In fuel cells, hydrogen and oxygen gases combine to form electricity, and pure water is the only byproduct. The electricity can then be used to propel a car, using the same power train system as an EV. In converting stored energy into electricity, hydrogen fuel cells are similar to batteries but rather than being recharged through electricity, they use hydrogen as input. Hydrogen, being a storable carrier, but not a primary source, can be derived from many sources including renewable energy sources, fossil fuels, electrolysis of water, coal and petroleum. Most early infrastructure focused on natural gas as the primary source, reformed into hydrogen at the fueling station. There were, however, critical growth barriers for HFCVs. Costs for hydrogen "at the pump", in 2010, were roughly $4–$9.50 per kilogram in the United States, although this cost was heavily dependent upon the source of energy.[40] On the other hand, HFCVs were much more energy efficient than conventional ICE vehicles, making them competitive on a per mile cost basis. Yet low energy density of on-board stored hydrogen meant that drivers would find themselves refueling much more often.

Like many other alternative fuels, hydrogen was incompatible with most existing transmission, storage and retail infrastructure for petrol, and required a dedicated network of hydrogen pipelines and refueling stations. Nonetheless, believing that many of the obstacles could be overcome through cumulative efforts, auto manufacturers including GM, Honda, Daimler AG and Toyota engaged actively in the development of fuel cell cars. The German government was working with RWE, a German utility, and Linde AG, a major producer of industrial gases, to develop infrastructure to support the use of hydrogen fuel cell vehicles.[41] Similarly, the

---

37 2008 Toyota Prius.
38 Electric Power Research Institute, 2009.
39 Petersen, 2009.
40 Blenco, 2009.
41 Ohnsman, 2009.

Japanese government and Toyota were working together to develop affordable hydrogen vehicles as well as an abundant supply of hydrogen.[42] Shell was also investing heavily in research and development as a precursor to installing hydrogen stations in California, estimating the cost at roughly $1–5 million per station.[43]

In addition to alternative fuels and power trains, some manufacturers were looking at reducing the weight to be transported, thereby increasing per-person efficiency. For example, lightweight materials, such as carbon fiber body frames, formed an alternative to heavy steel bodies that were the industry standard. By using lighter materials to build cars, less energy would be needed to propel it, thus offering consumers higher fuel efficiency. The cost of carbon fiber was dropping continuously as the material became more commonplace, making it more attractive to use in mass production models. Consumer concerns with safety had inhibited the widespread adoption of carbon fiber models, despite the fact that high performance vehicles such as race-cars were built primarily of carbon and withstood high-velocity impacts extremely well.

Another way of making cars lighter—and thereby more fuel efficient—simply required making them smaller. The Tata Nano, launched in 2008, was the world's cheapest automobile, costing only $2,000. It was 1.4 meters wide and just over 3 meters long, weighed 1,400 pounds and had a fuel tank capacity of 4 gallons. It was first launched in India and other developing countries with high population densities and lower household incomes. Renault entered the small car industry with the launch of the Logan in 2009. At a price of $6,000, the car was being launched in the Indian market to compete with the Tata Nano.[44] Small cars remained very popular in Europe, where vehicles like the Fiat 500 and the Mini were hugely successful, many decades before global warming was recognized as a threat.

All told, a significant number of alternative designs were being explored by automakers in a quest to reduce petrol dependence. It was within this context of multiple potential alternatives that Shai Agassi and others were attempting to transform the EV into the preeminent choice for consumers.

Establishing the EV market

Although production of EVs had halted in the 1930s, the idea of an electric vehicle lived on. General Motors sparked a short-lived revival of electric automobiles in the late 1990s when the company launched the EV1 in California. The 1,100 cars produced by GM came equipped with the choice of a lead acid battery or a nickel-metal hybrid battery offering drivers a range of anything between 55 and

42 Adams, 2010.
43 Ohnsman, 2009.
44 Naughton, 2008.

130 miles per recharge.[45] The car consumed roughly 11 kWh per 100 kilometers,[46] where only 10 percent of the energy was lost in conversion, compared to 65 percent energy losses in petrol-fueled ICEs.[47] GM provided users with EV recharging devices installed in their homes, whereby batteries could fully recharge each night, over an 8 hour time span. The EV1 was favored by drivers because it was quiet; did not create tailpipe emissions; and was easy and cheap to maintain, primarily because it contained only one-fifth the number of moving parts found in an ICE. The 100 percent recyclable, lightweight body panels also meant that less electricity was expended to move the car itself.[48] Even though the EV1 was hailed as a technological success and was popular among users, GM voluntarily recalled its cars in 1999 due to alleged low consumer demand and the company's inability to turn a profit from the initiative.

Although GM's withdrawal from electric vehicle production was a major step back for proponents of the technology, as the new millennium dawned, numerous other, smaller companies began developing new models. Tesla Motors, a California startup headed by Elon Musk, co-founder of PayPal, began marketing $100,000 luxury electric roadsters. The initial model catered to the high end of the market but Tesla subsequently announced that they would be working toward developing a more affordable model, the Model S. Entrepreneurial EV developers, focusing mainly on micro-cars, sprang up outside the United States, notably the affordable REVA developed in India, Norway's TH!NK city, and an electric version of Daimler's Smart Fortwo. Large manufacturers re-entered the fray with Renault-Nissan, Mitsubishi, Subaru, Toyota, Ford and others all announcing plans to mass-produce electric cars within a few years.

Infrastructure and standards

Competition began to emerge not only among and within the various vehicle platforms, but around other components of the system. For example, several battery producers ranging from large corporations to startups and auto manufacturers themselves started developing different products for EVs. The Johnson Controls and Saft partnership developed a lithium, nickel, cobalt and aluminum chemistry for Mercedes-Benz. LG Chem, AESC, Bosch-Samsung, Hitachi and NEC were investing in manganese-spinal batteries, attracting the interest of companies such as GM, due to their cost effectiveness and the larger amount of proven mineral reserves used in the production of these batteries.[49] Nissan announced plans to construct a battery manufacturing facility for their all electric EV, the Leaf, in

---

45 EV1 Specifications.
46 US Department of Energy.
47 Fung, 2009.
48 EV1 Specifications.
49 Petersen, 2009.

Smyrna, Tennessee.[50] Although Better Place favored lithium ion batteries, featuring an expected life span of approximately 8 years, several other designs offered alternative price points, energy densities, weights and life spans. As range, safety, recyclability and costs improved and battery standards converged, experts were forecasting a dramatic reduction in the number of global battery manufacturers.[51]

Of course, Better Place realized that the mere provision of an electric vehicle would not fully satisfy consumer needs for a coherent transportation solution. Direct competition had emerged in the form of alternative recharging infrastructures. Through its $37M "ChargePoint America" program, Coulomb Technologies, an electric car service provider founded in 2007, planned to provide nearly 5,000 charging stations to nine regions in the United States. Pilot charge stations providing free energy had already been unveiled in New York City, Houston and Seattle, as well as outside the United States, in Ireland and Australia. Coulomb Technologies planned on earning revenues based on provision of access to electricity, as opposed to selling the electricity themselves. Every time a driver wanted to use a charge point they would pay a fixed amount, for a certain amount of time, for example $2 for 30 minutes. On top of that, consumers would pay for whatever electricity they consumed, based on prices charged by the utility company. Elektromotive, a UK company, was pursuing a similar strategy and had established partnerships with Renault-Nissan and Mercedes-Benz to deploy EVs in Europe.

Some auto manufacturers decided to examine the viability of vertical integration, and took on additional roles to ensure that an electricity infrastructure, including batteries and charging stations, would be able to provide the energy needed to propel their customers' cars. Toyota, for example, announced that it would be installing roughly 20 solar-powered recharge stations in Toyota City, site of Toyota Motor Corporation's main plant. The stations would be compatible with both PHEVs and EVs and powered by the company's storage batteries as well as energy from the grid. GM was planning to launch its Chevy Volt in the UK (under the Opel Ampera name), together with a number of charging points at work places and in parking lots.[52] Nissan had partnered with Portland General Electric in developing smart grid technology to support a network of electric vehicles in several states, including Oregon, and in the Canadian province of British Columbia.[53] Nissan's Leaf and the Chevy Volt were featured in the United States Department of Energy sponsored "EV Project", in which some 15,000 fast chargers would be installed in five states with the aim of collecting data on vehicle use and charge infrastructure effectiveness in diverse topographic and climatic conditions.[54]

Tesla Motors had partnered with SolarCity, a photovoltaic company that installed recharge stations on buyers' roofs to ensure that electricity for vehicle propulsion

50 Caolgera, 2010.
51 Petersen, 2009.
52 Pickard, 2010.
53 Groom, 2008.
54 The EV Project, 2010.

originated from a clean source. At a cost of $2,000 to $6,000, Tesla owners would be able to have the peace of mind of recharging at home, including a free and renewable energy source.[55] Furthermore, Tesla had announced plans to develop cars with potentially removable batteries. Yet, the company was not deploying its own swapping infrastructure and had mentioned the possibility of integrating recharge ports with other electric car service providers, such as Better Place, to be able to expand its product line and ensure its compatibility with the rest of the EV market. Other manufacturers were trying to bypass the swapping procedure entirely, and were creating partnerships with utilities and governments directly, calling into question the value of ERGOs. Mercedes, for example, who had experimented with battery swapping in the 1970s, decided to pursue a fixed (non-swappable) battery technology.[56]

As the race to establish a dominant infrastructure design heated up, Better Place advocated consistently for EV infrastructures to be completely standardized, and called for utilities, car manufacturers and battery developers to adhere to international standards. Specifically, the International Organization for Standards (ISO) and International Electrotechnical Commission (IEC) were setting standards concerning EV battery modules, plug connectors and communication protocols to accelerate the transition to electric vehicles. As noted by Agassi: "What we ask governments to do is to force everybody that comes into this business, the electric recharge grid networks, to be bound by international standards, ISOIC standards, so we don't use a connector that is unique, that will lock anybody out. And we will provide open access across networks, because we want to optimize for speed of adoption. So, I'd rather have a second competitor that comes in and installs more of the network with their own money but with the same connector."[57]

Japan was demonstrating leadership in standardization as its top car manufacturers including Toyota, Nissan, Mitsubishi as well as their major utility company, Tokyo Electric Power Co, and battery manufacturer, Fuji Heavy Industries Ltd. engaged in talks to set a national standard. Standardization proceeded more slowly in Europe, and agreement was reached on only two issues—spot connectors and voltage requirements.[58] However, European Union industry commissioner Antonio Tajani launched an EU green vehicles strategy which attempted to catch up quickly with standards being developed in the United States, Japan and China[59].

Scaling up the EV market

Hurdles in growing the EV market stemmed not only from the challenge of reshaping the supply-side. Questions loomed regarding how fast the demand-side of

55 Woody, 2009.
56 Hybrid Cars, 2009.
57 Steenstrup, 2009.
58 Better Place, 2010.
59 Harrison, 2010.

the market would materialize. Assuming Better Place managed to get the infrastructure and vehicles in place, factors related to consumer adoption could still potentially constrain rapid uptake of EVs. A quick comparison between EVs and iPods illustrated the key challenge facing EV sales. With an average lifespan on the order of 15 years, vehicle turnover is much slower than for MP3 players. Moreover, the single biggest consumer investment—after the purchase of a house—is a car, thereby guaranteeing conservatism in choice for most buyers, unlike the relatively inexpensive iPod. Simply put, to achieve production numbers like those of MP3 players, that would generate economies of scale for producers and accumulate into a large installed base necessary to generate electricity demand and favorable exposure, EV market shares would have to attain critical mass very quickly.

While alternative power train technologies, and especially the various EVs, had received significant media attention, it was far from clear how consumers would respond when products were introduced into the market in large numbers. An Ernst and Young report examining the level of understanding of and interest in PHEVS and EVs in the United States validated these concerns.[60] The report indicated that familiarity with EVs was based primarily on conjecture, and that consumers had high expectations regarding EVs' increased fuel economy and environmental impact. However, the report suggested that consumer willingness to consider EVs as viable options remained very weak across the United States. Among the most significant concerns were vehicle cost and driving/battery range, even though most consumers did not need to cover long distances regularly. The report concluded that the majority of consumers would not be willing to compromise vehicle capabilities when considering the purchase of an EV. In part to address these psychological barriers and to create greater acceptance of EVs, Better Place launched a pilot project in Japan to demonstrate that the perceived tradeoffs inherent in the EV could be overcome. The project involved four taxis driving in Tokyo nonstop for 100 days, with the purpose of showcasing the long-range capabilities of EVs.[61]

The Better Place rollout strategy

For its initial launch sites, Better Place had sought regions with high consumer consciousness and strong demand for EVs. In Israel, Better Place's first site, 57 percent of drivers said they wanted their next vehicle to be powered with electricity. In Denmark, Australia, Canada and the United States, the numbers were 40, 39, 35 and 30 percent respectively.[62] In order for its business model and technology to be rolled out in the most congenial settings possible, Better Place had selected several small

60 Ernst & Young, 2010.
61 Agassi, 2010.
62 Better Place, 2009.

countries and "islands". Islands were conceptualized as regions with high population densities and limited traffic to "off-island" destinations. Israel's population, for example, is concentrated within roughly 10,000 square kilometers. Ninety percent of drivers commute less than 70 kilometers each day and urban centers are generally less than 150 kilometers apart. Vehicle travel outside the country's borders is negligible. Denmark was expected to become the second Better Place island in early 2011. In Denmark, DONG energy was expanding its renewable energy mix while the government had committed to EV incentive programs. The CEO of Better Place Denmark, Jens Moberg, had already announced the company's plans for rolling-out its charging infrastructure in the capital, Copenhagen.[63]

Better Place had engaged with other islands as well, including Hawaii and the San Francisco Bay Area. Hawaii was importing oil to meet 90 percent of its energy needs and had the highest gasoline prices of any US state. The state had launched its Hawaii Clean Energy Initiative (HCEI) to work with the US Department of Energy to develop clean energy alternatives for meeting 70 percent of the state's energy needs by 2030.[64] Australia, the largest island in the world, was also attractive for Better Place, which perceived it to contain three major urban centers connected by a single freeway, making it particularly suitable for the Better Place model. Spain and Portugal were also prospective locations as Better Place projected a demand for 50,000 plug-in electric cars in the region by 2011.[65] As of early 2010, the company had begun establishing partnerships and carrying out market research to assess the feasibility of entry into regions with fewer boundaries and more factors inhibiting the transition to EVs.

Establishing networks

> This is a massive integration project; everything needs to happen roughly at the same time. In other words, the cars need to show up at the same time that batteries need to produce in scale, at the same time as the infrastructure is in the ground...[66]

Better Place envisioned that utility companies would play a key role in mainstreaming EVs and provide much needed support by laying underground electric cables, providing lighting fixtures, and installing other infrastructure. In order for ERGOs and utilities to reap the greatest benefit from the model, ERGO software would need to be synchronized with utility software, allowing the local grid to determine optimal allocation of energy to vehicles during peak and off-peak hours. Better Place had begun developing software to track data, communicate with the grid and dispense electricity as demand fluctuated, thus minimizing costly spikes

---

63 Global Progress: Denmark, 2010.
64 Barron, 2008.
65 Day, 2008.
66 Pogue, 2009.

in electricity demand.[67] In order to manage this data flow process, the cars' on-board computers would be linked to a data system that would recognize when a car was hooked up to the grid. By establishing communication, the ERGO would have the capacity to complement the grid so that the bulk of recharging could take place during off peak hours.[68]

Based on its perception that it could add value to utilities, Better Place was working closely with utilities to develop long term investment plans in renewable and clean energy. Israel, for example, had set a goal to have 10 percent of its electricity sourced from solar power and renewable energy by 2020.[69] Israel Electric Corporation established a committee led by the senior vice president of engineering projects, Yakov Hain, to facilitate ongoing conversations between IEC and Better Place.[70] Hawaii Electric Company announced a non-exclusive agreement with Better Place to invest in renewable energy and establish a recharging network connected to the grid,[71] yet the utility noted its open-mindedness to engaging with similar companies. In Toronto, Canada, Better Place held talks with Bullfrog Power, an electricity provider that provided 100 percent renewable and clean energy.

To assist utilities in attaining renewable energy goals, some governments were offering tax rebates on electric vehicles. Israel, which typically taxed ICEs at 70 percent, agreed to tax EVs at 10 percent until 2019. Instead of the 180 percent ICE tax in Denmark, drivers would be able to purchase EVs at zero percent until 2015.[72] As of 2010, the United States was offering rebates ranging from $3,200 to $7,500, depending on the battery's capacity.[73]

Finally, Better Place was in talks with the Big Three auto manufacturers in Detroit, but no partnerships had materialized. Toyota's manager of environmental communications, John Hanson, went on the record expressing his views on developing a car compatible with Better Place technology. "What good does it do if we only sell 500 a year? We sell 175,000 Priuses alone in North America."[74] In fact, Renault-Nissan was the only car manufacturer that committed to providing automobiles compatible with Better Place specifications. Renault-Nissan had already started manufacturing an electric version of the Fluence in Bursa, Turkey, and had committed to producing 100,000 units by 2016.[75] The company planned to build a second plant outside of Paris, France, when demand increased,[76] and began designing EV versions of the Kangoo Z.E. Van, and the Laguna Sedan, as well

67 Woody, 2009.
68 See Exhibit 5.
69 Ritch, 2009.
70 Baron, 2008.
71 Markoff, 2008.
72 Lettice, 2008.
73 Voelcker, 2009.
74 Thompson, 2009.
75 Reed, 2010.
76 Jolly, 2010.

as the new two-seater Twizy.[77] Flexing its muscles, Renault-Nissan threatened to withdraw from the Danish project if the Danish government reduced the 180 percent sales tax they had previously set on ICE automobiles.[78] Renault-Nissan was on record, however, suggesting that as production reached 500,000–1 million vehicles per year government incentives would become unnecessary.[79]

The Israel launch

Israel's President Shimon Peres; Carlos Ghosn, the CEO of Renault-Nissan; and Agassi announced that Israel would be the world's first Better Place country, and that the venture would launch in 2010. Renault-Nissan would supply the Renault Fluence, compatible with Better Place infrastructure. Agassi claimed that 20,000 Israeli subscribers were already fully committed to purchasing EVs. Better Place planned to install 100,000 charge spots and 100 switching stations in the country and had invested $200 million. At the opening of the demonstration center in February 2010, the company announced the signing of 92 corporate fleet owners as subscribers, including FedEx, IBM, Microsoft, and Orange. Better Place also announced a partnership with Dor Alon, one of Israel's leading gas station operators, for the deployment of battery switching stations at Dor Alon's facilities.[80]

Clearly, Better Place's plan to radically transform personal transportation was revolutionary, and naysayers encountered little difficulty in unearthing potential flaws in the business model. These hurdles included technological obstacles, such as standardization of battery size and location in vehicles, necessary for automated battery switching. Others called into question the freedom of movement that Better Place customers would really enjoy, citing the high costs of roaming that often characterized mobile telephony. Yet others cautioned that widespread adoption of EVs would place unbearable loads on the electric grid, causing large scale power failures. More fundamentally, critics questioned whether Better Place could actually turn a profit, and the extent to which it required subsidization from governments and utilities. By piloting the concept in several small regions, Better Place hoped to iron out the wrinkles that would undoubtedly surface as the first cars were deployed. However, as the launch in Israel loomed near, the main questions the company needed to answer were its capacity to create value and its capacity to capture it, especially over the long term.

77 Better Place, 2010.
78 Renault Threatens Electric Car Withdrawal, 2010.
79 Bailey, 2010.
80 EarthTimes, 2010.

EXHIBIT 1
World map of automobiles per capita

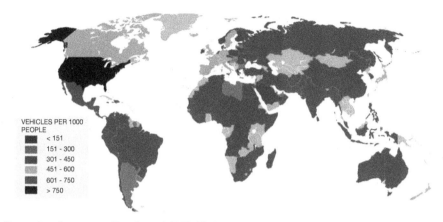

Source: http://commons.wikimedia.org/wiki/File:World_vehicles_per_capita.png.

EXHIBIT 2
United States energy consumption (2011)

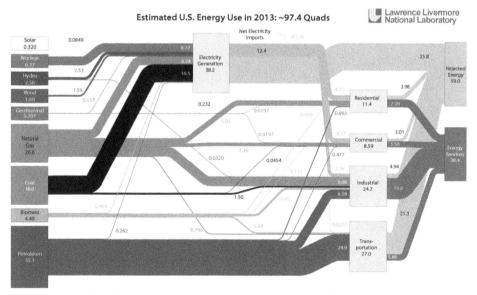

Source: https://flowcharts.llnl.gov/.

EXHIBIT 3
Electricity generation by fuel type, United States and global

US Electric power industry net generation by fuel, 2008

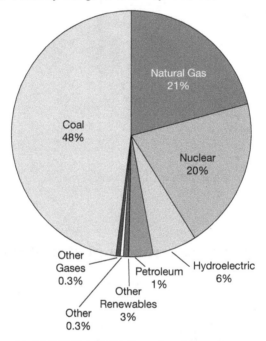

Source: US Energy Information Administration, *Electric Power Annual*, 2010.
   http://www.eia.gov/about/copyrights_reuse.cfm

World electricity generation by fuel type

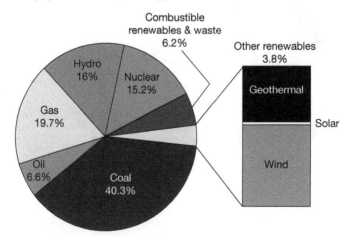

Sources: http://www.eia.doe.gov/steo and Earth Trends, using data from EIA 2007.

EXHIBIT 4
Renewable energy cost trends

Levelized cents/kWh in constant $2000[1]

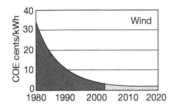

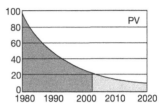

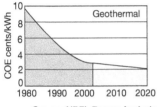

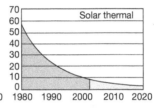

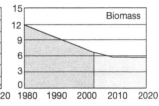

Source: NREL Energy Analysis Office (www.nrel.gov/analysis/docs/cost_curves_2002.ppt)
[1]These graphs are reflections of historical cost trends NOT precise annual historical data.
Updated: October 2002

EAO Energy Analysis Office
Understanding Energy Issues

⚡NREL NATIONAL RENEWABLE ENERGY LABORATORY

Source: Greentech History.

EXHIBIT 5
Load curve for a typical electric grid

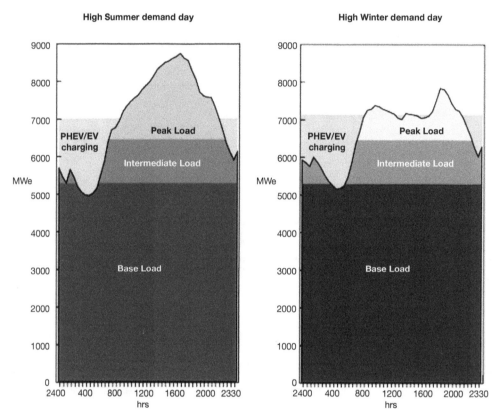

Source: http://www.world-nuclear.org/WNA/About-WNA/Annex/Non-exclusive-permission-for-reuse-of-WNA-material/

EXHIBIT 6
Gasoline vs. Electric Car Cost per Mile Comparison

$3.00	Price of one gallon of gas
30	Miles per gallon (gasoline car)
$0.10	Cost per mile (gasoline car)
25%	Efficiency of conversion, gas to mechanical energy
120	Miles per gallon (gasoline car, if 100% efficiency were attainable)
80%	Efficiency of conversion, grid to battery to electrical motor
96	Miles per gallon (electric car equivalent)
33	Kilowatt-hours (energy) stored in one gallon of gas
2.9	Miles per kilowatt-hour (electric car)
$0.10	Cost per kilowatt-hour (electric car)
$0.03	Cost per mile (electric car)

Compiled from various online resources, including www.ecoworld.com and www.cleantechnica.com.

EXHIBIT 7
Costs for fuel and electricity

Country	Cost of gas (USD/Gal)	Cost of electricity (Cents/kwH)	Primary source of electricity
Israel	6.76-7.00	12-54[81]	Coal, natural gas, diesel oil, fuel oil
Denmark	7-8[82]	10-11[83]	Coal, wind
Australia	6.40[84]	2.8-3.9[85]	Coal, natural gas, hydro
Toronto, Canada	3.86	4.4-9.3[86]	Hydro
Hawaii, USA	4.39-4.65[87]	26.05-32.50[88]	Coal
Japan	4.24[89]	19-27[90]	Nuclear, coal, gas, oil, hydro[91]

81 Israel Electric Corporation, 2008.
82 http://www.aaireland.ie/petrolprices/.
83 http://www.cbs.nl/en-GB/menu/themas/prijzen/publicaties/artikelen/archief/2006/2006-1945-wm.htm.
84 http://www.homebiznotes.com/rising-gas-prices-in-australia-affect-business-owners-where-will-it-stop/.
85 http://www.world-nuclear.org/info/inf64.html.
86 http://www.torontohydro.com/sites/electricsystem/residential/smartmeters/Pages/TOURates.aspx.
87 http://www.findingdulcinea.com/news/Americas/2008/December/Hawaii-Plans-Switch-to-Electric-Cars.html.
88 http://www.eia.doe.gov/cneaf/electricity/epm/table5_3.html.
89 http://money.cnn.com/pf/features/lists/global_gasprices/.
90 http://www.etaiwannews.com/etn/news_content.php?id=908024&lang=eng_news&cate_img=35.jpg&cate_rss=news_Business.
91 http://www.world-nuclear.org/info/inf79.html.

EXHIBIT 8
A graphical representation of the Better Place concept

Source: Roth, 2008.

EXHIBIT 9
Components of the Better Place business model

The Solution

| cars | batteries | charging |

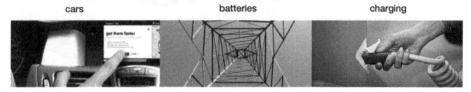

| ev driver services | ev network software | standards |

Source: http://www.betterplace.com/solution/.

EXHIBIT 10
Better Place battery swapping stations

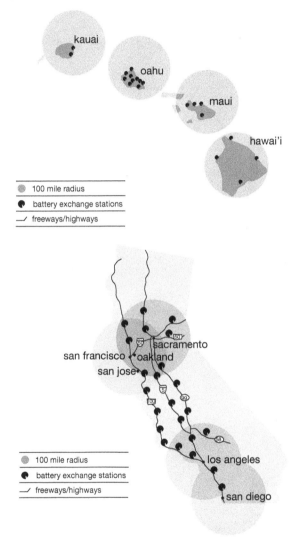

Source: www.betterplace.com.

EXHIBIT 11
Photographs

Charge spot.

Demo electric vehicle in position.

Battery moving into position.

Renault Fluence concept.

EXHIBIT 12
Better Place partners and investors

Governments	Battery manufacturers	Utility companies	Investors	Automobile manufacturers	Other private companies
Israel	A123 Systems	Israel Electric Corporation	Acorns to Oaks II	Renault-Nissan Alliance	Ahuzat Hof's Parking Lots, Israel
Denmark	Automotive Energy Supply Corporation	Dong Energy (Denmark)	Esarbee Investments Canada		Dor Alon Gas Station, Israel
Hawaii		Hawaiian Electric	GC Investments LLC		
Toronto		Bullfrog Power (Toronto)	HSBC Group		92 Corporate Fleet Partners, Israel
Japan			Israel Cleantech Ventures		Nihon Kotsu, Taxi Operator Japan
Australia		Australia Gas Light Company	Israel Corp		Microsoft
		Company	Lazard Asset Management		Intel
		Tokyo Electric Power Company	Macquarie Capital		
			Maniv Energy Capital		
			Morgan Stanley Investment Management		
			Musea Ventures		
			Ofer Group		
			VantagePoint Venture Partners		
			Vayikra Partners		
			Wolfensohn & Co.		

Source: www.betterplace.com.

EXHIBIT 13
Consumer surveys of automobile preferences

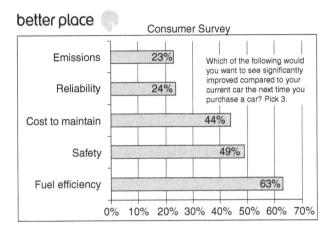

Source: www.betterplace.com.

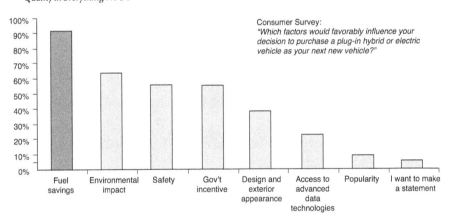

Source: Ernst & Young Automotive Survey January 2010.

References

Adams, Jonathan. "Japan leads the race for a hydrogen fuel-cell car." *Christian Science Monitor*, 1 Feb. 2010. http://www.csmonitor.com/World/Asia-Pacific/2010/0201/Japan-leads-the-race-for-a-hydrogen-fuel-cell-car.

"Advanced Diesel Technologies." *Energy Technology System Analysis Program*, Jun. 2009. http://www.etsap.org/E-techDS/EB/EB_T02_Adv_diesel_eng_gs-gct%20_TP_.pdf.

Agassi, Shai. "Climate Leaders Summit." 17 Dec. 2009. http://www.betterplace.com/cop15.

Agassi, Shai. "Transforming Transportation Globally." Beyond Oil Conference. Seattle. 2009. http://planet.betterplace.com/forum/topics/video-shai-agassi-speaking-at

Agassi, Shai. "Why Electric Vehicles Work." 2010. http://www.thomascrampton.com/china/shai-agassi-electric/.

Arnott, Sarah. "New Nissan Battery Plant to Create 350 Jobs." *The Independent*, 21 Jul. 2009. http://www.independent.co.uk/news/business/news/new-nissan-battery-plant-to-create-up-to-350-jobs-1754582.html.

Bailey, David, "Nissan: electric cars could shed government aid in 4 years". Planet Ark, 28 May, 2010. http://planetark.org/wen/58214.

Bar-Eli, Avi. "Solar energy could raise electricity prices." *Haaretz*, 6 Aug. 2008. http://www.haaretz.com/hasen/spages/1008854.html.

Barkat, Amiram. "Israel Corp to Triple Electricity Production to 1200MW." *Globes*, 23 Feb. 2010. http://planet.betterplace.com/group/betterplaceIsrael.

Baron, L. & Gedalyahu, D. "IEC in Better Place Talks." *Globes*, 26 Aug. 2008

Barron, Rachel. "Better Place Yet to Close Hawaii Electric Car Deal." *Greentech Media*, 10 Jun. 2008. http://www.greentechmedia.com/articles/read/better-place-yet-to-close-hawaii-electric-car-deal-1538/.

"Better Place research reveals Australian interest in Electric Vehicles in response to climate change concerns." Better Place, 23 Jul. 2009. http://australia.betterplace.com/assets/pdf/Better_Place_Australia_Consumer_Research_Release.pd.

"Better Place and Renault launch Fluence Z.E., the first "unlimited mileage" electric car together with innovative eMobility packages, in Europe's first Better Place Center." Better Place, 3 March 2011. http://www.betterplace.com/the-company-pressroom-pressreleases-detail/index/id/better-place-and-renault-launch-fluence-z-e-the-first-unlimited-mileage-electric-car-together-with-innovative-emobility-packages-in-europe-s-first-better-place-center.

Blanco, Sebastian. "Coulomb Technologies will legally "sell" energy for electric cars by not selling energy at all." *Autoblog Green*, 14 Aug. 2009. http://green.autoblog.com/2009/08/14/coulomb-technologies-will-legally-sell-energy-for-electric-car/.

Blenco, Greg. "Cost of hydrogen from different sources." *Hydrogen Car Revolution*, 9 Nov. 2009. http://www.h2carblog.com/?p=461.

Bossel, Ulf. "Does a Hydrogen Economy Make Sense?" Institute of Electrical and Electronics Engineers, Oct. 2006. http://www.efcf.com/reports/E21.pdf. Retrieved 1 Feb. 2010.

Carroll, Rory, and Schipani, Andres. "Multinationals eye up lithium reserves beneath Bolivia's salt flats." *The Guardian*, 15 Jun. 2009. http://www.guardian.co.uk/world/2009/jun/17/bolivia-lithium-reserves-electric-cars.

Caolgera, Stephen. "Department of Energy Announces Closing of $1.4 billion loan to Nissan to build Leaf EV in U.S." *EGM CarTech*, 28 Jan. 2010. http://www.egmcartech.com/2010/01/28/department-of-energy-announces-closing-of-1-4-billion-loan-to-nissan-to-build-leaf-ev-in-u-s/.

"Cars." Worldwatch Institute. Washington, 2008. http://www.worldwatch.org/node/1480.

"Celebrating the Ford Model T, Only 100 Years Young!" *Auto Atlantic*, 2008. http://www.autoatlantic.com/Sept08/Sept08_Ford-Model-T-is-100.html.

"CNG price to shoot to Rs48.90." *The Nation*, 15 Jan. 2009. http://www.nation.com.pk/pakistan-news-newspaper-daily-english-online/Business/15-Jan-2009/CNG-price-to-shoot-to-Rs4890.

"Danish Wind Power Export and Cost." Coherent Energy and Environmental System Analysis. Department of Development and Planning, Aalborg University, Feb. 2010. http://www.windpower.org/download/541/DanishWindPower_Export_and_Cost.pdf.

Day, Paul. "Spain and Renault study electric car plan." *Reuters*, 21 Oct. 2008. http://www.planetark.com/dailynewsstory.cfm/newsid/50686/story.htm.

Dubois, Shelly. "Shai Agassi: China is the EV Tipping Point." *Wired Magazine*, 15 Jul. 2009. http://www.wired.com/epicenter/2009/06/shai-agassi-china-is-the-ev-tipping-point/.

"Eco Tech: Toyota Industries develops solar-powered EV charging stations."*Ecofriend* 26 Dec. 2009

Ernst & Young. "Measuring the understanding of and interest in plug-in hybrid and electric vehicles in the US." Automotive Survey. 2010.

"North American Grid Operators Assess Impact of Electric Vehicles." *Electric Energy*, 24 Mar. 2010. http://www.electricenergyonline.com/?page=show_news&id=130216.

"Smart Grid Demonstrations." Electric Power Research Institute. Sept. 2008. http://www.smartgrid.epri.com/doc/EPRI%20Smart%20Grid%20Overview.pdf.

"Electric Cars—How much does it cost per charge?" *Scientific American*, 13 Mar. 2009. http://www.scientificamerican.com/article.cfm?id=electric-cars-cost-per-charge.

"Electric Vehicles: Assessing U.S. Consumer Demand." Better Place, 13 Jul. 2009. http://www.betterplace.com/images/news/usareshighlightsslideshare-090714120442-phpapp01.pdf.

The EV Project http://www.theevproject.com/overview.php

"EV1 Specs." General Motors Corporation, 2001. http://www.evchargernews.com/CD-A/gm_ev1_web_site/specs/specs_specs.htm.

Fineren, Daniel. "Spain Needs Electric Cars, Links for Wind Boom." *Reuters*, 2 Mar. 2010. http://planetark.org/wen/56930.

"Forecast: 17M Natural Gas Vehicles Worldwide by 2015." *Green Car Congress* 19 Oct. 2009. http://www.greencarcongress.com/2009/10/forecast-17m-natural-gas-vehicles-world-wide-by-2015.html.

Frank, A et al. "What are Plug-In Hybrids?" Team Fate, U of California, 2007. http://www.team-fate.net/wordpress/?page_id=11.

Fung, Derek. "How Better Place plans to revive the electric car." *CNET Reviews*, 20 Feb, 2009. http://reviews.cnet.com/8301-13746_7-10168501-48.html.

Gerson Lehrman Group. "Overview of ethanol and flex-fuel auto industry: past & present." GLG Expert Contributor. 16 Jul. 2009. http://www.glgroup.com/News/Overview-of-ethanol-and-flex-fuel-auto-industry--past--present-41502.html.

"Better Place drives through $83m." *Globes*, 25 Mar. 2010. http://archive.globes.co.il/searchgl/Better%20Place%20drives%20through%20$83m_h_hd_2L34oC3CrCbmnC30mDJGvE34rBcXqRMm0.html.

"Renewable Energy Cost Trends." *Energy Analysis Office*, Oct. 2002. http://www.greentechhistory.com/2009/03/renewable-energy-cost-curves-1980-2020/.

"Alternative Fuels and CNG." *Gas Fueling Technology*, 2006. http://www.gasfuellingtech.com/alternative_fuels_cng.php.

Global Progress: Denmark. "Better Place presents the environmental case for EVs during COP15." Better Place, 20 Dec. 2009. http://www.betterplace.com/global-progress/denmark/.

Global Progress: Israel. "Better Place opens first electric vehicle demonstration center." Better Place, 11 Feb. 2010. http://www.betterplace.com/global-progress/israel/.

Groom, N. & Krolicki, K. "Automakers detail electric car plans at L.A. show." *Reuters*, 19 Nov. 2008. http://www.reuters.com/article/idUSTRE4AJ0Z720081120.

Gutman, Lior. "Domestic electricity prices to rise by 3.5%." *Y Net News*, 12 Nov. 2009. http://www.ynetnews.com/articles/0,7340,L-3816896,00.html.

Harrison, Pete. "Europe Charts Route For Electric Car Roll-out". Planet Ark, April 29, 2010. http://planetark.org/wen/57773.

"Mercedes Rejects Electric Car Battery Swapping." *Hybrid Cars*, 9 Mar. 2009. http://www.hybridcars.com/news/skeptics-question-electric-car-battery-swapping-25627.html.

"The History of the Automobile: The Internal Combustion Engine and Early Gas-Powered Cars.". http://inventors.about.com/library/weekly/aacarsgasa.htm. Retrieved 31 Jan. 2010.

"The History of Diesel.". http://www.talktalk.co.uk/motoring/diesel/history.html.

Jolly, David. "Renault Pledges to Build New Electric Vehicle in France." *New York Times*, 17 Jan. 2010. http://www.nytimes.com/2010/01/18/business/energy-environment/18renault.html.

Khal, Martine. "Mass market electric vehicles: there is much to be done." *AutomotiveWorld*, 31 Mar. 2010. http://www.automotiveworld.com/news/environment/81494-mass-market-electric-vehicles-there-is-much-to-be-done.

Kim, Chang-Ran. "Japan Firms to standardize electric car rechargers." *Reuters*, 15 Mar. 2010. http://www.reuters.com/article/idUSTOE62E04S20100315.

Kitman, Jamie L. "The Secret History of Lead." *The Nation*, 2 Mar. 2000. http://www.thenation.com/doc/20000320/kitman.

Krauss, Clifford. "Global Demand Squeezing Natural Gas Supply." *New York Times*, 29 May 2008. http://www.nytimes.com/2008/05/29/business/29gas.html?pagewanted=1&_r=3.

Lettice, John. "Israel electric car project aims to wipe out oil." *The Register*, 22 Jan. 2008. http://www.theregister.co.uk/2008/01/22/israel_electric_car_project/.

Levinson, Yoni. "Better Place Interview: Mile Plans, Cost and Compatibility." *EcoGeek*, 27 Apr. 2009. http://www.ecogeek.org/component/content/article/2713.

Markoff, John. "Hawaii Endorses Plan for Electric Cars." *New York Times*, 2 Dec. 2008. http://www.nytimes.com/2008/12/03/technology/start-ups/03hawaii.html.

Moriarty, Patrick and Honnery, Damon. "The prospects for global green car mobility." *Journal of Cleaner Production*, Nov 2008. 16, 16: 1717-1726

"Monthly US Natural Gas Vehicle Fuel Consumption." U.S. Energy Information Administration, 2 Mar. 2010. http://tonto.eia.doe.gov/dnav/ng/hist/n3025us2m.htm.

Natural Gas Background. *Natural Gas Org*, 2004. http://www.naturalgas.org/overview/background.asp.

Naughton, Keith. "Small, It's The New Big." *Newsweek*, 16 Feb. 2008. http://www.newsweek.com/id/112729/page/1.

"Powertrends, 2010." New York Independent System Operator, 2010. http://www.nyiso.com/public/webdocs/newsroom/power_trends/powertrends2010_FINAL_04012010.pdf.

Ohnsman, Alan. "GM, Toyota Fuel-Cell Plans Clash With U.S. Battery Car Push." *Bloomberg*, 9 Oct. 2009. http://www.bloomberg.com/apps/news?pid=20601087&sid=az48qD9Cl_kQ.

OICA. "2008 Production Statistics.". http://oica.net/category/production-statistics/.

"On goats and exploding emotions in the gasoline retail sector." *Haaretz*, 22 Jan. 2010. http://www.haaretz.com/hasen/spages/1144135.html.

Pogue, David. "Electric Cars for All! (No, Really This Time)." *New York Times*, 19 Mar. 2009. http://pogue.blogs.nytimes.com/2009/03/19/electric-cars-for-all-no-really-this-time/.

Petersen, John. "Debunking the PHEV Mythology. *Alt Energy Stocks* 19 Aug. 2009. http://www.altenergystocks.com/archives/2009/08/debunking_the_phev_mythology.html.

Pickard, Jim. "Electric Car Buyers to Receive Subsidy." *Financial Times*, 25 Feb. 2010. http://www.ft.com/cms/s/0/3ccf8b9e-2168-11df-830e-00144feab49a.html.

Reed, J. Arnold, M. "Better Place draws investors to 'clean-tech'." *Financial Times*, 25 Jan, 2010. http://www.ft.com/cms/s/0/9dad5b84-090e-11df-ba88-00144feabdc0.html?nclick_check=1.

"Renault Nissan Alliance Signs Partnership with Saitama City to Promote Electric Vehicles." *Japan for Sustainability*, 9 Feb. 2010. http://www.japanfs.org/en/pages/029696.html.

"Renault Threatens Electric Car Withdrawal." *The Copenhagen Post*, 22 Jan. 2010. http://www
.cphpost.dk/business/119-business/48036-renault-threatens-electric-car-withdrawal.html.

Ritch, Emma. "Israel allows first solar power plants." *Cleantech Group LLC*, 9 Jan. 2009. http://
cleantech.com/news/4042/israel-allows-first-solar-power-plants.

Romero, Frances. "A Brief History of the Electric Car." *Time*, 13 Jan. 2009. http://www.time
.com/time/business/article/0,8599,1871282,00.html.

Roth, Daniel. "Driven: Shai Agassi's Audacious Plan to Put Electric Cars on the Road."
Wired Magazine, 22 Aug. 2008. http://www.wired.com/print/cars/futuretransport/
magazine/16-09/ff_agassi.

Roth, Hand & Gohla-Neudecker, Bodo. "Analysis of Renewable Energy Power Demand
for Specifically Charging EVs." Munich Technical University, 9 Nov. 2009. http://www
.betterplace.com/images/news/TUM_Research_Report_FNL.pdf.

Schafer et al. "Transportation in a Climate Constrained World." *The MIT Press*, 2009. http://
mitpress.mit.edu/books/chapters/0262512343chap1.pdf.

"Service Station Retailing in Denmark." *Datamonitor*, 29 Jan. 2010. http://www.datamonitor.
com/store/Product/toc.aspx?productId=BFEN0466.

Shirouzu Norihiko "Renault, Nissan Weigh Lithium-Ion Battery For Electric Car Projects" *Wall
Street Journal*, 11 Mar. 2008. http://online.wsj.com/article/SB120111595837510587.html.

"Siemens: If At First You Don't Succeed." *Business Week*, 5 Sept, 2005. http://www.business
week.com/magazine/content/05_36/b3949077_mz054.htm.

Slavin, Matthew. "Portland may be Better Place down the road." DJC Oregon, 15 Jul. 2009.
http://djcoregon.com/news/2009/07/15/portland-may-be-better-place-down-the-road/.
Retrieved 4 Nov, 2009.

Squatriglia, Chuck. "Better Place Unveils an Electric Car Battery Swap Station." *Wired Magazine*, 13 May, 2009. http://www.wired.com/autopia/2009/05/better-place/. Retrieved 11
Nov. 2009.

Squatriglia, Chuck. "GM Fires Up Its Chevrolet Volt Battery Factory." *Wired Magazine*, 7 Jan.
2010. http://www.wired.com/autopia/2010/01/chevrolet-volt-battery.

Schwartz, Ariel. "Toyota Challenges Coulomb, Better Place With Solar-Powered EV Charging
Station." *Fast Company*, 30 Oct. 2009. http://www.fastcompany.com/blog/ariel-schwartz/
sustainability/toyota-challenges-coulomb-better-place-ev-charging-station.

Steenstrup, Kristian. "Professional Profile: Better Place." *The Gartner Fellows*, Feb. 2009.
http://www.gartner.com/research/fellows/asset_221489_1176.jsp.

Thompson, Clive. "Batteries Not Included." *New York Times*, 16 Apr. 2009. http://www
.nytimes.com/2009/04/19/magazine/19car-t.html.

"Oil for Natural Gas Engines – On the Rise in the US." *NGV Global News*, 19 Mar. 2010. http://
www.ngvglobal.com/oils-for-natural-gas-engines-on-the-rise-in-the-us-0319

Voelcker, John. "Driving Electric To Cost No More Than Using Gas, Says Better Place."
Green Car Reports, 28 Sept. 2009. http://www.greencarreports.com/blog/1035839_driving-
electric-to-cost-no-more-than-using-gas-says-better-place.

Woody, Todd. "SolarCity makes electric cars an even smarter investment." *Grist*, 6 Oct. 2009.
http://www.grist.org/article/2009-10-05-solarcity-electric-vehicles-california.

Woody, Todd. "Shai Agassi: Green's Steve Jobs." *Grist*, 1 May 2009. http://www.grist.org/
article/2009-05-01-shai-agassi-better-place/.

Yarrow, Jay. "The Cost of a Battery Swapping Station: $500,000." *Business Insider*,
21 Apr. 2009. http://www.businessinsider.com/the-cost-of-a-better-place-battery-swap
ping-station-500000-2009-4.

"1999 General Motors EV1.". http://www1.eere.energy.gov/vehiclesandfuels/avta/pdfs/fsev/
eva_results/ev1_eva.pdf.

"2008 Toyota Prius." *Hybrid Car*, 21 Oct. 2007. http://www.hybridcar.com/index.php?option=
com_content&task=view&id=521&Itemid=103.

Part III
Corporate social entrepreneurship

CASE 9

How to establish and manage a social business at the bottom of the pyramid
The case of OSRAM in Africa[1]

Pia von Nell

1 The case study was prepared in 2010 under the supervision of Prof. Dr. Holger Ernst. It was developed solely as the basis for class discussion. It is not intended to serve as an endorsement, source of primary data, or illustration of effective or ineffective management. Due to OSRAM's IPO in 2013 and associated major changes, the group's financial ratios were updated in 2014. I would like to thank Jochen Berner, Project Manager of the Off-Grid Project at OSRAM, for his support and the interviews.

The photo shows a Kenyan woman using the OSRAM lantern. Source: OSRAM.

Otto Beisheim School of Management

Company background

Having its headquarters in Munich, Germany, OSRAM GmbH was already registered in 1906. Since then, it has developed into one of the two leading lighting manufacturers in the world being active in the fields of general lighting, automotive
lighting, ballasts and luminaires, opto semiconductors, precision materials and
components and display/optics (Exhibit 1).

Currently, the lighting market is at a crossroads. Energy-efficient technologies and
LED lighting, making a significant contribution to climate protection, are on the
march. This trend is supported by legislations such as the EU directive, which came
into force on September 1, 2009, and which indicates the end of incandescent lamps.[2]
Thus, OSRAM sees its future growth markets in products and processes that contribute to solving global sustainability issues, address economic needs and protect the
environment. In order to be able to react to the new challenges and to meet the future
demand, innovation plays a crucial role. Following its slogan of "Light is OSRAM",
OSRAM spends 6.5 percent of its sales on R&D. In 2008, the company's portfolio of
energy-efficient products was acknowledged with the German Sustainability Award.
Today, these products already generate the largest share of the company's revenue
and are expected to gain more and more shares of the total sales in the next few years.

Also, international markets have become increasingly important for OSRAM. In
its 36 production and manufacturing facilities the company manufactures lighting products that shine in over 120 countries. While sales in Europe and America
declined during the financial downturn and have stagnated since then, revenues in
emerging markets grew to 25.8 percent of OSRAM's total revenue and continue to
grow.[3] Now focusing on those countries due to the growth potential, OSRAM tries
to further expand its production capacities and to explore new markets such as the
Asia–Pacific region and Africa.

Historically, OSRAM's first activities in Africa date back to 1971, when the company opened a first sales office in South Africa. Since then, it has developed into
an independent organization serving the southern part of Africa with OSRAM
products. Step by step, sales offices in Kenya, serving the East African market, and
Tunisia, serving the North African market, were opened. However, the West African
business is still run by the German or Dubai office, while the Angolan market is
handled from Portugal.

In the fiscal year 2013, OSRAM employed more than 35,000 people and generated
a revenue of €5.28 billion together with an EBITDA of €413.6 million (Exhibit 2).
Thereof, business outside Germany accounted for 86 percent[4] and is expected to
become even more important in the next ten years (Exhibit 3).

2 See Annual Report 2013. Available at www.osram.com.
3 See Annual Report 2013. Available at www.osram.com.
4 See Annual Report 2013. Available at www.osram.com.

The pilot project "Energy for All"

Since September 2008, OSRAM has run a pilot off-grid project in the form of a social business in Kenya. The prevailing view on social businesses (Exhibit 4) is that they are enterprises with a social goal, targeting a need that is not yet satisfied by society, government or non-governmental organizations (NGOs). However, they have to act along the triple bottom line,[5] which means that they have to be not only socially or environmentally sustainable, but also financially.

The idea for the project in Kenya came from different directions. The Global Nature Fund (GNF), an international NGO for environmental protection, observed Lake Victoria being heavily polluted by the fishermen's kerosene, which is used for illumination in order to attract fish at night. When the GNF finally found a solution to counteract the pollution, namely a battery box in combination with a lamp, it asked OSRAM to provide the technology. For OSRAM, however, this was not sufficient because it had the necessary preconditions such as size, resources, technical knowledge and connections in order to found a proper social business itself. Hence, it would be able to develop corporate social responsibility (CSR) and to explore new markets in developing economies such as Kenya. With this idea, it felt that it could materialize the theory of a self-sustaining social business and target people living at the bottom of the pyramid (BOP).

Therefore, OSRAM's corporate innovation management in cooperation with experts from various functions across the company developed a holistic approach to tackle this issue and to meet people's needs. Thus, the company decided to pursue a feasibility study at three different locations in order to test the developed concept, the products and the technology which were all completely new to the company.

After a trial phase of one year, the project team recently presented the status quo to OSRAM's board, which has now to decide upon the project's future and whether to continue it at all. Even though the pilot phase was successful overall, the project is not yet able to compete with other OSRAM projects from a financial point of view. Therefore, and especially now during an economic downturn, where cost saving measures have to be undertaken everywhere, the decision whether to further invest in the project is not easy. A continuation in the form of expansion, however, would require valuable resources.

The market

Market size

OSRAM found out that 77 billion liters of kerosene per year are used for off-grid lighting worldwide resulting in 190 million tons of CO_2 emissions. Depending on

---

5 The concept of the triple bottom line refers to the three pillars of a sustainable organization, being people, planet and profit.

the actual market price of kerosene this consumption creates a market size of about €30 to €50 billion per year, nearly twice the size of OSRAM's normal illuminating market, which is about €22 billion worth.[6] Thus, neither OSRAM nor Philips but rather big oil companies represent the actual world market leaders for illumination.

Having conducted further research OSRAM found that out of 1.6 billion households without access to power supply worldwide 78 percent live in India and Africa.[7] Africa has about 105 million households without electricity, with 30 million people living in the area around Lake Victoria.[8] Feeling that this could become a very important market where a lot of revenues could be generated, OSRAM decided to initiate a pilot project in this region by establishing three presences in Mbita, Sindo and Nyandiwa, all being very close to Lake Victoria (Exhibit 5).

OSRAM chose the proximity to the lake for another reason as well: naturally, there are many fishermen who spend about 75 percent of their income on kerosene for lighting the boats to attract fish at night (Exhibit 6). As light is of central importance for work around Lake Victoria, each fishing boat uses about 1,200 liters of kerosene annually, amounting to a total of 20 million liters and emitting 50 tons of CO_2 per year.[9] This represents a great and clustered additional demand for illumination, where OSRAM could easily test its business model.

The market's character

Despite those promising numbers, the market shows the typical drawbacks of a BOP market, such as the inconvenience of reaching the people via common distribution and communication channels. Since people are rarely educated at all and live in rural villages that are dispersed over the country, physically reaching people is difficult and usual advertisement and marketing strategies are less effective.

However, OSRAM identifies other aspects as the greatest constraints for its social business: firstly, the local culture, which is completely different to the western culture OSRAM is normally used to. Nevertheless, the company gives itself time to learn from experiences and additionally cooperates with a local partner, who supports OSRAM in any related issues. As a second market drawback, OSRAM names corruption. For compliance reasons, OSRAM decided not to engage in bribery. This created a difficult start, but after some time local authorities recognized that they would not receive bribe money from OSRAM. When local authorities also saw the community benefits, OSRAM's prestige increased and it is now granted the rights in the official way and without hesitation. A final major disadvantage of the market is the political instability. During December 2007, for example, adherents from two different political leaders, Mwai Kibaki and Raila Odinga, started to fight and two

6 See Rybak, 2008.
7 See Gregor, 2008.
8 See Dewald, 2009.
9 See Gregor, 2008.

months of violence followed in which business had to be put on hold.[10] As a result, OSRAM decided to remain independent and not to cooperate with politicians, as they can change very quickly and the risk of a successor breaking a cooperation is too high.

The O-Hub as the core of the off-grid project

Need for a holistic business model

When OSRAM entered the market there were already many off-grid lighting solutions which were rather unsuccessful on a large scale because providers did not think "beyond the product". OSRAM noticed that in order to be successful and to overcome income and distribution constraints of people living at the BOP it had to develop a holistic concept considering infrastructure and communication as well as engineering and maintenance issues.

Very quickly OSRAM discovered that its new customers live at or below the poverty line. This means that they have only very low or irregular income, which does not allow for major investments. Consequently, they are forced to live from day to day unable to calculate their expenses over a week's time. Therefore, it is obvious that they cannot afford €400—the cost for an access to modern power supply in Kenya—even if this is the least expensive solution in the long run. Additionally, they cannot receive any credit for this investment. Thus, OSRAM developed a new way that would supply its products with electricity. By investigating why kerosene is so commonly used OSRAM revealed the fact that it has one crucial advantage in comparison to any other solution: it can be bought in very small portions whenever the customer needs it and has enough money to spend, thus allowing consumption despite the low and irregular income.[11] Following this idea, OSRAM decided to create a similar off-grid model that delivers energy in very small quantities not requiring any up-front investment.

With this new approach, OSRAM does not only pursue its core business by providing lighting devices but also supplies the energy in the form of charged batteries. For several reasons, which are discussed later, OSRAM decided to lease out charged lamps and later replace the empty devices with charged ones again. Thus, only the price for the charging, which is low and therefore affordable for many BOP consumers, has to be paid in order to receive high quality products.

The O-Hub

In order to reach people without access to the grid-based power supply, OSRAM bases its new concept on a charging station called O-Hub. This is a building with 48 solar panels on the roof (Exhibit 7). Of these, 42 big panels are used for charging

---

10 See Zeug, 2009.
11 See Gregor, 2009.

batteries and lanterns for illumination, which are then leased out. In times of good weather, 112 batteries can be recharged concurrently in two to three hours[12] (Exhibit 8). The remaining six small solar panels are used for recharging mobile phones, as well as for cleaning and purifying rain water in order to make it drinkable. OSRAM decided to use solar energy, because as a renewable and inexhaustible energy source, it does not have CO_2 emissions and is delivered for free by the sun. Since Kenya is located close to the equator, the sun rays hit the panels at a 90-degree angle making the energy generation very efficient.[13]

Independent on site

The pilot project's three O-Hubs, located in Mbita, Sindo and Nyandiwa, are operated by a local partner called Thames Electricals Ltd.[14] This partnership is necessary for legal as well as for other practical reasons, such as too high European wages. During construction and the first few weeks of operation, OSRAM experts flew to Kenya in order to train the local staff and to transfer all knowledge concerning the underlying technologies. Thus, local employees are now able to operate, repair and maintain the technologies, as well as to pursue daily operations themselves. Hence, OSRAM experts only have to come to Kenya for major repairs, general checks or to give further training.

However, due to the fact that there are only three O-Hubs, the social business's administration, organization and management are still conducted in Munich, because OSRAM's available resources are still sufficient to cover the project's current degree of complexity. However, an increasing number of O-Hubs would require a higher administrative effort, which could not be conducted from OSRAM in Germany any more, but would require an own local venture to carry out this function.

Leasing as the core concept

The O-Hub's products are leased out instead of being sold for the following reasons: firstly, local customers do not have the burden of paying the price for owning the products (e.g. about 8,000 KES[15] for the battery), but have only to pay a deposit fee for the duration of usage. This fee is paid back once the contract ends and the product is properly returned. For many people though, the deposit of 1,000 KES for the lamp's battery or 750 KES for the lantern is still unaffordable. Cooperation with a local financial institute that offers microcredits, which can be paid back stepwise, however, allows every customer to disburse the expense of the deposit.[16] Therefore, because the O-Hub bills only small fees for the recharging, customers can now

12 See Rybak, 2008.
13 See Mair, 2009.
14 See Mair, 2009.
15 100 Kenyan Schilling (KES) currently equal about one Euro.
16 See Gregor, 2008.

afford the products and profit of the approximately 50 percent cost savings.[17] A second motivation for the leasing model is the fact that OSRAM remains the owner of the products. This enables an all-inclusive service, which includes the complex maintenance and repair of batteries and lamps. Thus, empty or broken devices can be replaced directly by sound and recharged ones without causing idle time. The service is offered for free as long as customers do not destroy the products on purpose. A final reason is that OSRAM wants to prevent its lamps and batteries, containing toxic materials, to end up on a normal garbage dump. This would not only counteract the project's environmental benefits by polluting the soil, but would also throw a bad light on the company's reputation. For these reasons, OSRAM decided to remain the owner of the products and to be responsible for disposing and recycling it in a correctly manner.

The budget

With the decision of owning the lighting devices and to lease instead of selling them, the initial investment per O-Hub increases by 34 percent to a total of approximately €190,000 (Exhibit 9). Technology and power also contribute a major cost block, namely about 40 percent. However, when the hub is finally set up, there are only marginal operational costs, because the sun delivers energy for free and the costs for maintenance and local staff are relatively low.

Initially, the budget for the pilot project was €1.2 million. This included the construction of three pilot hubs in Kenya and one year of operations. Due to the political crisis, repairs and underestimated costs for logistics, however, the total costs increased and additional €1 million were granted to the project.[18]

When the first O-Hub started its operations in September 2008, it quickly proved that the business model successfully pursues the triple bottom line paradigm. The project is not only advantageous for the environment and the local customers, but also promises positive financial returns for the second year, if a capacity utilization of 80 percent is achieved. Finally, the social business contributes a major part to OSRAM's corporate social responsibility and catches great attention in the media.

The products

With the O-Hub and the leasing concept, OSRAM manages to imitate the only USP of kerosene-based lighting namely the ability to be sold in small portions, overcoming income, maintenance and distribution constraints. Furthermore, kerosene-based lighting has several crucial disadvantages in comparison to OSRAM's products that are charged with solar energy: firstly, it emits great amounts of CO_2, which is not the case with solar energy. Secondly, as the kerosene price shows a great correlation

17 See Dewald, 2009, and Iken, 2009.
18 See Iken, 2009.

with the oil price, it gets increasingly expensive, and households have to spend more and more of their income on it. Contrary to that, people can calculate with stable and low prices when they use OSRAM's devices, which cost only half the price of the kerosene solution because they do not heavily depend on factors other than the sun. Furthermore, while OSRAM's products are completely safe, using kerosene for lighting is dangerous because of the open flame, risking fires and substantial health damages through toxic smoke. A final advantage of the OSRAM products is the higher lighting quality in comparison to kerosene-based lighting.

Currently, the social business's product portfolio consists of two illuminating products, namely the O-Box in combination with the O-Lamp and the O-Lantern, a water treatment system that produces purified drinking water, as well as a mobile phone charging station. These products were all launched during the first year and help local people at the bottom of the pyramid to satisfy basic needs and to tremendously increase life quality.

The O-Hub's most important product is the O-Box, a rechargeable battery, together with the O-Lamp (Exhibit 11). This combination illuminates small houses, restaurants and shops for approximately 18 hours. As it is water and dust resistant, as well as comparatively inexpensive, it is the perfect solution for the local conditions and therefore attracts many diverse customers ranging from housewives to fishermen. The second illumination product is the O-Lantern (Exhibit 12), which has an integrated rechargeable battery and is therefore easy to carry around and perfect to use in small households. The mobile charging station (Exhibit 13) uses the O-Hub's abundant energy to recharge mobile phones with electricity of higher quality than any other local alternative and therefore supports the lifetime of the mobile phones. Finally, OSRAM offers drinking water (Exhibit 14), rain water that is purified via different filtering and illuminating processes and therefore free of any bacteria and viruses.

Customers and communication

Customers

As already described, OSRAM's off-grid project targets people living at the BOP in rural villages, having no access to the power supply or to clean and safe drinking water and living on very low and irregular incomes.

For these people, the O-Hub represents a possibility of satisfying a basic need. Therefore, the hub targets all people who need electricity for their daily lives or jobs but did not get it before. This makes not only households and fishermen but also restaurants, farms, and shops into OSRAM's clients, because they see that less expensive light and energy imply longer business hours and more customers, resulting in higher revenues. This effect was already proven within the first weeks of the O-Hubs' existence.[19] Consequently, the O-Hub also supports self-employment,

19 See Dewald, 2009.

the most efficient way of escaping poverty, and improves families' asset bases and therefore an area's overall economy.

Communication

From the beginning, OSRAM was thinking about an effective marketing strategy for its O-Hubs. As normal media such as radios, TVs and magazines are lacking in the areas around the O-Hubs, usual advertisement would have been very ineffective. Seeing the local community as an elementary part of people's lives, OSRAM decided to build its approach upon the impact of word of mouth. Therefore, it firstly chose popular and inquisitive opinion leaders among the fishermen and convinced them of the products' benefits. Due to their business thinking and the immense cost block the kerosene consumption represented, they quickly recognized the saving potential, as well as the positive impact on their daily income. As a consequence, other fishermen saw and heard of the products' benefits and more and more of them became O-Hub customers. Today, fishermen still represent OSRAM's greatest customer group. Households and others, on the other hand, are more reluctant and harder to convince. Therefore, OSRAM employs people who walk from door to door, demonstrating the products' benefits by calculating the cost advantage and explaining the increased security through the eliminated fire risks and health damages caused by toxic gases.

Assessment of the project's first year

OSRAM's strategy for the first year

Looking at the social business's first year, OSRAM is very satisfied with the pilot phase. Initially, it did not have great expectations for the project and considered the pilot phase more as a feasibility study testing the market, the demand and the fit of the products.

Even though the "Energy for All" project is OSRAM's first social business, it instantly followed some major recommendations for a successful social business that can be found in the literature. Through cooperation with a local financial institute, it supports the locals' buying power and insures that people are able to receive a credit in order to afford the rental rate and the charging fees for their products. Secondly, OSRAM innovated along the whole value chain, used new technologies and tailored solutions that fit the local habits and the environment, because it saw that its normal devices were not adequate for the different needs, infrastructures, environmental conditions, culture and habits. By reviewing its products and by creating a new business model, it is now able to meet the challenges of the bottom of the pyramid market in Kenya. Consequently, it offers high quality products, focusing on functionality and sustainability, for a price that is affordable for the people living at the poverty line. In addition, it takes care of the proper disposal of its recyclable products.

Performance evaluation

As in any of its other businesses, OSRAM also has to evaluate its social business in order to decide upon its future. However, a social business's profitability is hard to measure, as it seeks more than just financial profit. OSRAM's primary goal was founding a social business that acts along the triple bottom line, which means maximizing social, environmental and financial profit. In order to assess whether it achieved its aim, social and environmental, as well as financial profits are assessed separately and then summed up.

Social profit

Firstly, the social business affects people by creating benefits for the community, its employees and its customers. Already during the construction phase, OSRAM was anxious to employ local companies using local material and employing local workers. Also nowadays, Thames Electricals, the Kenyan firm that is operating the O-Hub, only engages local staff as technical experts, security and sales personnel. Thus, the workforce is able to learn from OSRAM experts in the beginning so that the know-how concerning the products, the installation and business know-how is completely transferred (Exhibit 15). Moreover, OSRAM tries to avoid importing from Germany, but rather to source from the African surroundings, which reduces local poverty by stimulating production.

Consumers can benefit from OSRAM's products not only because of lower costs, but also for the following reasons. Firstly, light and energy represents a means for work and education. Thus, children having to work during daytime are now able to study in the evening with high quality illumination, which may help them reach higher educational levels. In addition, the products support longer business hours and ideally more revenues. Thus, the O-Hub creates an infrastructure that has not been there before and helps the poor to be able to improve their situation themselves.

Finally, OSRAM's products contribute to health and safety through clean energy and water. During the first year, OSRAM has seen enough demand and customers accept and even appreciate the O-Hubs products. Within that period, OSRAM managed to distribute about 3,180 products that were already recharged about 88,000 times across the three hubs. This equals a CO_2 abatement of approximately 400 tons.

Obviously, the total social profit of the project has various social and environmental sources and is therefore nearly impossible to be put together and finally to be objectively calculated by means of a standardized measure such as, e.g., the social return on investment.

Financial profit

Looking at the financial benefit, OSRAM had a new experience. Before it started the social business, OSRAM did not think about any marketing effects the project might bring along. Nevertheless, newspapers and magazines became more and more interested and published articles about it. When calculating how much money OSRAM would have spent on marketing in print media in order to reach the same level of publicity, the company found that the equivalent value for the marketing expenses would have been €1 million. Being stunned by this remarkable effect and the attention the project draws upon itself and OSRAM, the company decided to put the project on a more concrete basis, because it started to see this as another payback of its social business.

Research has found a positive correlation between social activities and the financial profit of a company, as well as the fact that consumers are willing to switch to companies engaging in social and environmental activities. Bearing in mind those two findings, one can only assume that the social business also convinces new consumers in the developed world to buy OSRAM products and thus stimulates sales. Furthermore, due to the social business, OSRAM gained valuable know-how in areas where it did not have expertise before, such as water, battery and solar technology. These technologies will play a major role in the next few years, and the new knowledge may offer OSRAM a golden business opportunity, which it would miss out on otherwise.

As showed in Exhibit 16, every O-Hub recorded losses during the first year. However, if everything turns out as calculated and the social business manages to lease more of its products and to hit the critical capacity utilization of 80 percent, first returns are expected for the second year, which would result in an amortization period of roughly 8.5 years.

During the first year, the average capacity has constantly grown, but it is still around 50 percent and subject to a strong cyclical volatility, having a low bottom point every four weeks (Exhibit 17). This is because fishermen do not go fishing during the week of full moon and therefore do not need to recharge their O-Boxes, resulting in a tremendous decline in sales. Therefore, OSRAM needs to find a way to smoothen the volatility and to lift the lowest points in order to achieve the critical value.

Assessing the products' performance

In its mobile charging station, OSRAM does not see an important means either for substantial revenue generation or for further growth. In fact, it quickly gained a lot of customers, but then stagnated and stabilized on a constant level. Nevertheless, the charging station attracts a lot of foot traffic, because customers understand that charging their phones in the O-Hub with constant electrical flows is better for the lifetime of their batteries than any other option. Therefore, the O-Hub has emerged as the number one mobile charging destination in the entire region and is famous for its high quality mobile charging. Thus, even though OSRAM is not able to generate important revenues with it, it is a good way to attract customers and to cross sell other products, but also to serve a basic need and to use the abundant energy effectively.

Of the total sales, the charging station and the purified water hold only a 10 percent share. However, in comparison to the former, OSRAM faces an immense demand for clean and safe drinking water and expects great revenue potential. Hence, it plans to expand its water business into the second main pillar in its product portfolio and to make it another top seller. This undertaking, however, still faces various difficulties: as the O-Hubs are located close to Lake Victoria, many local people feel that they have enough water in close proximity and therefore do not understand why they should buy clean water instead.

The O-Box in combination with the O-Lamp was certainly the top seller in OSRAM's product portfolio during the first year. In the beginning, initial results had shown small maintenance issues and technical adjustments, but after minor improvements have been made, the robust water and dust resistant O-Box and O-Lamp are the perfect solution for rural use. Within the first 12 months, OSRAM had more than 1,900 O-Boxes in circulation and found that not only fishermen, but also more and more households, restaurants, shops and farms used it for illumination and as energy source for other electronic devices.

The first-year result for the O-Lantern was less successful, because OSRAM faced major technical problems concerning the quality and lifetime of the batteries. The necessary adjustments and improvements in order to fit the rough surroundings took longer so that the lantern has not long been on the market yet. Hence, it is still less known and less popular, but OSRAM expects a great demand and is confident about the lantern's future.

Future challenges and a possible roll-out plan

To summarize the first year, the social business reached its initial aim by getting to know the market and its customers properly, to build up new infrastructures and to develop adequate products suitable for BOP customers. Above that, it was able to generate a considerable social profit not only affecting its customers, but also the environment and the community.

Also, OSRAM confirmed that there is a great demand for its products and it is therefore conducting minor product improvements in order to better tackle customers' needs. If it succeeds, OSRAM aspires to constantly hit the critical capacity utilization of 80 percent and to equalize the volatility of the demand for the second year. Hence, it would be able to cover its cost and to generate first profits, resulting in compliance with the triple bottom line paradigm.

Overall, however, an objective evaluation of the project's total profit has not been conducted yet. This does not represent a major issue for the small-scaled pilot phase, but may become inevitable for any expansion using more resources and therefore becoming more meaningful within the company. Additionally, such an evaluation might add credibility and competitiveness to the social business's status within OSRAM.

After the successful trial phase, expansion would be one logical way to continue the project. Nevertheless, this would impose several difficulties upon OSRAM. Firstly, an expansion requires its own local organizational structure with its own administration, because more O-Hubs need too many resources and would become too complex to manage from OSRAM's headquarters in Germany. The profitability of such an independent venture, though, highly depends on the number of O-Hubs, in order to cover overhead costs and administration with the small revenue streams that are earned with the products. Overall, new hubs and building their own organizational structures require very high investments, e.g. about €4 million for the first five years for ten new hubs. These are assets with long pay-back periods that require more standardization of products and processes. Secondly, these assets are also urgently needed for other projects within OSRAM (especially during the financial crisis), which promise higher financial returns. However, expanding the project and building more O-Hubs would tremendously boost the project's social profit, as well as all the other positive side effects, which were already recorded during the pilot project.

Suggested questions for class discussions

1. What do you think is the predominant logic of multinational corporations (MNCs) as it relates to BOP? Is it reasonable nowadays—why yes or why not?

2. Why are social businesses gaining importance for MNCs to access the BOP? Which of these reasons apply to OSRAM?

3. What do you think are the "best practices" for managing such a project that other companies could learn from? Is there something OSRAM could improve in the future?

4. Should OSRAM continue the project? Why yes or why not? In which form?

EXHIBIT 1
OSRAM's reporting segments[20]

Lamps & Components (LC)

Accounting for 49.16 percent of the group's revenue, the LC segment comprises the product business with lamps, light engines, and ballasts. This segment therefore includes both traditional lamps and SSL-based lamps for private and professional use as well as electronic ballasts, components for LED systems, and light management systems. The products thus cover a number of application areas, such as residential, office, industrial, gastronomy, outdoor, and architectural.

Luminaires & Solutions (LS)

The LS segment comprises OSRAM's project and solutions business. The portfolio comprises luminaires for professional applications such as street lighting and architectural lighting as well as solutions for private end users. In addition, LS offers lighting solutions and associated light management systems that are used in internal and external lighting. Installation and maintenance services for the LS product portfolio are covered by the Service business. LS accounts for around 10 percent of the revenue.

Specialty Lighting (SP)

The SP segment offers light sources and systems for the automotive sector as well as special applications in the display/optic area. In the automotive sector, the spectrum ranges from interior and exterior lighting all the way to sensing. Display/optic covers the areas of projection and entertainment/architainment as well as medical and industrial applications. The products are sold via the wholesale trade and original equipment manufacturer (OEM) channels as well as directly to commercial customers. This segment accounts for around 27.5 percent of the total revenue.

Opto Semiconductors (OS)

OS offers a broad portfolio of optoelectronic semiconductors for external customers and for other OSRAM businesses. The products offered include LED components for visible light, infrared components, laser diodes, and sensors. The application spectrum extends from the automotive industry, industry electronics, general lighting, and consumer and communication electronics to medical technology, materials processing, and measurement and printing technology. OS accounts for around 19 percent of the group's revenue.

Source: Annual Review, 2013. Available at www.osram.com.

20 The reporting structure for external reporting purposes has consisted of four reportable segments since the beginning of fiscal year 2013: Lamps & Components (LC), Luminaires & Solutions (LS), Specialty Lighing (SP), and Opto Semiconductors (OS).

EXHIBIT 2
OSRAM at a glance

OSRAM Licht Group in € million, if not stated otherwise		2013
Revenue		5,288.7
Revenue growth (comparable)[1,2]	in %	
EBITA[2,3]		99.5
as % of revenue (EBITA margin)		1.9%
therein special items[2,3]		(309.9)
Transformation costs		(299.5)
Costs associated with the separation/for going public (net)		(10.4)
Legal and regulatory matters		–
EBITDA[2]		413.6
Income (loss) before income taxes		50.1
Net income (loss)		33.6
Basic earnings per share[2]	in €	0.26
Diluted earnings per share[2]	in €	0.26
Return on capital employed (ROCE)[2]		1.9%
Free cash flow[2]		284.3
		2013
Cash and cash equivalents		522.1
Total equity		2,169.3
Total assets		4,425.3
Equity ratio (total equity in % of total assets)	in %	49.0%
Net debt/net liquidity[2,4]		(172.0)
in relation to EBITDA		(0.4)
Adjusted net debt[2]		186.5
in relation to EBITDA		0.5
Employees	FTE	35,108
of which in Germany	FTE	9,727
of which outside Germany	FTE	25,381

[1] Adjusted for currency translation and portfolio effects.

[2] See the glossary.

[3] Special items of 2013: 580 bps (2012: 490bps).

[4] Net liquidity existed as of September 30, 2013 and is presented as a negative value.

Source: Annual Review, 2013. Available at www.osram.com.

EXHIBIT 3
Revenue by regions in 2013

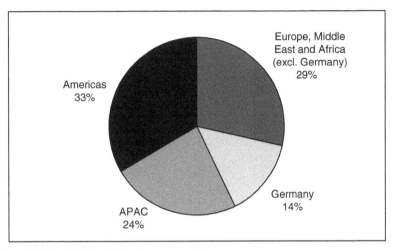

Source: Annual Review 2013. Available at www.osram.com.

EXHIBIT 4
Other successful social businesses

The idea of social businesses is relatively new and has developed since the technology boom in the 1990s. Nowadays, it has emerged as a trendy expression, which can be heard everywhere and suddenly new journals, competitions and courses at universities are addressing that issue.

The unchallenged role model of social businesses is the Grameen Bank, which lends micro credits to the poor. It already works in 37,000 out of a total of 68,000 villages in Bangladesh and its credits amount to $2 billion.[21] The founder, Muhammad Yunus, who received a Nobel Peace Prize for his work, founded further organizations, such as Grameen Cybernet, Grameen Shakti and Grameen Phone. They all started as not-for-profit organizations, but were quickly converted into social businesses not only addressing social and environmental issues but also being financially independent.[22]

A second example is BSH Bosch und Siemens Hausgeräte GmbH, a worldwide operating company for household appliances. It saw the need for safe, environmental friendly and more effective stoves in Indonesia, where many people cook with kerosene stoves that do not only produce excessive CO_2 emissions but are extremely dangerous too. Therefore, BSH founded a social business, which

21 See Yunus, 1998.
22 See Yunus, 1998.

developed a plant oil stove that is innocuous, more effective and only has a tenth of the CO_2 emissions of a high quality kerosene stove. From the very beginning, it was very innovative in order to assure sustainability and to make profits and to reinvest them into organic growth. By 2012, BSH is going to complete the standardization process and to expand its business concept to other developing countries.

A final example initiating a successful social business is Allianz Deutschland AG, one of the leading insurance companies in the world. After the Tsunami in the end of 2004, Allianz only faced small financial burdens due to destruction even though it was the century's worst natural catastrophe with incredible damage. Since Allianz is one of the largest insurance companies in the world, a huge financial loss should have actually occurred. This revealed a need for structural change, because people who needed protection most, namely the poorest of the poor, were not insured.[23] As a solution Allianz found a social business offering affordable micro insurances, which are adjusted to the locals' major risks. Thus, for example, it has life and accident insurances, costing a premium of €1.5 and paying for accidental deaths or flood damages a maximum of €380 and €75 respectively—a fortune and a lifesaving measure for people living at or below the poverty line.[24] After its fourth year, the social business counted about 3.5 million customers and expects a further future growth.[25]

EXHIBIT 5
The first three O-Hubs around Lake Victoria

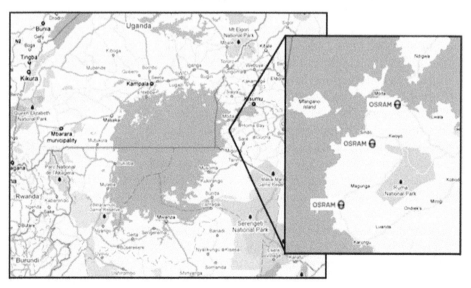

Source: Google Maps, 2010.

23 See Jarke, 2008.
24 See Jarke, 2008.
25 See Anthony, 2009.

EXHIBIT 6
Fishermen using OSRAM products for night fishing

EXHIBIT 7
The O-Hub with solar panels and water tanks

EXHIBIT 8
The O-Hub's O-Box and O-Lantern charging station

EXHIBIT 9
Initial investment for an O-Hub

Initial Investment per Hub	K€
Land, Construction and Installation (incl. Labour)	36
Power and Tech. Parts	76
Phone Charging Station/Water Treatment System	18
Lighting Products	65
DtC (Design to Cost)	–3
Total	**192**

EXHIBIT 11
O-Box and O-Lamp

Source: Mair, 2009, p. 79.

The O-Box, a 4.5 kilogram heavy metal box, contains a rechargeable battery made out of lead.[26] Together with the O-Lamp, an energy saving lamp, these two parts represent the core product of the off-grid project. The O-Lamp is dimmable and has a 6W and an 11W output level, which can spend light up to 18 hours.[27] Especially with the higher output level, the lamp gives enough light and is the perfect solution for fishermen, small restaurants, hotels and shops. In addition, two plugs on each side of the O-Box allow customers not only to use it for illumination, but also to supply other electrical devices such as fridges, mobile phones, TVs, radios or a second O-Lamp with energy. Adapted to the local customs and needs, OSRAM developed the O-Box to be water and dust resistant, as well as easy to use. Thus, it is now perfectly suitable for night fishing and working in other rough conditions, and fishermen as well as housewives quickly understand how to handle it.

Every O-Hub has an inventory of about 1,000 O-Boxes, which cost about €80 and need about three hours to be recharged.[28] The safety deposit for leasing this combination is 1,000 KES and customers have the possibility of financing this amount via a micro credit. Exchanging an empty storage battery with a full storage battery costs 75 KES resulting in an average price per hour of 4.2 KES for a dimmed light and 7.5 KES for the full light.[29]

26 See Dewald, 2009.
27 See Mair, 2009.
28 See Mair, 2009 and Rybak, 2008.
29 See Mair, 2009.

EXHIBIT 12
The O-Lantern

Source: Mair, 2009, p. 80.

The O-Lantern is the second illumination product in OSRAM's product portfolio. Instead of being plugged into the O-Box, the O-Lantern has an integrated recharge-able battery. Thus, the lantern can be brought back to the O-Hub and can be replaced by a charged one if the battery is empty. In comparison to the O-Lamp, the O-Lantern is rather intended for small households and small shops. With a 7W compact fluorescent lamp, the O-Lantern shines for about eight hours and with a low energy LED light source it works considerably longer still giving enough light to read a book.[30]

The safety deposit for the O-Lantern amounts to 500 KES and here again, people have the opportunity to finance this amount with a micro credit. For exchanging an empty lantern with a charged one, customers have to pay 50 KES, resulting in an average lighting price of 6.25 KES per hour.[31]

30 See Gregor, 2008.
31 See Mair, 2009.

EXHIBIT 13
The mobile phone charging station

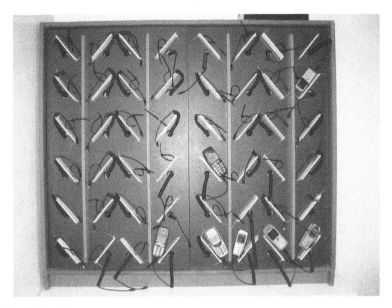

Source: Mair, 2009, p. 84.

At the moment, mobile phones are the latest trend in Africa because they are the only medium that is able to connect rural villages having no ground line. Thus, they recorded a double digit growth rate in Kenya and other African countries in the last few years helping the local economy to grow.[32]

When Nokia, the market leader with a 70 percent market share in the mobile phones sector in Kenya, heard about OSRAM's social business, it approached the company and proposed a deal. As it does not sell its products in Kenya itself, but through independent distributors, Nokia has no possibility to establish own infrastructures or to get to know the market at all. To improve its situation and to understand its customers and their needs, Nokia suggested establishing an "Official Nokia Recharge Station" in the O-Hub. As a consequence, it pays a share of the marketing expenses for the O-Hub on one hand, while it receives information about the Kenyan market and OSRAM's experience on the other hand.

The idea for the charging station is that people bring their empty mobile phones to the O-Hub and get it recharged for 15 KES. Concurrently, the hub can charge 48 mobile phones.[33] The alternative for local people possessing a mobile phone and having no access to the electricity grid is going to other mobile phone charging stations that use small diesel generators. This, however, is more expensive and of lower quality.

32 See Gregor, 2008.
33 See Mair, 2009.

EXHIBIT 14
Purified water

In 2009, about 2.4 billion people, 50 percent of the world population, did not have reasonable sanitation and out of them, about 1.1 billion used unimproved water sources. This number is forecasted to rise to 2.3 billion by 2015, Africa accounting for a third. Unclean water is the reason for many child deaths and therefore the reduction of the number of people suffering from the effects is one of the Millennium Development Goals.[34]

OSRAM identified the short supply of safe drinking water in Kenya very quickly and found that this was a further challenge it could easily address with its solar technology. It therefore developed a water purification station that produces 3,000 liters of clean and safe drinking water per day.[35] Sterilized by OSRAM Puritec UVC lamps instead of chemicals, the water keeps its usual taste and does not adapt a chemical flavor.

The rain water from the panels and the roof is collected in three tanks with a capacity of 6,000 liters per tank. OSRAM filters the water in several steps in order to eliminate the viruses and bacteria. The received drinking water is then stored in another tank being illuminated by a UVC-lamp so that the growth of microorganisms is prevented and clean water can be pumped into the sales room, where it is sold for 2 KES per liter.[36]

34 See UN, 2000.
35 See Gregor, 2008.
36 See Mair, 2009.

EXHIBIT 15
Local workers constructing the O-Hub under guidance of OSRAM experts

EXHIBIT 16
OSRAM's financial calculation per O-Hub for the first five years

One Hub view in K € Year	1	2	3	4	5
Initial Investment	192	0	0	0	0
Sales	119	174	191	206	219
Profit/EBIT (hub)	−11%	9%	14%	15%	19%

EXHIBIT 17
Average capacity utilization for the lighting devices

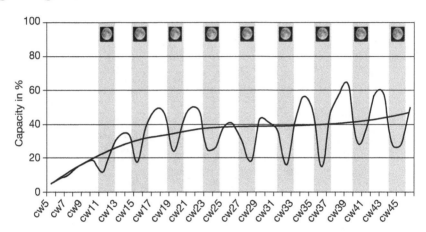

Bibliography apart from personal interviews

Anthony, M. (2008) Speech at Utopia Konferenz 2008. Available at: http://www.utopia.de/magazin/lauschmittel-die-sprecher-der-utopia-konferenz-zum-nachhoeren-michael-anthony (accessed June 17, 2010).

Dewald, U. (2009) "Licht für Afrika". *Bild der Wissenschaft*, 2: 96-104.

Google Maps (2010) Available at www.maps.google.de (accessed September 22, 2010).

Gregor, W. (2008) "Seeing the Light". *The Environmentalist*, 69: 14-15.

Iken, J. (2009) "Little Noticed Markets are Developing". *Sun & Wind Energy*, 6: 80-84.

Jarke, P. (2008) "Schutz gegen Armut". *WirtschaftsWoche*, 2: 67-69.

Mair, G. (2009) "Sustainable Development Through Efficient Energy Use: Impact Assessment of the OSRAM Off-Grid Project in Kenya". Master Thesis. University of Natural Resources and Applied Life Sciences, Vienna.

OSRAM (2010) Available at: www.osram.de (accessed September 15, 2010)

Prahalad, C.K. and S.L. Hart (2002) "The Fortune of the Bottom of the Pyramid". *Strategy and Business*, 26(1): 1-14.

Rybak, A. (2008) "Osram—Kundenfang in Afrika. *Financial Times Deutschland*, January 5.

Siemens (2010) Available at: www.siemens.de (accessed September 15, 2010).

UN (2000) United Nations Millennium Declaration. Available at: http://www.un.org/millenniumgoals/ (accessed June 23, 2010).

Yunus, M. (1998) "Poverty Alleviation: Is Economics Any Help? Lessons From the Grameen Bank Experience". *Journal of International Affairs*, 52.1: 47-65.

Zeug, K. (2009) "Kein Licht für Afrika". *Die Zeit*, January 8.

CASE 10

Vodafone M-PESA (A)

"Unusual innovation"—from a corporate social responsibility project to business model innovation[1]

Loïc Sadoulet and Olivier Furdelle

> **One billion consumers in the world have a mobile phone but no access to a bank account.**[2]

"Nick, how did giant multinational Vodafone manage to come up with the most successful mobile money service ... and in Kenya!"

1   This case is intended to be used as a basis for class discussion rather than to illustrate either effective or ineffective handling of an administrative situation. 05/2014-5693

Additional material about INSEAD case studies (e.g. videos, spreadsheets, links) can be accessed at cases.insead. edu. Copyright © 2014 INSEAD.

2   Gavin Krugel, Director of Mobile Banking Strategy at GSM Association, February 2010.

INSEAD

The Business School for the World®

"12.6 million users? More transactions daily in Kenya than Western Union worldwide??"

"What's the impact on the Kenyan economy?"

"And why don't *we* have this in Germany?"

Chuckles resounded in the Warburg Haus library during the annual INSEAD–Harvard Africa Club meeting in September 2010 in Hamburg. The audience was riveted by the presentation that Nick Hughes had just given and the question-and-answer session

Nick Hughes, a former Vodafone executive and now a founding partner of Signal Point, had been until recently the Head of Global Payments at Vodafone, where he started M-PESA, the pioneering mobile money service rolled out in 2007 by Vodafone in partnership with its Safaricom subsidiary in Kenya. Nick had initiated the M-PESA concept in 2004 and by September 2010, M-PESA had attracted an unprecedented 12.6 million registered users, tens of millions of transactions per month, and over 30 billion Kenyan shillings of transfers per month (US$375 million; about 15% of Kenya's monthly GDP).[3] M-PESA has revolutionised payment systems in Kenya (and soon, hopefully, worldwide).

M-PESA—"M" for mobile, "Pesa" for cash in Swahili—is a simple service that allows registered users to transfer money from their mobile phone to another mobile phone user. Users do not need to have a bank account; they simply register with Safaricom for an M-PESA account, bring cash to one of the 28,000 authorised M-PESA agents (typically small shopkeepers who sell cell phone top-up cards among other things) who will credit the M-PESA account with the amount of cash received. The user can then use their phone to transfer any part of the balance at any time to another person simply by entering the desired recipient's phone number, the amount to be sent, and a PIN code for security reasons (like on bank cards). An application on the user's SIM card instantaneously transfers the balance from the sender's M-PESA account to the recipient's M-PESA account.[4,5] The user

---

3 By April 2011 (the latest figures available at the time of writing), the numbers had grown to 14 million users, 29,000 agents, and US$570 million monthly money transfer volumes. M-PESA revenues increased by 46% year-on-year to reach US$135 million in fiscal year 2011. M-PESA accounts for 12% of Safaricom's total revenues, making it the largest non-revenue stream (twice that of SMS and 50% more than all other data service revenues). (Safaricom FY11 Annual report, April 2011) See Exhibit 7 in the Appendix. For the latest figures, see Safaricom's website: http://www.safaricom.co.ke/.

4 If the recipient is not a registered M-PESA user, a temporary account is created.

5 The first version of M-PESA had a program lodged on the user's SIM card in their telephone (a STK–SIM Tool Kit-based system), requiring users to exchange their SIM for a new one. The newer version of M-PESA works on USSD (Unstructured Supplemental Service Data), a two-way real-time information exchange system between the telephone and the server, thus allowing the service to operate with a program on the user's phone: users type in information on their phone, but the program is hosted on Safaricom's servers.

and the recipient receive an SMS confirming the transaction. Typical uses include peer-to-peer transfers (to pay for services, reimburse debts, or send money home, for instance), paying bills with partner companies, buying Safaricom air time, or simply storing money rather than carrying cash.

Vodafone's success was the result of a project with a clearly defined objective—contributing to making a positive impact on society—which has been relentlessly pursued since 2004. While M-PESA is not the first mobile money service launched in the world, it is the most successful (so far).

Why was M-PESA so successful in Kenya? What were the most crucial internal and external factors that came into play? In what other countries could similar mobile payment services be launched to replicate the Kenyan success on a broader international scale? What other compelling products or services might operators consider launching as extensions to a mobile payment service? Are there interesting lessons from Vodafone's experience with the development of M-PESA that could help other (non-telecom) companies in their "unusual innovation" strategies?

It was going to be an interesting evening.

Background

In 2000, the United Nations' Millennium Development Goals (MDGs), endorsed by 192 nations at the Millennium Summit, pledged to reduce poverty by 50% by 2015. As part of this ambitious objective, information and communication technologies (ICT) were designated an important lever to improve social and economic conditions in the world's poorest countries:

> In cooperation with the private sector, [we should] make available the benefits of new technologies—especially information and communications technologies.[6]

In the ICT industry, mainstream opinion at that time was best captured by the likes of Bill Gates, when he said in early 2001, "What good is a cell phone to someone who is starving or dying from a disease?"[7] Most industry players were still struggling simply to define a role they could or should play in such a context.

In 2001, when establishing its Corporate Responsibility (CR) team, Vodafone recruited Nick Hughes to help the company work out a potential role and action plan in addressing issues such as the MDGs. Vodafone's objective was to position its CR efforts outside the scope of traditional charities or foundations, and identify ways to support its business while generating a positive social impact.

---

6 United Nations Millennium Development Goals, goal 8, target 18.
7 World Economic Forum, January 2001.

Socio-economic impact studies

In this context, Vodafone CR conducted research on the socio-economic impact of mobile (SIM) in 2004, aiming to provide a systematic analysis of the impact of mobile phones in key areas such as economic empowerment and social interaction. The objective was to help policy-makers provide a regulatory environment that would stimulate growth and economic development.[8]

Other studies conducted at the same time highlighted that while mobile phones in developing countries were playing the same role that fixed telephony played in developed countries in the 1970s and 1980s, the growth impact of mobiles was about twice as large in developing countries: a 1% rise in mobile penetration yielded GDP growth of 0.6%.[9] Another study[10] found that mobile phone penetration was positively correlated to foreign direct investment (FDI): the same 1% increase in mobile penetration led to a 0.5% increase in FDI.

Vodafone's own research findings confirmed the impact of mobile phone usage on economic development in African countries. Their final report[11] concluded:

> Differences in the penetration and diffusion of mobile telephony certainly appear to explain some of the differences in growth rates between developing countries. If gaps in mobile telecoms penetration between countries persist, then our results suggest that this gap will feed into a significant difference in their growth rates in the future.

New uses for the mobile

Importantly, the research also highlighted that people wanted to use their mobile phones in many other ways than simply making calls or texting (see Exhibit 1 below). The early views of Nick Hughes and the CR team that they "could do a lot more" and turn corporate responsibility issues into real business opportunities were confirmed.

---

8 http://www.vodafone.com/start/responsibility/access_to_communications/emerging_markets/sim_research.html.

9 The Impact of Telecoms on Economic Growth in Developing Countries, Waverman, Meschi, Fuss, 2005.

10 Mobile Networks and Foreign Direct Investment in Developing Countries, Williams, 2005.

11 Africa: The Impact of Mobile Phones, March 2005.

EXHIBIT 1
Vodafone findings on "Socio-Economic Impact of Mobile"[12]

Areas of possible engagement	
• Finance • M-banking • M-payments	• Civic engagement • Monitor elections • Electoral registration
• Education • M-school—info to students/parents • School registration facilities	• Entrepreneurship • Job search • Mobile "yellow pages" • Market prices
• Health • Permanent link between remote locations and hospitals • Vaccination / awareness campaigns via SMS • Remote monitoring for chronic diseases (HIV, TB, Malaria, etc.) • Medicine-taking reminders	• Security • Social alarms • Disaster relief

Hughes believed that Vodafone could play a substantial role in tackling these development challenges. In particular, given that a telecom operator could adapt mobile technology to deliver financial services quickly, securely and cheaply, Vodafone could provide a more effective way to deliver funds (e.g. from donors and microfinance institutions) to the targeted recipients. A mobile network provider could enable efficient financial services even in areas with poor infrastructure and low banking penetration. He indicated to his team that the mobile finance area was a "low hanging fruit" opportunity that should quickly be captured.

From ideation to pilot case selection

The initial concept was to design a simple mobile service to improve access to microfinance for an unbanked population. The platform would allow borrowers to receive and repay loans remotely by using their mobile phones and the operator's extensive network of airtime resellers. All transactions between the microfinance institution (MFI) and their clients would be done electronically through simple encrypted SMS texting for authentication, authorisation and transfer, and translated into physical money transactions (cash deposit or withdrawal) using familiar airtime resellers. Integration into the MFI's management information system

12 Provided by Joaquim Croca, Vodafone, May 2009.

would thereby relieve it of the need to dispatch loan officers to distribute and collect loans, record the transactions in a ledger, and ultimately enter the content of the ledger in an electronic database, thereby increasing the loan officers' ability to serve a larger client base.[13]

Hughes' initial concept was to design a simple mobile service to support local microfinance transactions and make MFIs more efficient. The platform would allow customers to both receive and re-pay microfinance loans using their mobile handset. The value proposition to MFIs would lie in the process automation of their (paper-based) operations, hence increasing their efficiency and ability to "circulate" funds to a largely unbanked customer base.

Search for initial funding

Hughes began to look for internal support from key stakeholders in Vodafone to finance his project, but the business was entirely focused on the imminent launch of 3G. Although a couple of the senior executives in Vodafone at the time saw the potential, he struggled to raise funding. Three factors were behind the lack of initial backing for this concept:

1. Core business focus: while already present in some emerging markets, in 2002–2003 Vodafone was a fast-growing company (resulting from the 2000 mega-merger of Vodafone AirTouch and Mannesmann in Germany) with a prime focus on Europe and the USA, where high market growth was still being captured.

2. Benchmark: other mobile money experiences to date were limited, such as Globe Telecom's (2004) G-Cash, and Smart's (2003) Smart Money in the Philippines, Paybox's (2001) cash transfer system in Austria, and Celpay's (2001) payment solution in Zambia. But the results were not (yet) convincing.[14] Indeed Vodafone's previous foray into payment systems with other European multinationals had been unsuccessful (a project called Simpay was never brought to market despite large cross-operator teams being set up and operational for over a year).

---

13 Typically, loan agents go to local markets on a weekly basis, to visit borrowers and collect loan repayments. Part of the visit is spent talking to the clients to better assess the business conditions and needs and build a bond of trust between the bank and its clients, but a disproportionate of time is spent on purely transactional purposes. Alternative systems have borrowers travelling to their local MFI office to repay their loan instalments. Either way, the opportunity costs are significant. (Source: author's experience with loan officers in Guatemala).

14 For background information about mobile money experiences, please see the GSMA's project on Mobile Money for the Unbanked (MMU) (www.gsmworld.com).

3. Economics: traditional margins (mainly on voice calls and SMS texting) were high, above 38%,[15] creating a significant hurdle for new product introductions, which would pale in comparison.

But the main issue at Vodafone was "overcoming the internal fight for capital expenditure"[16]—as it was in the vast majority of (listed) companies where the view prevailed that private capital should be used to deliver maximum short-term returns to shareholders, rather than to fund "non-core" longer-term products that achieved sustainability benefits.

Based on this, Hughes decided on an alternative route for getting his project funded. He recalled a discussion he had at the World Summit for Sustainable Development in 2003, where he had been approached by a representative of the UK Government with the concept of a "Challenge Fund" set up by the Department for International Development (DFID). This proposed a new approach for funding sustainability innovations: instead of relying on its internal R&D resources, what if a private company could access public funds to overcome the internal competition for capital expenditure?

In 2000, the DFID had set up a £18.5 million Financial Deepening Challenger Fund (FDCF) built upon the recognition that the private sector could make a major contribution to poverty reduction and development. The Fund provided grants of £50,000 to £1 million, on a risk-sharing basis with private sector companies, to projects that met clearly defined criteria, reflecting the DFID's priority to improve access to financial services.

The hope was that such a fund would not only meet the DIFD's objectives, but also change the behaviour of private companies—both those who received support as well as others wanting to replicate the success observed. Grant recipient companies had to be willing to at least match the money, and, more importantly, engage in projects that would otherwise not have been pursued, and demonstrate their potential to be commercially sustainable after the support ended, thus providing more solid financial support to the poor.[17]

Hughes submitted a proposal in mid-2003 to the DFID which was approved and awarded £910,000, conditional on Vodafone finding the remaining 50%. He returned to his Chief Marketing Officer who agreed to support the project on the grounds that the funding requirements were lower, and that the matched funding could take the form of people and time as well as capital.

---

15 Vodafone Group mobile EBITDA margin for the year ending in March 2003.
16 Source: authors' conversation with Joaquim Croca, Vodafone's global Head of Corporate Responsibility Performance & Reporting, May 2009.
17 Source: DFID website.

Selection of the test market

The overlap between FDCF's regional focus and Vodafone's own commercial activities suggested Kenya and Tanzania would be Vodafone's prime candidates. The support of Safaricom CEO, Michael Joseph, was a key factor in the choice. Joseph had been hired as an independent consultant with four other expatriates from Vodafone in 2000 to set up Vodafone's operations in Kenya with the incumbent state-owned telecom operator, Telkom Kenya. It was not an easy job: Telkom was inefficient and corrupt—and owned 60% of Safaricom. Moreover, a new operator, Kencell, had entered the market with a newly built top-class network.[18]

Michael Joseph had spent the previous three years (1997–2000) in Hungary launching the country's third operator, Vodafone Hungary, but as he acknowledged, "We did not make the right decisions because our strategy [as a third operator] was to copy our competition."[19] Adopting the same strategy in Kenya would have meant following Kencell and drawing blood in shark-infested waters fighting for big corporate customers and heavy phone users where Kencell had already fished the pool of dissatisfied Safaricom customers.

He therefore focused on building a differentiated service. Inspired by MTN's innovations in South Africa,[20] Safaricom launched four radical simultaneous moves: it commercialised an armada of inexpensive phones; it launched a series of pre-paid phone cards in various affordable denominations; it moved to per-second billing (the norm was per-minute billing, with a fixed three-minute minimum charge); and it launched Sambaza, a service that allowed family and friends to share phone credit through text messages. By 2005, Safaricom had a 60% market share and three million customers. It was highly successful in building a strong Kenyan brand.

Another key criterion behind the choice was Kenya's favourable local regulatory environment; the government was "agnostic" about mobile money and open to the idea of a trial.

Initial pilot design and lessons

About the same time as the trial commenced in Kenya, another subsidiary in the Vodafone group, Vodafone Egypt, had started a mobile money experiment with HSBC bank in Cairo. A service called Vodafone Cash was launched in 2004, designed to allow money transfers between HSBC customers. Despite approval from the Egyptian regulator, the service quickly failed because of its limitations: being a "mono-bank" it lacked sufficient customer appeal, and the unbanked population was simply left out of the equation.

---

18 Source: "He built a Sh250bn empire from scratch," *Daily Nation*, August 13, 2010.
19 Michael Joseph, quoted in *Daily Nation*, August 13, 2010.
20 MTN, the second largest South African mobile operator behind Vodacom, increased its market share by aggressively targeting poor workers by selling cheap phones and low-denomination pre-paid top-up cards.

The M-PESA team took a different approach. They focused on organisations that were currently providing access to finance—the microfinance sector—and seeing how technology might help them reach deeper and more efficiently. Although MFIs provided access to finance to people who were typically unbanked, the transactions cost involved were high: visits to disburse loans, visits to collect loan instalments, the security of carrying large amounts of cash, and paper ledger entries that then needed to be entered into the digital management information system of the lending organisation. By designing a system by which transfers could be made by mobile phones and where local Safaricom airtime resellers could be used as local cash-access points, loan officers could focus on improving their outreach and better servicing their client base.

A partnership thus formed between Safaricom, microfinance organisation Faulu Kenya, and a technology consulting firm Sagentia, with Nick Hughes and his team as the overall coordinator of the project. Hughes kept the executive team at Vodafone informed and engaged, and dispatched a mobile commerce expert, Susie Lonie, to Kenya to lead and coordinate all the local aspects and the collaboration with Safaricom and Sagentia.

A key decision in the design was to leverage the existing Safaricom distribution network of airtime resellers, from which customers already bought prepaid airtime credit, as "windows" where clients could go to deposit or withdraw cash from their electronic accounts. The resellers were entrepreneurs or independent companies, who usually sold other telecom (e.g. mobile handset) as well as non-telecom goods (small drugstores, for example). Safaricom had several hundred of these resellers, with outlets spread across the country (although there was less coverage in rural areas), some of whom would be hired and trained to become agents for the pilot programme.

Agents were the kingpins in the mobile money system. Incentivising agents appropriately, keeping them liquid, and deterring fraud was a major concern for mobile money operators. While M-PESA users did not particularly trust the M-PESA agents, their trust in Safaricom and in the system sufficed to reassure users that confirmations received by SMS were a reliable check on fraud. However, for the system to work, agents had to retain a sufficient cash float in their stores to provide a reliable supply of available cash for customers coming to withdraw, and a sufficient amount of cash in their M-PESA bank account to have enough M-PESA e-float on hand to credit clients' accounts. The cost of maintaining liquidity was reported to be the number one cost for agents.[21]

The pilot[22] finally started in October 2005 in three selected locations (Nairobi city centre, Mathare, a nearby slum, and Thika, a market town 80 km from the capital); 500 customers were enrolled (each was given a free phone) and eight agents were trained to perform their tasks. Safaricom opened a dedicated customer service line

---

21 For more detail about the issues of agents, please refer to the Appendix.

22 For a detailed account of the trial, please refer to the article "M-PESA: Mobile Money for the Unbanked", Nick Hughes and Susie Lonie, *Innovations*, 2007.

for the pilot project and its Finance Department managed the cash flows of the M-PESA accounts.

Teething troubles

The very early tests were done with Safaricom staff. Early "pain points" were identified and (wherever possible) mitigated, via customer training in using the handset interface and agent support, as well as via additional support to Faulu processes, transactions backlog and reconciliation.

Interestingly, the usage of M-PESA services was not confined to loan repayments. People could use some of the M-PESA float received from the MFI to purchase Safaricom credit which they sent to relatives. Many of the pilot customers did business with each other (being in the same MFI credit group) and started using the system to pay each other. Others travelling between pilot areas would load their M-PESA account in one area and withdraw it when they arrived in the other. Some deposited cash in their M-PESA accounts overnight to avoid holding the cash. The analysis of transaction patterns thus supported the extension of the concept from simply a microfinance disbursement and loan reimbursement tool, to a payment and low-cost remittance service in Kenya (where domestic remittances are often sent from urban to rural locations), which was more attractive than other riskier or more expensive alternatives (e.g. transporting cash or giving cash to someone travelling[23]).[24]

By October 2006, at the end of the trial, Safaricom and Vodafone were satisfied with the results:

1. The service worked well and had proved compelling to end-users and agents.

2. The business model looked viable (fees were being paid by the sending consumer, commissions were being paid to the agent, and there as additional airtime and customer retention for the mobile operator).

3. The economic inclusion and social objectives seemed to be served (e.g. remittances between urban and rural family members, trading between businesses, greater security of travelling "cashless")

However, for Faulu Kenya, the microfinance institution, the ability of borrowers to repay their loans from anywhere weakened attendance at weekly group meetings, which led to some unease about the long-term impact of M-PESA on the

---

23 Erik Bekker, formerly of the International Finance Corporation's Nairobi office, estimates the cost of business transfers to be close to 50% of the remittances. Western Union had 590 agencies, a 2% fee with a minimum fee of KSh 100 (about $1.5, but at a GDP per capita of around $850 per capita. In comparison, the fee for M-PESA is 30 KSh for transfers up to 35,000 KSh (see Exhibit 6 in Appendix).

24 It should be noted that there were no inter-bank transfers in Kenya and that the largest bank of Kenya, Equity Bank, only had 300 branches country-wide.

cohesion of the credit groups and the detection of potential risks. Furthermore, further process and technology integration would be necessary between M-PESA and Faulu for the system to work seamlessly.

However, Faulu's involvement in the pilot phase had been critical. Mobile payment systems are network economies, requiring a critical mass of users for the system to be useful. The loan repayment service had enough participants for the community of these participants to find other uses for M-PESA amongst themselves, not just for transactions with Faulu. The entry value proposition was easy loan repayment; the extended usefulness of M-PESA was discovered through the network effect.

Revamp of the consumer proposition

To lighten the process, the mobile money team decided to remove the micro-loan repayment functionality and simplify the service offering for the full commercial launch. Customers would be able to deposit or withdraw cash at M-PESA agent outlets, transfer money person-to-person, and send prepaid airtime remotely. This revised consumer proposition translated into a simple and efficient communication campaign, "Send Money Home",[25] which purposely came without reference to a "banking" service (see Exhibit 2).

25 The TV campaign commercial can be viewed at: http://www.youtube.com/watch?v=nEZ30K5dBWU.

EXHIBIT 2
Safaricom's print advertisement of the "Send Money Home" campaign

As Nick Hughes recalled at a 2008 industry roundtable:[26] "We never positioned this as mobile banking. We said: 'Do you send money home, or do you want to send money between A and B very quickly? Then M-PESA is the answer.'" With such a message, M-PESA was on its way to address the target market of 80% of Kenyan adults who lacked a bank account to make easy transfer but did own a mobile phone.

For the full-scale roll-out, agents attended a one-day workshop and incentives were built in so that agents would get customers to sign up and use the system. In order to keep the focus and momentum, the dedicated M-PESA team at Safaricom got additional staffing for the ramp-up to the full-scale launch.

---

26 CGAP, December 2008. The video can be watched with the following link: http://technology.cgap.org/2008/12/18/watch-the-video-mobile-banking-for-poor-people-pioneer-perspectives/.

Getting the regulatory green-light

In the absence of pre-existing regulations on mobile financial services, Vodafone and Safaricom took a proactive stance in addressing the potential risks and issues for the Kenyan regulator. Although M-PESA involved accepting repayable funds from the public, Safaricom structured the product in such a way that it fell outside the definition of "banking business". Specifically, the proceeds from issuing "e-money" were held by M-PESA Trust Company Limited in trust for the customers in a pooled account with the Commercial Bank of Africa.

It had the following features:[27]

- No interest paid to customers—no borrower/lender relationship.

- Funds were moved according to instructions received via the M-PESA service.

- No use of float funds by Vodafone or Safaricom—funds were held in a deposit account for customers, with no lending or investment of funds, not used for any other business.

- Funds were fully redeemable upon request.

In addition, caps on the maximum account balance (about US$750) and maximum transaction size (about US$530) provided the Commercial Bank of Africa with additional comfort because they limited the risk of money-laundering and the amount any individual customer could lose in case of the mobile operator's insolvency.

These preventive measures, alongside the platform's inherent security (e.g. PINs, data protection through encrypted SMS) and compliance with the applicable "Know Your Customer" requirements (e.g. customer ID number registered at account opening), ensured the Kenyan regulator would adopt a flexible and pragmatic approach when it came to launching M-PESA.

From full launch to country-wide success

Safaricom launched M-PESA in full in March 2007. The consumer appeal was quickly confirmed on a wide scale, and its commercial success overtook Safaricom's business plan. In just 4 years, close to 14 million customers were registered by M-PESA, while 29,000 agents were servicing the product across Kenya.

---

27 M-PESA: Regulating Transformational Branchless Banking, Vodafone, March 2008.

EXHIBIT 3
M-PESA Kenya customer and agent adoption[28]

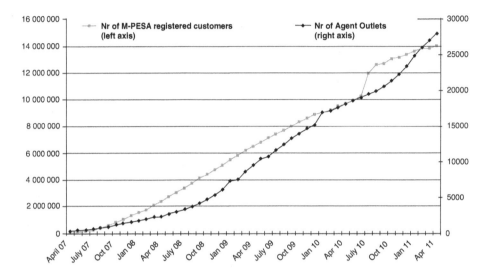

Despite a lack of either cash or e-float from time to time with some agents,[29] the ease of use ("anytime anywhere" with no need to travel),[30] speed (almost instantaneous), safety (no carrying of cash) and cost-efficiency of M-PESA were overwhelmingly endorsed by its customers.

In this respect it is worth noting that, after the Kenyan elections in 2008, the new acting Minister of Finance, John Michuki, ordered an audit of the service and warned that M-PESA could be a disaster waiting to happen,[31] stating: "I am not sure M-PESA will end well." A public outcry ensued and the audit, carried out by the Central Bank of Kenya, concluded that M-PESA was a secure service that had proved valuable to thousands who had been locked out of the formal banking system. The unpopular Minister was thereafter relieved of his duties.

28 Safaricom data, April 2011.
29 See Appendix on M-PESA Impacts and Learnings.
30 Mark Pickens (CGAP) and Frederik Eijkman (PEP Intermedius) estimated that M-PESA was saving Kenyans over US$4 million per week in travel expenses (CGAP document: "Building viable agent networks: Driving to scale with mobile money", Feb 2009.)
31 "Unmasking the storm behind M-PESA", *East African Standard*, December 30. 2008.

Financial success

The overall value of the transfers made on M-PESA on a monthly basis steadily increased over time, reaching the equivalent of $570 million at the end of Safaricom's 2011 fiscal year (which ended in March 2011).[32]

The average monthly value of transfers made per registered customer fluctuated more over time: after decreasing until early 2008, it steadily increased to reach $35–$40 by March 2009 (Exhibit 4).

EXHIBIT 4
M-PESA Kenya value of transactions[33]

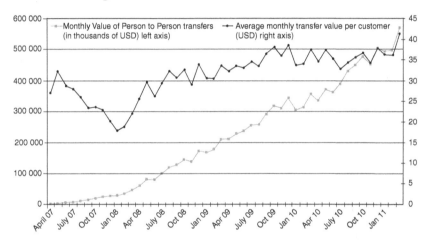

With this high volume of transactions, M-PESA reportedly broke even after only 14 months and became profitable from the transaction fees. In addition, and even more importantly, M-PESA contributed to a reduction in churn of Safaricom's customer base. Safaricom remained the undisputed mobile telecom leader in Kenya with more than 80% market share, despite the presence of two other mobile operators, including Zain, which launched its own "Zap" mobile money service in February 2009, 30% cheaper and using its "One Network" its borderless mobile service offering free of roaming charges to offer international transfers between the countries it operates in,[34] and Orange rolling out Orange Money in November 2010.

32 Full Year 2011 Results Presentation and Press Release Commentary March 2011 in the Investor Relations section of Safaricom's website.
33 Safaricom data and INSEAD analysis (based on KSh/EUR = 0,0096), September 2010.
34 Bharti Airtel bought Zain's African operations in 2011 and rebranded Zap as Airtel Money in April 2011.

These results underlined the exceptional success of this innovative service for Safaricom and Vodafone. They also attracted telecom peer recognition: Safaricom and Vodafone received the GSM Association's "Best Mobile Money Service" in 2009 for M-PESA and 2010 for M-PESA's extension to bulk payments and utility bill payments, and the "Best Mobile Money for the Unbanked Service" in 2011 (with Roshan, Vodacom, and Vodafone Essar for M-PESA's extension to Afghanistan, South Africa, Fiji, Qatar and India).[35]

Yet mobile money was still in its infancy. Despite mobile operators introducing clones of M-PESA, few of them went beyond payment. In October 2009, the M-PESA International Money Transfer service between the UK and Kenya was launched in partnership with KenTV, Western Union and Provident Capital Transfers at a very competitive price (£4–£7 compared to the average £10 cost of a bank transfer) allowing for frequent transfer of smaller amounts. In March 2010, Safaricom partnered with Equity Bank to offer an interest-bearing savings account accessible directly by mobile phone: users could transfer money instantly to an M-KESHO account via mobile phone from anywhere. Safaricom also partnered with the Syngenta Foundation for Sustainable Agriculture and UAP Insurance to provide point-of-sale micro crop-insurance for Kenyan farmers based on local rainfall levels and M-PESA payment systems (Kilimo Salama). And Safaricom introduced bulk payment systems, allowing companies to pay their employees by M-PESA, and bill paying services (for utility bills, school fees, etc.).

How many other spaces could be revolutionised by mobile phones? Could location-based individualised services foster socio-economic development on a more inclusive basis?

"This is the reason I left Vodafone," explained Nick Hughes as the last group reluctantly ended the conversation in the hotel bar much (much!) later that evening. "I want to find the next M-PESA".

Appendix: M-PESA impacts and learnings

Customers' perspective

Research[36] conducted by CGAP in two communities in Kenya shows that M-PESA users fall into two categories: urban senders, who are usually men, and rural recipients, who are mostly women. Their transactions are generally either small, regular

---

35 Interestingly, Zain's Zap service received in turn the "Best Mobile Money for the Unbanked Service" award in February 2010, and Airtel Africa (who bought Zain's Africa operations in 2010) received the "Best Mobile Money Product or Solution" award in 2011 for the Airtel Card which is a single-use debit card number backed by Airtel Money accounts, allowing Airtel Money customers to conduct on-line shopping on any website that accepts MasterCard.

36 *Poor People Using Mobile Financial Services: Observations on Customer Usage and Impact from M-PESA*, Olga Morawczynski and Mark Pickens; CGAP, August 2009.

transfers that act as income support for rural users, or lump sum transfers which are often used to pay school fees.

Transactions are deemed 27% cheaper than remittance services offered by the postal network, and 68% cheaper than sending money by bus companies.

Rural users declare increases of 5% to 30% in their income thanks to transfers received via M-PESA. By making smaller, more frequent transfers, urban workers on average send more money home than they did before. This represents a significant boost for rural beneficiaries, for whom remittances can account for up to 70% of household income.

In addition, more than 20% of M-PESA customers in urban areas store small amounts of money in their "mobile wallets", a use that goes beyond the original positioning for remittances. Frequent users make on average 15 small deposits to their M-PESA accounts each month. Some of these savings are used to invest in their (rural) homes, while others move the money to their bank accounts to earn interest. This latter finding may come as a surprise. Contrary to common expectation it turns out[37] that 70% of M-PESA customers have a bank account (sometimes several). This echoes a study[38] by CGAP that estimates that less than 10% of current mobile money users in the world are low-income and unbanked.

Urban users are sometimes frustrated by failed transactions,[39] which are often the result of network congestion. Because it is often difficult to get through to Safaricom's busy customer call centre, a failed transaction may require the user to go to an agent to seek support.

As M-PESA becomes critical for conducting daily business without outage, users are enticed into using a second service (e.g. competitor's Airtel Money). While non-M-PESA users can be recipients of transfers (and withdraw transferred cash at M-PESA agents), different operator services are not yet interoperable, i.e. an M-PESA user cannot send money to an Orange Money or Airtel Money user (or vice-versa).[40]

Money transfers typically flow from urban centres to rural areas. Rural users complain that agents sometimes lack cash on hand. M-PESA customers whose agents cannot meet their withdrawal requests are often forced to travel to cities to get their money. Overall, 20% of users report at least once not being able to withdraw money from an agent when they wanted to,[41] and 69% of these instances were due to the agent having insufficient cash on hand (cf. 12% due to technical problems in

---

37 FSD Kenya, 2009.
38 Ivatury and Mas, CGAP, 2008.
39 Safaricom data and INSEAD analysis (based on KSh/EUR = 0,0096), March 2010.
40 An article by Ovum cites that the lack of interoperability among different operators' offer and Safaricom's 80% market share (and therefore Safaricom's lack of incentive to participate in an interoperability agreement) is the primary reason why the other operators have found it difficult to replicate M-PESA's success in Kenya ("StraightTalk Opinion: Other operators find M-Pesa's success hard to replicate," by Angel Dobardziev, *Ovum*, 7 June 2011)
41 "Mobile Money: The Economics of M-PESA", William Jack and Tavneet Suri, October 2009.

the agent system or Safaricom mobile network). Nevertheless, when asked "What would be the effect of losing M-PESA?", 84% of users said it would have a "large negative impact" on their lives.

One unexpected outcome[42] is that some men working in cities have cut back on the number of visits to their rural homes—visits they made frequently before M-PESA was available to deliver funds to their wives and relatives—as they no longer need to make the trip to hand over the money. Their wives fear their husbands may leave them for urban spouses, which could put to a stop to remittances or, worse, lead to competing claims for their houses and land.

The agents' perspective

EXHIBIT 5
M-PESA Kenya average agent metrics[43]

#Transaction/day	Commission/day (USD)	Profit/day (USD)
87	16,11	5,01

A typical agent generates more than twice as much commission from M-PESA than through the sale of airtime. Also, particularly among rural agents, M-PESA brings cash into the village, where it is spent locally, usually in the agent's shop

Several agents, however, report having trouble keeping a sufficient float to maintain service continuity. This is particularly a problem for rural agents, where cash withdrawals are prevalent, and who are located further away from bank outlets. Many rural agents find it costly to pay for trips to the nearest town to acquire float, which can use up a large part of the profit they get from operating M-PESA in a day. The cost of maintaining liquidity is the number one expense for agents,[44] as it represents on average 30% of total expenses (including bank fees, transport to location where cash and e-float can be converted, and commissions to aggregators who advance funds immediately).

42 Safaricom data and INSEAD analysis (based on KSh/EUR = 0,0096), March 2010.
43 "Building viable agent networks", Mark Pickens, CGAP, February 2010.
44 "Agent Economics: M-PESA", Mark Pickens, Sarah Rotman, Ignacio Mas and Olga Morawczynski, CGAP, 2009.

M-PESA fees

EXHIBIT 6
M-PESA tariff[45]

M-PESA Tariff

Transaction type	Transaction range (KShs)		Customer Charge (KShs)
	Minimum	Maximum	
Value Movement Transactions			
Deposit Cash	100	35,000	0
Send money to a registered M-PESA user	100	35,000	30
Send money to a non-registered M-PESA user	100	2,500	75
	2,501	5,000	100
	5,001	10,000	175
	10,001	20,000	350
	20,001	35,000	400
Withdraw cash by a registered M-PESA user at an M-PESA Agent outlet	100	2,500	25
	2,501	5,000	45
	5,001	10,000	75
	10,001	20,000	145
	20,001	35,000	170
Withdraw cash by registered M-PESA user at PesaPoint ATM	200	2,500	30
	2,501	5,000	60
	5,001	10,000	100
	10,001	20,000	175
Withdraw cash by a non-registered M-PESA user	100	35,000	0
Buy airtime (for self or other)	20	10,000	0
Pay Bill Transactions	–	–	0 - 30
• Transaction fees of between KShs 0-30 applicable depending on the organization you are paying to			
• Confirm that the company you intend to pay to accepts payment via M-PESA before transacting			
Information Transactions			
Show Balance			1
Change Secret Word			0
Change PIN			20
Update Menu			0
Change Language			0
SIM Replacement			20

- FREE REGISTRATION
- No minimum balance required
- Maximum Account Balance KShs 50,000
- Maximum daily transaction value KShs 70,000
- No monthly fees / No hidden charges
- All SMS sent to and from M-PESA are FREE
- To use M-PESA, your Safaricom phone needs to be ACTIVE

- All charges are deducted by M-PESA from your M-PESA account
- To send PESA you must first deposit money into your own M-PESA account. You cannot deposit money directly into another person's M-PESA account.

To register or transact at any M-PESA agent you will need your original identification document:
National ID, Passport, Military ID, Diplomatic ID or Alien ID.

Safaricom

45 From the Safaricom website.

M-PESA contribution to Safaricom revenues

EXHIBIT 7[46]

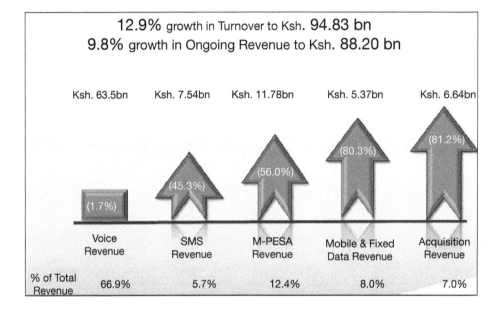

46 From the Safaricom full year 2010–2011 results presentation (available in the Investor Relations section of Safaricom's website).

A wide network of agents

EXHIBIT 8

Niko na Safaricom

We have built the widest network in the country,
ensuring that you enjoy our peerless products
and services wherever you are in Kenya

About the oikos Case Writing Competition

Concept

The annual oikos Case Writing Competition promotes the development of new, high-quality teaching case studies reflecting on sustainability within the fields of management, entrepreneurship and finance. Consequently, the competition hosts three different tracks, namely on 'Corporate Sustainability', 'Social Entrepreneurship' and 'Sustainable Finance'.

The competition welcomes entries from scholars from all continents to any of the three tracks. The case studies should be suitable for use in management education and should be related to managerial issues faced by organizations and individuals. Applicants may be teachers, research assistants or students of business administration (or related areas) at a registered university. Case entries may have more than one author, and each applicant may submit one case per track only. The case studies and associated materials should concentrate on corporate sustainability, social entrepreneurship or sustainable finance, be presented in English, be based on real cases, be focused on a recent situation or development (not older than two years before the launch of the call for cases for each edition) and be released by management of the subject organization/company for use by other business schools. A completed case submission form and a comprehensive teaching note must accompany each case.

Accepted submissions are subject to a two-step double blind review process. For all of the three competition tracks the judging committee pays particular attention to:

- Concept and content: the integration of the different sustainability dimensions (economic, social and environmental), the topic relevance and its ability to create a learning experience.

- Teaching note: a comprehensive teaching note must accompany each submission and include a thorough analysis of questions suggested as well as strategies and teaching approaches recommended in the class room.

- Form: the style of writing, quality of presentation and clarity of data.

In each track the top three cases are awarded with prize money. The annual first prize is 5000 Swiss Francs (CHF), second place is 2000 CHF and third 1000 CHF.

Copyright ownership remains with the author(s) and/or their employer(s). Inspection copies (without teaching notes) are published in the oikos online case collection.

List of the Award Committee Members

Since the inception of the competition in 2006, oikos has been fortunate to have leading international faculty members join the jury of the oikos-Ashoka Case Writing Competition. This volume is based on a selection among the best cases that took part in the Social Entrepreneurship Track between the editions of the competition of 2010 and 2013. Within this period the following list of scholars actively participated as reviewers and members of the award committee of the oikos Case Writing Competition.

- Prof. Dr. Alfred Vernis, ESADE, Spain

- Prof. Dr. Cheryl Kernot, Centre for Social Impact (CSI), Australia

- Prof. Dr. Chris Steyaert, University of St. Gallen, Switzerland

- Prof. Dr. Dror Etzion, McGill, Canada

- Prof. Dr. Ezequiel Reficco, University of San Andres, Argertina

- Prof. Dr. Felipe Santos, INSEAD, France

- Prof. Dr. Francesco Perrini, University of Bocconi, Italy

- Prof. Dr. Gabriel Berger, University of San Andres, Argentina

- Prof. Dr. Heiko Hosomi, University of Innsbruck, Austria

- Prof. Dr. Imran Chowdhury, Pace University, USA

- Prof. Dr. Jan Lepoutre, ESSEC Business School, France

- Prof. Dr. Johanna Mair, University of Stanford, USA

- Prof. Dr. Madhukar Shukla, XLRI Jamshedpur, India

- Prof. Dr. Marie Lisa Dacanay, Asian Institute of Management, Philippines

- Prof. Dr. Michael Pirson, Fordham University, USA

- Prof. Dr. Minna Halme, Helsinki School of Business Administration and Economics, Finland

- Prof. Dr. Roberto Gutiérrez, Universidad de los Andes, Colombia

- Prof. Dr. Saurabh Lall, Aspen Institute, USA

Short Biographies of the Award Committee Members

Prof. Dr. Gabriel Berger
University of San Andres, Argentina

Gabriel Berger is an associate professor in the Department of Administration at the Universidad de San Andrés (UdeSA), Buenos Aires, Argentina. In 2007, he launched UdeSA's Center for Social Innovation, which coordinates training, research and teaching activities for nonprofit organizations, corporations and individual philanthropists. Dr. Berger is the academic director of the Graduate Program in Nonprofit Organizations launched in 1997, with the collaboration of CEDES, with 560 alumni (as of 2011) working with the main nonprofit organizations and corporate foundations in Argentina. Dr. Berger's teaching and research focuses on strategic management and governance of nonprofits, social businesses, corporate social engagement, and philanthropy. He was a co-editor of *Social Inclusive Business in Latin America* (Cambridge, MA: Harvard University Press, 2010). He has collaborated as adviser to NGOs, businesses and foundations in several Latin American countries and in the USA. He has served as general coordinator of Social Enterprise Knowledge Network (SEKN) from 2008 to 2011, a collaborative group of ten business schools in Ibero-America engaged in joint research and writing on social initiatives by corporations and nonprofit organizations, and was one of its founding members in 2001. He has been a member of several advisory boards in Argentina, including Fundación Compromiso and Help Argentina. He obtained a PhD in Social Policy and a Master in Management of Human Services from the Heller School of Social Policy and Management at Brandeis University (USA).

Prof. Dr. Imran Chowdhury
Pace University, USA

Imran Chowdhury is Assistant Professor of Management at the Lubin School of Business, Pace University. His current research focuses on social entrepreneurship, social responsibility, and business in emerging economies, and has been published in *Academy of Management Learning and Education, AOM Best Papers Proceedings*, and in several edited volumes. He received his PhD from ESSEC Business School, an MSc from INSEAD, and a BA in Anthropology and Geography from Hunter College (CUNY).

Prof. Dr. Marie Lisa Dacanay
Asian Institute of Management, Phillipines

Marie Lisa M. Dacanay joined the faculty of the Asian Center for Entrepreneurship (ACE) after completing a two-year assignment at the Philippine Department of Agrarian Reform (DAR). She was designated Program Director for Social and Development Entrepreneurship. Prof. Dacanay was manager of the DAR-ADB ARCP, the department's largest foreign-assisted project funded by the Asian Development Bank. She also served as adviser to the DAR Secretary on countryside development. Before joining government, Prof. Dacanay was vice president of the Philippine Rural Reconstruction Movement (PRRM). As manager she worked on the operationalization of PRRM's Sustainable Rural District Development Program (SRDDP) with farmers, fisher folk and indigenous communities. She spearheaded the National Affairs Committee of the University of the Philippines Student Council and other youth organizations during the martial law era in the late '70s and early '80s. She was Deputy Secretary General of the Asian Students' Association (ASA) based in Hong Kong from 1983 to 85. She was the working group leader and editor of Pathways (1999), a research-book project of the Conference of Asian Foundations and Organizations (CAFO). She continues to be part of CAFO's leadership as Executive Committee member at the regional level and as country coordinator for the Philippines. Her recent published works include *Citizenship and Sustainable Development in the Philippines* (1999), *What Makes a Practice Exemplary?* (1999) and *Strategic Planning for Sustainable Area Development Intervention* (1999). Prof. Dacanay holds a Master in Development Management (With Distinction) from the Asian Institute of Management (1996). She received a Bachelor of Science in Statistics from the University of the Philippines (1983).

Prof. Dr. Dror Etzion
McGill, Canada

Dror Etzion is an associate professor of strategy and organizations at the Desautels Faculty of Management, and an associate member of the McGill School of the Environment. He joined McGill in 2008, after completing his PhD studies at IESE Business School in Barcelona, Spain. Previously, Dror worked for five years in the Israeli software industry, and also spent a year at The Natural Step, an international non-profit research and consultancy organization focused on sustainable development. Dror's research program focuses on environmental metrics: how we decide what we measure, how new metrics diffuse in the organizational landscape, and how accurately the measures used actually capture the reality of business impacts on the environment. This research integrates areas of scholarship as diverse as economic sociology, signaling theory, behavioral economics and social psychology. In other research, he examines the effects of industry affiliation and geographic location on firm environmental performance. A third stream examines the social context of business and critically investigates the intersection of corporations, democracry and the public good. In 2013 Dror received the Organizations and the Natural Environment (ONE) Division Emerging Scholar Award, presented at the Academy of Management (AoM) Business Meeting. The ONE Emerging Scholar Award recognizes early career academics who have already made outstanding research contributions in the area of organizations and the natural environment, and who appear to have a strong potential to continue making such contributions in the near future. Earlier in his career, his work was awarded the Booz Allen Hamilton/Strategic Management Society Fellowship and the Aspen Institute's Business and Society Program Dissertation Proposal Award. His research has been published or is forthcoming in *Organization Science, Strategic Management Journal, Sloan Management Review, Academy of Management Perspectives, Journal of Management* and other outlets. Currently, Dror teaches the MBA core course on Markets and Globalization, an elective on Strategies for Sustainable Development, and in the not-for-profit consulting program.

Prof. Dr. Roberto Gutierrez

Universidad de los Andes, Colombia

Roberto Gutiérrez chairs the Social Enterprise Knowledge Network (SEKN), an alliance of ten universities throughout Ibero-America, and directs the Social Enterprise Initiative in the School of Administration at the Universidad de los Andes where he is an Associate Professor. He received a PhD in Sociology from Johns Hopkins University and, in 2000, an Academic Excellence Award from the school for his research and teaching. He has published articles about alliances, social enterprises, education, and development in popular media and academic journals—among them the *American Sociological Review*, the *Review of Educational Research*, the *Journal of Management Education* and the *Stanford Social Innovation Review*. Recently he was co-editor of the book *Effective Management in Social Enterprise: Lessons from Business and Civil Society Organizations in Ibero America* (Cambridge, MA: Harvard University Press 2006).

Prof. Dr. Minna Halme

Helsinki School of Business and Economics, Finland

Minna Halme is an assistant professor at Helsinki School of Economics (HSE). Her areas of specialization include: developing environmental corporate cultures, actor networks and sustainable development, environmental communication and marketing, sustainable tourism, and sustainable business strategies in forest industry. Minna was the scientific coordinator of a recently concluded sustainable tourism research project EMPOST-NET (The Emerging Paradigm for Sustainable Tourism: A Network Perspective), funded by EU-DGXII. At present she concentrates on eco-efficient services study in an HSE-based team working on a project: Demateralization: The Potential of Service-Orientation and Information Technology. Since 1994, she has taught Master's degree courses on corporate environmental management and qualitative research methods. She is an associate teacher of corporate environmental management at the Business School of University of Tampere, Finland, and the International Institute for Industrial Environmental Economics, University of Lund, Sweden. Since 1994 she has published in several peer-reviewer journals on the topics of corporate environmental management and business ethics, in a number of edited books and written two monographies. She is a member of the editorial board of Business Strategy and the Environment and of the Action Planning Committee of the Greening of Industry Network.

Prof. Dr. Heiko Hosomi Spitzeck

Universidad Fondacao Dom Cabral, Brazil

Heiko Hosomi Spitzeck received his Master in Economics (European Studies) at the University of Bamberg, Germany in 2001. While working as Director of International Issues and President of the St. Gallen Chapter of Oikos International, Switzerland from 2004 to 2007 he worked on his doctoral thesis, which he finished in 2008 (Dr. oec.) at the University of St. Gallen, Switzerland. Heiko Hosomi Spitzeck currently works as Professor at Fundação Dom Cabral in the fields of sustainability, business ethics and corporate social responsibility, as well as at Cranfield University's School of Management, Doughty Centre for Corporate Responsibility, UK.

Prof. Dr. Cheryl Kernot
CSI, Australia

Cheryl Kernot is an Australian politician, academic, and political activist. She was a member of the Australian Senate representing Queensland for the Australian Democrats from 1990 to 1997, and the fifth leader of the Australian Democrats from 1993 to 1997. In 1997 she resigned from the Australian Democrats, joined the Australian Labor Party, and won the seat of Dickson at the 1998 federal election. She was defeated at the 2001 federal election. Kernot later stood as an independent candidate to represent New South Wales in the Australian Senate in the 2010 federal election. Kernot worked in the United Kingdom as Programme Director at the Skoll Centre for Social Entrepreneurs at the Said Business School at Oxford University and as the Director of Learning at the School for Social Entrepreneurs in London. Kernot is currently the Director of Social Business at the Centre for Social Impact, based at the University of New South Wales. She has also expressed support for Australia becoming a republic.

Prof. Dr. Saurabh Lall
Aspen Institute, USA

Saurabh Lall leads ANDE's research initiative, which focuses on understanding the impact of small and growing businesses on poverty and economic development. Saurabh was previously the Research Officer of the New Ventures program at the World Resources Institute, where he studied the investment potential of environmental entrepreneurship in developing countries. Originally from Mumbai, Saurabh has also worked on rural water and sanitation issues in several states across India. He has a Master of Public Policy degree from George Washington University and a Bachelor of Engineering degree from the University of Mumbai. He is currently pursuing a PhD in Public Policy and Administration at the George Washington University, focusing on impact investing and program evaluation.

Prof. Dr. Jan Lepoutre
ESSEC Business School, France

Jan Lepoutre is Research Fellow at Vlerick Business School. Since 2012 he has been Assistant Professor at ESSEC Business School in France. Jan Lepoutre has an MSc in Bioscience Engineering (KU Leuven, 2001), a Postgraduate in Applied Economics (Ghent University, 2004) and obtained his PhD in Applied Economic Sciences at Ghent University in 2008. In his PhD "Proactive Environmental Strategies in Small Businesses: Resources, Institutions and Dynamic Capabilities", he explored how small firms can successfully overcome the difficulties associated with pursuing green strategies. He has published several articles, including in the *Academy of Management Journal*, *Journal of Business Ethics*, *Small Business Economics* and *Journal of Cleaner Production*. Current research interests are focused on the psychological and institutional antecedents of entrepreneurial initiatives that promote social and economic development, such as the effects of education on entrepreneurship and the institutional dynamics of environmental strategy development.

Prof. Dr. Johanna Mair

Hertie School of Governance, Germany

Johanna Mair is Professor of Management, Organization and Leadership at the Hertie School of Governance. She is also the Hewlett Foundation Visiting Scholar at the Stanford Center on Philanthropy and Civil Society and the Academic Editor of the Stanford Social Innovation Review. From 2001 to 2011 she served on the Strategic Management faculty at IESE Business School. She has held a visiting position at the Harvard Business School and teaches regularly at the Harvard Kennedy School and INSEAD. Before earning her PhD in Management from INSEAD (France), she was directly involved in executive decision-making in international banking. In 2008 she was recognized as a "Faculty Pioneer" for Social Entrepreneurship Education by the Aspen Institute. Her research focuses on how novel organizational and institutional arrangements generate economic and social development and the role of innovation in this process. She is the co-editor of three books and has published in leading academic journal. Today, alongside her academic responsibilities, she serves as the vice-chair of Global Agenda Council on Social Innovation of the World Economic Forum and carries out advisory and board work for multinational companies, the United Nations, governments, foundations and social venture funds.

Prof. Dr. Francesco Perrini

University of Bocconi, Italy

Francesco Perrini is professor of management and CSR at the Institute of Strategy, Department of Management and Technology, Università Bocconi, Milan, Italy. He is also SIF chair of Social Entrepreneurship and senior professor of corporate finance at the Corporate and Real Estate Finance Department, SDA Bocconi School of Management. He is director of the Università Bocconi Center for Research on Sustainability and Value (CReSV), head of Bocconi CSR Unit, Department of Management and Technology, Università Bocconi, and coordinator of CSR Activities Group at SDA Bocconi. His research areas are management of corporate development processes, from strategy implementation (acquisitions and strategic alliances) to financial strategies and valuation; small-and medium-sized enterprises; and social issues in management: corporate governance, corporate social responsibility, sustainability, social entrepreneurship, social innovation and socially responsible investing.

Prof. Dr. Michael Pirson

Fordham University, USA

Michael Pirson joined the Fordham Schools of Business as an associate professor of management systems in 2008. A scholar of humanistic management, which holds that business and commerce ought to advance human dignity and society, Professor Pirson helped to establish an undergraduate sustainable-business concentration at Fordham. He teaches courses such as Social Entrepreneurship, Fundamentals of Management and Principles of Management, and his work spans the undergraduate and graduate levels. A native of Germany, Professor Pirson has worked and lived in Switzerland, France, China, Costa Rica and the United States. Before beginning his academic career, he worked for an international consulting group for several years and then started his own private consultancy. He has worked for and with businesses, nonprofits, embassies, political campaigns and local and national governments. Professor Pirson is the social entrepreneurship track chair for the oikos-Ashoka Global Case Writing Competition in Social Entrepreneurship. He is also a founding partner of the

Humanistic Management Network, an organization that brings together scholars, practitioners and policymakers around the common goal of creating a "life-conducive" economic system. In that capacity, he is the co-editor of the Humanism in Business book series, published by Palgrave-McMillan. Professor Pirson is a research fellow at Harvard University and serves on the board of three social enterprises in the United States.

Prof. Dr. Ezquiel Reficco
University of San Andres, Argentina

Ezequiel Reficco has been a professor of management at the University of the Andes, since 2009. Since 2001, he has served as a researcher and post-doctoral fellow for the the the Social Enterprise Initiative at Harvard Business School. He was also a visiting professor at ESADE Business School (Barcelona), affiliated with the Institute for Social Innovation, and the University of San Andrés (Buenos Aires), as a member of its Center for Social Innovation. His research agenda focuses on issues of social and environmental sustainability of corporate strategy, inclusive business and social entrepreneurship. He is co-author of *Social Partnering in Latin America* (Harvard University Press, 2004) and co-editor of *Effective Management of Social Enterprises* (Harvard University Press, 2006). He has published articles in various publications of the United States, Europe and Latin America, including the *Harvard Business Review, INCAE Business Review* and the *Stanford Social Innovation Review.*

Prof. Dr. Felipe Santos
INSEAD, France

Filipe Santos is Associate Professor of Entrepreneurship at INSEAD and is based in the Abu Dhabi campus. He is the Academic Director of the INSEAD Social Entrepreneurship Initiative since 2007. His research lies at the intersection of strategy, organization theory, and entrepreneurship. His focus is the emerging field of social entrepreneurship and social innovation. He is particularly interested in understanding the processes through which entrepreneurs construct new firms and markets. He is also interested in the growth and scaling up processes of new ventures in order to maximize economic and social impact. Related research interests are on business model innovation, impact investing, corporate social entrepreneurship, and family business. His research has been published in journals such as *Academy of Management Journal, Academy of Management Review, Organization Science*, as well as several books and book chapters. Professor Santos teaches courses on entrepreneurship and social entrepreneurship in the INSEAD MBA, EMBA and Executive Education programmes and co-directs the INSEAD Social Entrepreneurship Programme (ISEP) since 2007. He also developed the INSEAD Social Entrepreneurship Bootcamp that has been adopted by partners worldwide. He regularly speaks on topics of entrepreneurship and innovation from both a commercial and a social perspective. He also mentors entrepreneurs and advises venture investors. A native of Portugal, Professor Santos holds a PhD in Management Science and Engineering from Stanford University. He also holds an MSc degree in Industrial Strategy and Management from Lisbon Technical University and an Economics degree from Lisbon New University. He was the recipient of the Lieberman Fellowship at Stanford University, an award recognizing outstanding scholarship and institutional contributions. He also received in 1996 the award for best MSc student. His doctoral thesis "Constructing Markets and Shaping Boundaries: Entrepreneurial Action in Nascent Markets" was finalist for the Heizer 2004 Entrepreneurship Award. He received an Honourable Mention for Best Paper at the 2006 Strategic Management Society Conference and the 2008 IDEA award for Research Promise from the Academy of Management Entrepreneurship Division. He also won the 2008 award for Best Teacher in Elective Courses at the INSEAD GEMBA program. He was the finalist for the same award in 2009, 2010 and 2011, and received the Deans' commendation for excellence in MBA teaching in 2010. He also received the EFMD 2012 award for best case in the Africa category with the Nuru Energy case series.

Prof. Dr. Madhukar Shukla
XLRI Jamshedpur, India

Madhukar Shukla is Chairperson, Fr Arrupe Centre for Ecology & Sustainability, and Professor of Strategic Management & OB, XLRI Jamshedpur. Madhukar has served as a member of the Advisory Council of University Network for Social Entrepreneurship (founded by Ashoka: Innovators for the Public and Skoll Center for Social Entrepreneurship, Oxford University), and is also a Member, Livelihood India Advisory Board. He has served on the Jury for the Microfinance Award '07, instituted by PlaNet Finance, and was a lead assessor for the India NGO Awards 2007, 2008 and 2009. He has been the Conference Coordinator for the annual National Conference on Social Entrepreneurship since 2009. Prof. Madhukar is a Villgro Awardee for his Academic Contribution for the Social Entrepreneurship Ecosystem in 2011.

Prof. Dr. Chris Steyaert
University of St. Gallen, Switzerland

Chris Steyaert is a Professor of Organizational Psychology at the University of St. Gallen, Switzerland. Professor Steyaert's research and teaching focus on creativity and newness, diversity management and difference, language and translation, and aesthetic and political implications of organizational life. His work has been published in leading academic journals such as *Human Relations*, *Organization*, *Journal of Management Studies*, *European Journal of Work and Organizational Psychology*, *Journal of World Business*, and *International Studies of Management and Organization*.

Prof. Dr. Alfred Vernis
Esade, Spain

Alfred Vernis is a member of the Institute of Public Management (IDGP). He co-directs the courses The Managerial Function in Non-Governmental Organizations, and Leadership and Social Innovation, with the collaboration of Fundació "la Caixa". He currently manages the Social Enterprise Knowledge Network (SEKN) research at ESADE, led by the Harvard Business School and supported by Fundación Avina. He has published various articles and books on management in the third sector. He is a co-author of *La gestión de las organizaciones no lucrativas* (Deusto, 1998), *Los retos en la gestión de las organizaciones no lucrativas* (Granica, 2004), *Nonprofit organizations: Challenges and Collaboration* (Palgrave, 2006), and *Effective Management of Social Enterprises* (Harvard University, 2006). In recent years he has collaborated on strategic planning tasks with Intermón-Oxfam, Medicus Mundi, the Centre Excursionista de Catalunya and the Fundació Jesuites Educació. He is a member of the Board of Trustees of the Fundació Catalana de l'Esplai (Barcelona) and of the Fundación Lealtad (Madrid). Since 2002 he has formed part of the Social Council of the Inditex Group (Arteixo, Galicia).

About oikos

oikos is an international student-driven organization for sustainable economics and management. Founded in 1987 in Switzerland, we today empower future leaders to drive change towards sustainability worldwide.

Our programs embed environmental and social perspectives in faculties for economics and management. They comprise conferences, seminars, speeches, simulation games and other initiatives to transform teaching and research. They promote the integration of sustainability in curricula. And they provide platforms for learning, creating and sharing solutions.

The heart of our organization is our student members who turn ideas into action in currently close to 40 oikos chapters around the world. They are supported by a global community of oikos alumni, advisors, faculty and partners, as well as an international team based in Switzerland.

For more information about our programmes please refer to our website (www.oikos-international.org) or contact us at via mail or e-mail at the address below.

oikos
Tigerbergstrasse, 2
9000 St. Gallen
Switzerland

Telephone: +41 71 224 25 90
Email: info@oikos-international.org

About the authors

Manish Agarwal is currently designated as Research Scholar in IBS, Hyderabad (Constituent of IFHE University), India. He has about 13 years of rich cross functional experience in teaching, company valuation, industry research, financial research and case study development. He has developed around 50 case studies including teaching notes, and structure assignments on a range of topics including financial services, financial management, financial risk management, enterprise risk management, mergers and acquisitions, social entrepreneurship, investment banking and financial services, wealth management. His area of interest includes corporate finance, wealth management and social entrepreneurship.

Catherine Bédard is a food safety specialist in the retail grocery industry. She earned her MBA from the John Molson School of Business at Concordia University and her BSc in Human Nutrition from McGill University.

Darrell Brown has a BS in Forestry from University of Montana, an MBA from University of Montana, and an Accounting PhD from the University of Utah. Dr Brown is a Certified Public Accountant (Montana, inactive) and teaches accounting information systems and managerial accounting. His current research interests include measurement issues related to organizational impacts on social and natural systems. In particular, he studies corporate social and environmental reporting, the relationship business reporting and business transparency, and the relationship between social and environmental reporting and firm performance. He serves on the editorial boards of *Issues in Accounting Education*, the *Journal of Information Systems* and the *International Journal of Information Systems*.

Min Cai has a BA in English Language from Beijing Foreign Studies University and an MBA in International Business from Portland State University. Her career aspiration is to help businesses implement sustainable supply chain practices. She currently works with the sustainability program in a coffee roaster based in Portland, OR, focusing on carbon accounting. She also volunteers with a non-profit organization promoting human education on animal protection, human rights and environmental ethics to children, educators, administrators and community leaders.

Charles Corbett, PhD, is Professor of Operations Management and Sustainability at the UCLA Anderson School of Management. He served as Chairman and Deputy Dean of Academic Affairs from 2009 to 2012. He has received a number of teaching awards, as well as the Anderson School's J. Clayburn LaForce Faculty Leadership Award for 2012. He was an AT&T Faculty Fellow in Industrial Ecology, and is the founder and co-director of the award-winning UCLA Leaders in Sustainability graduate certificate program and founding director of the Easton Technology Leadership Program.

Sarang Deo is Assistant Professor of Operations Management at the Indian School of Business (ISB). His primary area of interest is health care operations with special emphasis on the impact of operations decisions on population level health outcomes. He has studied the influenza vaccine supply chain and ambulance diversion (in the USA), adult HIV treatment supply chains and infant HIV diagnosis networks in sub-Saharan Africa, and the TB diagnosis pathway in rural India. He frequently collaborates with agencies such as the Clinton Health Access Initiative and the Bill and Melinda Gates Foundation and his research has been funded by the US National Science Foundation and Grand Challenges Canada. Prior to ISB, Sarang was Assistant Professor at the Kellogg School of Management. Sarang has a PhD from UCLA Anderson School of Management, an MBA from IIM Ahmedabad and a BTech from IIT Bombay, and also worked as a management consultant in Accenture's Mumbai office.

Dror Etzion is an associate professor of strategy and organizations at the Desautels Faculty of Management, McGill University, and an associate member of the McGill School of the Environment. He received his PhD from IESE Business School. His research agenda focuses on the use of metrics and information in organizational settings, primarily metrics for sustainability. In other research, he examines the effects of industry affiliation and geographic location on firm environmental performance. His work has been published or is forthcoming in *Organization Science, Strategic Management Journal, Sloan Management Review, Academy of Management Perspectives, Journal of Management* and other outlets. At McGill, he teaches the MBA core course on Markets and Globalization as well as an elective on Strategies for Sustainable Development. Prior to his academic career, he worked in the Israeli high-tech sector.

Erin Ferrigno began cultivating an interest in the environment while growing up in the mountains of Park City, Utah. She earned a BS in Communication from the University of Utah and later went on to complete the MBA program at Portland State University with a focus on sustainability. It was there that her interest in sustainable business truly peaked, eventually taking her back to Park City to take part in the first EarthWell Festival, a weekend-long festival promoting sustainability and wellness. Erin recently relocated to the Napa Valley and is a member of the accounting team at a private winery where she hopes to bring her knowledge of sustainable business practices to a young and growing company.

Olivier Furdelle is an independent executive consultant in Social Innovation and Impact Investment. He has been affiliated with the INSEAD Social Innovation Centre since 2009. Olivier advises investment funds, development agencies and multinational companies with a focus on Sub-Saharan Africa. He has been involved in numerous projects and transactions across various geographies e.g. Senegal, Democratic Republic of Congo, Cameroon, Mali, Niger, Madagascar, Burundi. Previously, Olivier was Vice-President, Business Development & Planning at Belgacom, the leading ICT company in Belgium. Prior to that, he started up an internet company and worked as a management consultant at Accenture and KPMG.

He graduated with a Master of Science in Management from Solvay Business School (Belgium) and followed leadership development training at INSEAD (France).

Geneviève Grainger is a Strategic Planning and Business Development Coordinator at Valero Energy Inc. She has a diverse professional background, having held several operational and technical positions in the petroleum, defense (energetic materials) and agri-food industries. She earned her MBA from the John Molson School of Business at Concordia University and her Bachelor of Chemical Engineering from McGill University.

Magdalena Kloibhofer, research assistant at the Chair of Social Business at European Business School Wiesbaden, holds a Masters degree in Economic Geography from LMU Munich University and has completed a postgraduate program on adult education at Munich School of Philosophy. Her research focuses on leadership culture and organizational identity in social enterprises. She has several years of practical experience in the field of corporate sustainability and social business in Egypt and Germany including corporate responsibility rating and consulting, sustainability management, and supporting social entrepreneurs through business coaching and strategy workshops.

Karin Kreutzer holds the Chair of Social Business at European Business School Wiesbaden. She has practical and academic experience in the area of managing social mission-driven organizations. She holds a doctoral degree from University of St. Gallen, a Masters degree in International Business Studies from University of Passau and a Masters degree in Management of Nonprofit Organizations from Bocconi University. Karin Kreutzer has done research on social entrepreneurship and management of non-profit organizations. She has published in international journals including *Voluntas, Nonprofit and Voluntary Sector Quarterly*, and *Nonprofit Management and Leadership*.

Jan Lepoutre is Associate Professor at ESSEC Business School, France. Drawing on multiple disciplines, he has a passion for learning and teaching about entrepreneurial strategies that individuals and organizations develop to address complex and systemic, often societal issues. Using both qualitative and quantitative methods, this has taken him to a diverse range of settings, including horticulture, cleantech, banking and heavy manufacturing in both the developing as well as the developed world. He is the author of a number of articles published in the *Academy of Management Journal, Journal of Business Ethics, Small Business Economics* and *Journal of Cleaner Production*, as well as book chapters, case studies and reports.

Philippe Margery has extensive international business development experience and several successful entrepreneurial ventures under his belt in both Europe and South America. He worked for six years at IMD, four of them in Switzerland, mainly on innovation, entrepreneurship and learning, writing case studies and working on research projects. He also worked with executive coaching, being a certified NEO and Tavistock coach. He spent the last two years developing IMD's business in Brazil. French, he has lived and worked in Sweden, England, the Netherlands, France, Switzerland and Brazil.

R. Scott Marshall has a BA in business economics, Willamette University; an MA in international affairs, George Washington University; and a PhD in international strategy, University of Oregon. Dr Marshall is Associate Dean for Graduate Programs and Research at the School of Business. In this role, he has overall responsibility for accreditation, curricular, budgetary, marketing and personnel issues for the graduate programs. His research is in the areas of proactive environmental strategy, corporate governance and sustainability reporting. Dr Marshall has published in leading academic journals including *Business Strategy & Environment, California Management Review, Journal of Business Ethics, Journal of Information Systems, Journal of International Business Studies, Journal of World Business*, and *Organization & Environment*.

Raymond L. Paquin is an Associate Professor of management at the John Molson School of Business, Concordia University. His research focuses on the intersection of business and society, in particular around environmental strategy and collaborative environmental actions. He earned his doctorate from Boston University School of Management; MAEd from Virginia Tech; and Bachelor of Music from North Carolina School of the Arts.

Lisa Peifer is a 2010 alumna of Portland State University's Master of Business Administration program, having chosen the PSU MBA for its strong corporate sustainability curriculum. She went on to work for Tropical Salvage in the areas of sales and marketing, and is most proud of her role directing the development of a new website for the company.

Stuart Read was a Professor at IMD, Switzerland from 2005 to 2013. After a sabbatical year sailing the North Atlantic and West Indies with his family, he recently joined the faculty of Atkinson Graduate School of Management at Willamette University, USA.

His research is focused on effectuation. Derived from practices employed by expert entrepreneurs, effectuation is a set of heuristics that describe how people make decisions and take action in situations of true uncertainty. Stuart has nearly twenty years of industry experience, having participated in the creation of six high technology start-up firms, and serving in Oracle, Lotus and Sun Microsystems.

Loïc Sadoulet is Affiliate Professor of Economics at INSEAD, and Visiting Professor at CEDEP. Loïc holds a PhD in Economics from Princeton University. He has been teaching at INSEAD since 2000 in Executive Development Programmes, MBA and Executive-MBA programmes. In 2008, Loïc launched the INSEAD Africa Initiative, one of the initiatives of the INSEAD Social Innovation Centre. His research focuses on business development and expansion in emerging economies, both by local efforts and through entry by multinational companies. His interests lie in creating profitable agreements in environments with substantial information gaps. A major line of his research has concentrated on the design of financial services that can be extended (profitably) to traditionally neglected segments. Recently, he has also been involved in investigating ICT-based solutions to create new profitable markets for a range of activities: health, information services, financial services. Previously, Loïc has worked for the World Bank; in a microfinance institution in Guatemala; at the European Centre for Advanced Research in Economics and Statistics (ECARES) at the Free University of Brussels; and at the Solvay Business School (Belgium).

Bex (Rebecca) Sakarias has a BS in Mathematics from Southern Oregon University, a BS in Physics from Southern Oregon University, and an MBA from Portland State University. She is a supply chain professional with experience in the food and beverage industry. She is also a TEFL certified English teacher. Her current endeavors have taken her to rural Nicaragua where she is a community educator focusing on English language instruction. She also provide volunteer coordination services to a bilingual school start-up in the community.

D. Satish is currently working as Associate Professor at IBS Hyderabad (Constituent of IFHE University), India. He has around 15 years of experience in training, research and consulting. He has authored more than 125 cases and written more than 300 articles in Indian and international newspapers and magazines. His area of interest includes strategic financial management, international finance, risk management, alternate investment and entrepreneurial finance. He has conducted management development and leadership development programme for senior executives for both public sector enterprises and companies like Indian Railways, Hindalco and Intelligroup (now part of NTT group).

Jeroen Struben is Assistant Professor in the Strategy & Organization Area at the Desautels Faculty of Management Faculty and Fellow of the Marcel Desautels Institute for Integrated Management, McGill University. Jeroen holds a PhD from MIT at the Sloan School of Management and a graduate degree in physics from Delft University of Technology. Jeroen's work focuses on understanding the factors that contribute to successful market formation, while considering implications for firms and socio-technical trajectories. Empirically Jeroen studies energy, alternative fuel vehicles, and nutrition markets. Jeroen is particularly interested in the question: How do alternative products, ideas, and practices successfully penetrate in the marketplace or society at large, rather than falter? To examine this, Jeroen's research focuses on how social processes and evolution of the built environment jointly condition the formation of self-sustaining markets. His research combines empirical, analytical and systems science-based analysis, producing insights related to coordination, collective action and commitment across organizations, industries and governments.

Pia von Neil is an entrepreneur. She combines extensive start-up know-how (she did 3 years venture development for Rocket Internet) with experiences from social entrepreneurial projects in developing countries. Pia holds a Bachelor in Business Administration from WHU- Otto Beisheim School of Management and a Master of Law and Business from Bucerius Law School.